Managing Value in Organisations

Reviews of *Managing Value in Organisations*

'Managing Value in Organisations *is a terrific read. Donal Carroll offers a fresh perspective on organisation change, combining his experience as a consultant combined with a deep knowledge of theory and an irreverent and iconoclastic style. In Donal's world, there are no simple recipes – change is a journey, it requires experimentation, learning and self-reflection, and it happens most effectively when we are mindful of the tensions and trade-offs we are grappling with. If you are looking to shake up your workplace, this book provides a wealth of ideas and tools to help you.'*
Julian Birkinshaw, London Business School, UK

'Traditional approaches to the management of change at best produce results too slowly. Carrol offers an approach which enables faster adaptation to today's nasty surprise. Enormously valuable.'
Richard Chambers, lately Principal, Lambeth College, UK

'Entertaining and informative, this book aimed at "practical visionaries" has major relevance for third sector organisations facing significant challenges. The focus on value creation through integration of the three models of management, learning and business has an intuitive appeal as well as demonstrating its practical application. I found it a seriously entertaining consideration of managing complexity in uncertain times, providing a modern paradigm which challenges traditional management thinking. The use of the models as self improvement tools creates an innovative way of organisations understanding themselves and giving a sense of direction.'
Jan Jenkins, Director, Blenheim CDP

'In this book Donal Carroll explores so many layers of learning, including: his own encyclopaedic knowledge of modern management thinking, the creation of his new learning theory, the testing and development of that theory in real organisations and most of all how learning is the midwife to organisational development and productivity. If you're trying to find out how to move your organisation forward then dive in and start to unpeel your own learning onion.'
Tim Stranack, Head of Transformation and Project Management,
Westminster City Council, UK

'In a world where there are no quick fixes and even the more recent rules and models of management can prove obsolete or impractical when implemented, this book offers a fresh and refreshing approach. It provides a sturdy yet flexible framework for directors and managers to approach business and management strategy and their effective implementation for longer term success.'
Ian Dowds, Former Senior Vice President, Specific Media

'Donal's book is a fascinating journey into how a range of organisations fare through implementing a new agile management model. The model is based on a culture where leaders emerge when needed, where work is structured through self-organising and where overall control is – perhaps counter-intuitively – maintained through greater trust. This is a book about how it is done, not how it might be done. It tracks the changes and key learning points as these companies adopt the new approach. Recommended reading for anybody looking to escape the old ways of management and discover new trust-based approaches for the 21st century.'
Henry Stewart, Chief Executive, Happy Ltd

Managing Value in Organisations

New Learning, Management, and Business Models

DONAL CARROLL

Routledge
Taylor & Francis Group

LONDON AND NEW YORK

First published 2012 by Gower Publishing

Published 2016 by Routledge
2 Park Square, Milton Park, Abingdon, Oxfordshire OX14 4RN
711 Third Avenue, New York, NY 10017, USA

First issued in paperback 2016

Routledge is an imprint of the Taylor & Francis Group, an informa business

Gower Applied Business Research
Our programme provides leaders, practitioners, scholars and researchers with thought provoking, cutting edge books that combine conceptual insights, interdisciplinary rigour and practical relevance in key areas of business and management.

British Library Cataloguing in Publication Data
Carroll, Donal.
  Managing value in organisations : new learning, management,
  and business models.
  1. Organizational change--Management. 2. Reengineering
  (Management) 3. Organizational learning--Management.
  4. Intellectual capital--Management.
  I. Title
  658.4'06-dc23

Library of Congress Cataloging-in-Publication Data
Carroll, Donal.
  Managing value in organisations : new learning, management, and business
models / by Donal Carroll.
     p. cm.
  Includes bibliographical references and index.
  ISBN 978-1-4094-2647-9 (hbk.)
  1. Organizational change. 2. Organizational effectiveness. 3.
Value. 4. Management. I. Title.
  HD58.8.C363237 2011
  658.4--dc23

                                                                    2012002224

ISBN 13: 978-1-138-27125-8 (pbk)
ISBN 13: 978-1-4094-2647-9 (hbk)

Contents

List of Figures

About the Author

Donal Carroll was born in the Republic of Ireland. He left school early and did a TV Engineering Apprenticeship. After graduating as a mature student in the Arts, his first teaching post was in modern poetry at Clare College, Cambridge. He worked for over 20 years as a teacher and manager in Further Education, forming Critical Difference Consultancy in 1998. As a consultant, he has worked with many organisations in all sectors including NEC, Lufthansa, Ranger Oil, Lucas, NHS and over 100 Learning and Skills Providers. He has also worked for the past 10 years with the Open University Business School on their MBA programme 'Creativity, Innovation and Change' and is a poet, writer, blogger and tweeter on learning and management issues.

He produces Management Unplugged, innovative products and services, designed to 'refresh company energy, entertain and transform "management" thinking and bring a smile back to your business face'. Throughout his work as a teacher, manager and consultant, he has remained committed to developing critical, creative, independent individuals, teams and organisations.

Donal Carroll works for Critical Difference Consultancy: www.criticaldifference.co.uk

He can be reached at: d.carroll@criticaldifference.co.uk

His blogs are at: http://www.criticaldifference.co.uk/blog.php

Twitter: @donalcarroll1

Foreword

Conventional by-the-book management, still running blindly along rails laid down 100 years ago, is running on empty, out of ideas, track and steam. From how to do it to why to do it, all the things that managers took for granted have been blown away. Even before the crisis, Hamel and Birkinshaw were calling the end of the industrial management paradigm – fine for efficient replication of existing products but useless at innovation and initiative. When even the global head of McKinsey says that that paradigm's dominant ideology, shareholder value, can no longer keep the structure standing, we know it's time to move on out. The credit crunch of 2008 brought the roof down. Since then, individual pillars of the old order – BP, Nokia, RIM, even GE and Microsoft, have faltered. The greatest of today's successes, Apple, has done so by doing the exact contrary of what the business books tell you – in strategy, structure, focus on product and – especially – corporate governance.

With the tired old corporate exemplars no longer worth copying and traditional business models dissolving in the all-powerful solvent of the internet, today's managers need to look elsewhere for new sources of knowledge and inspiration. The dawning realisation of the post-crash era is that since the old rules don't work anymore (in fact, they never did work very well, but – to adapt Warren Buffett – it took a rapidly receding tide to show just how many people were bathing naked), it's up to them to invent, or at least make their own choice of new ones.

This is the positive message of the young entrepreneurs, and the businesses, represented here. Thank goodness for some new ones and the new thinking this work brings. Their year's journey is instructive. We owe to the social entrepreneurs and innovators the lesson that if the sense of purpose is strong enough, there is almost certainly a way of making the numbers add up. If it can't be done by traditional means, that's no reason to despair (look where traditional means have brought us). It does however put a premium on experimentation and iteration – and above all learning from that experience. Those lessons may seem elementary or unfocused at first – it was Reg Revans, the father of action learning, who wrote that 'The essence of action learning is to pose increasingly insightful questions from an origin of ignorance, risk and confusion'. But the effort is essential. Because, as Revans also noted, 'For an organisation to survive, its rate of learning must be equal to or greater than the rate of change in its external environment'. Given the acceleration of change, that insight has even greater gravitas than when he formulated it half a century ago.

As Douglas Board points out in another forthcoming Gower volume, management has to blend science, intuition and politics. An account that leaves out any of the three is incomplete and likely to mislead – each tempers and qualifies the others. What links them all is learning. Learning and reflecting on learning may be the most important thing that today's managers do.

However, this work also questions what learning is, in another radical form of 'blending'. It challenges organisations to live more *on purpose*: to develop faster by reinventing their (commonly default) models of management, business and learning, using a new model of learning as the midwife for this. These three models, along with an innovative value-creating method, offer all organisations a template for managing in an uncertain environment and creating sustainable change.

Simon Caulkin
Ex-*Observer* Management Editor and Business Columnist of the Year

Preface

The Story of a Title... and a Journey

A benefit of writing a Preface last is that you can indulge in some 'if I'd known then what I know now', as if it was a pretence that you now casually include things you nearly left out. Getting a title for the overall work looks easy. However, if the title is wrong, even a 'newspaper' can only get away with it for some time – like being called News *of the World* when it isn't...

Securing a 'fit' title runs all sorts of dangers: sticking with your starting one could mean ending up clinging to the wreckage when more apt stuff emerges, events bypass it or when what you thought was a detour along the journey turns out to be a destination. The title of this book has gone through various stages of dress and undress. It started off as *Rust, Trust and Gold Dust*, how different management models produced different organisational performance. Catchy, but a search engine might lead you to used cars. The next stage was *Trust, Engagement and Collective Learning* but far better writers have nailed that. Increasingly through the writing, what would not go away was something around 'value'.

This emerged in two different ways. One was the awareness that 'value' was depleted daily by big corporations (do we need any more evidence?) and 'big' people, while at the same time, there was much talk about being 'passionate' about business while a common experience was of service getting worse. The other was my claim that the work could produce 'new value' for both customers and organisations. Value creation did indeed occur (but you be the judge) but not in the way I had envisaged, *once the journey got started*. That then, was my first title-anchor – a journey. And, in turn, that meant starting even with the wrong clothes *and* a timescale (another anchor). Then there was the influence of social media, particularly Twitter which can be dangerously filling, with much more impact than many other forms of communication –particularly from good management and business writers (yes, there's narcissistic popcorn too but you can click that away). And finally, there was the mainstay idea itself, that organisations need to reinvent their management, learning and business models together to reach their next stage of development faster. This was the ultimate title-anchor. And even that is shorthand for the launch of a family of struggles: test tools, testing-forums, proof, arguing through 'what's wrong with what we already have', re-assembling ideas and constructing new choices. Eventually, through the journey, this emerged:

- **1 5 1 2** Testing one idea in five organisations over one year through two journeys. And somewhere, the larger heading, *Managing Value*.

As for search engines, why not bridge canyons of categories and grasp what can be found here: individual and collective morality, collective 'wealth', values, business, management, learning, social media and committed direction. And above all, hopeful travelling.

Welcome reader: this is a journey I hope you will experience as *different*.

Participant Organisations and the Relevance of the Work to Other Organisations

All the organisations involved in this work are real. For reasons of confidentiality some have been anonymised. The five participant organisations are from a range of sectors, public, private and not for profit, and are at different stages of development, three being established, one starting-up and one selling-on. Though they are all small, the largest with 20 staff, the overall approach easily applies to any organisation, whether established or starting-up which is struggling to grasp the next stage of development. It could be used in various sections or departments to identify blockages to higher performance though the logic is that eventually it would need to apply to whole organisations. The benefits are its holistic approach, bringing together management, learning and business models for rigorous assessment, and recognising their interdependence. The approach begins by identifying traditional 'limitations', then offers new pathways to build conditions for sustainable development. Also, the value-creating method enables organisations to improve practice *themselves*.

We have not found any other developmental tools which bring together key business 'enablers' in this way.

Acknowledgement

I would like to thank all the organisations who participated, and their staff. Also those who began the inquiry though did not stay all the way, and those small businesses that gave their time and experience.

As well, to Greg Palmer, *Critical Difference*, long-time ally and friend; Claudia Crawley, of *Winning Pathways Coaching*, a consummate nudger in the right direction; and Simon Caulkin, still among the best crafters of ideas on the business pages. At a greater distance, though no less influential, also two strong women: Judith and Rebecca.

'In no society is any product the exclusive result of one person's effort.' John Berger.

Finally: This is for anyone who has struggled … and kept going.

Donal Carroll

PART I
The Background

Introduction: What This Book is About and Who it is For

This is a learning journey over one year, an experiment in how to engage organisational effort, thinking and value for faster, sustained development.

What 'Can't Be Done'

Finbar went to Limerick determined to tackle the epidemic of people living on the streets, many alcohol-dependent. He had no money, and agencies who could have helped didn't because the 'victims' used alcohol. Through his networks, he quickly found a large empty building, got some beds from a local hospital and opened a hostel. That is why today people say 'there is no street homelessness in Limerick'.

During the Thatcher period, there were many community activists like Finbar. If you meet them today their business card says just one word: 'Organiser'. They would rather say that than 'manager' but it means manager too.

This work is for managers: to get excited about a purpose and new ideas, and get on the road with them.

Trusting the *Sense-makers*

This work uses ideas from a range of sources, for instance the history of small businesses, the increasing use of technology and social media, and other issues. The sources are what I call 'sense-makers'. These provide good ideas from reliable, enquiring minds which I trust so don't need to embark on a long trail of 'primary sources' all over again. They include those who write regularly, a demanding means of performance, those who provide surprise and insight to build and use an enquiring readership, like John Naughton and Simon Caulkin. Others are used more indirectly such as Seth Godin, Tara Brabazon, Martin Parker, Studs Terkel, John Berger and Edward Said. Intellectually, as Shelley says in his *A Defence of Poetry*, they provide 'the influence which is moved not, but moves'. At a time when public thinking about management and other key areas seems little more than an uncritical acceptance of an agenda set by market forces, these writers construct something more just. Or to paraphrase George Bernard Shaw, they ensure that if you don't know what you want you won't grow to like just what you get.

On Not Being Academically Safe

This work is not an academic analysis of management, learning and business. Rather it is a putting together of some old and new theories in fresh ways, to experiment with a new approach to find better ways of acting. It won't exhaustively re-examine issues like shareholder value, management, education or learning organisations, but will use a particular view of them to construct new approaches to tackle common and anticipated business problems. The arguments I make with these ideas and all their imperfections then become part of the history of management thinking: grist to the mill, to address problems which should be addressed, using perhaps what shouldn't even be considered.

How to Read This Book

As one manager said, the best metaphor for 'your models' in this work, is career coaching *for organisations*.

Tweeting the Work

1 5 1 2 Testing one idea in five organisations over one year through two journeys.

What is This Book About and Who is it For?

How fast does your world change? Nowadays, when somebody says something can't be done, they are likely to be interrupted by someone who is already doing it.

Here are some striking examples of 'what can't be done':

- For years the streets of Sao Paulo, South America's biggest city, were awash with advertising, so much so that the continent's biggest consumer market was a vortex of chaotic visual debris. Towards the end of 2006, the mayor came up with a solution – all outdoor advertising would be removed *within six months*. The campaign to combat pollution … would start with its most conspicuous form – visual pollution. Advertising companies argued that the ban would damage everything – freedom of speech, jobs, their sector, even the image of the city. Nonetheless, in early 2007, Lei Cidade Limpa (The Clean City Law) came into operation. The effect: the end of outdoor advertising, forcing advertising companies to find more innovative ways to operate and be more effective, including an exploding digital market.[1]

- 'Mobile phones will soon be able to diagnose sexually transmitted diseases … people can put … saliva into a computer chip the size of a USB chip, plug it into their phone and receive a diagnosis within minutes.'[2]

- Traveleyes: setup by a blind entrepreneur, this organisation matches non-sighted travellers with sighted ones who act as their 'eyes' on trips.[3]

- An electric car plugged into a lamp post – which city? Shenzen Huashi Future Parking trialled in Beijing in 2011 and coming to a city near you very soon.[4]

Maybe striking these days… but not that unusual.

Success is an Iceberg

What do these things tell us? Even in a climate of apparently intensifying uncertainty and mandatory austerity-wear, anything is still possible –if

---

1   *The Financial Times*, 7 September 2010.
2   'New test will diagnose sexual diseases via phones' *The Guardian*, 6 November 2010.
3   Graham Snowdon, 'Taking care of business' *The Guardian*, Work 4 December 2010.
4   'The 50 best inventions of 2010' *Time Magazine*, 22 November 2010, p. 55.

somebody believes in it *first*! Value creation, a central concern of this book, begins with somebody imagining the initial ideas which informed these businesses into existence.

The examples here are 'successful' ideas, ones that worked. 'Success' *looks* easy. It hides the scar tissue of its preparation, the flimsiness it can be based on, the ideas that didn't work, the scorching risk for its proposers – not just financial – and the self-inflicted silences which can be exited only through new actions. Not to mention the time it takes to get there: 'successful' entrepreneurs need to remember Jarvis Cocker's (of Pulp) comment, 'It took us 12 years to become an overnight success.'

'Success' has some flaky characteristics. It is invariably applied in retrospect, and has anything but a linear pathway: commonly 'success' claims intention where there is chance and improvisation, and causal lines where there is obliquity. This gives the illusion of control, which can blind us to the organic complexity of things. 'Organic' because problems do not simply repeat themselves, they emerge like a Stonehenge of drunks. Whether they live or die, are tackled or disappear, depends entirely on how they are *framed* by their owners. Crucially, 'success' involves the success–owner's response to all these uncertainties, including the very notion itself.

The examples above might provide promising practice for business builders and entrepreneurs. With hindsight, those involved no doubt knew what they were doing. But did they really? Given that the route to success is by definition uncertain, with considerable U-turns and re-routings, what were they doing when they didn't seem to know what they were doing? The builders of organisational 'success' described here had immense commitment and direction, knew where they were going, and their planning was more than matched with improvisation and, particularly at the initial stage, risk.

A highly successful college vice principal I had the good fortune to work for used to say that plans are tombstones, *planning* is being able to drive past the cemetery. What plan survives its first impact with the enemy (its market)? So these people *knew* all right. But they knew more than 'knowing' and knew 'knowing' is not enough. Man plans, God laughs. What they had was something else, which was crucial: they were able to *increase their rate of learning* when it most mattered – this is not so much what they learned but how they could hurry it into action when they needed to – for instance when significant change occurred in their strategic environment.[5]

Franklin Roosevelt, described by John Kay as the 'most successful US president', understood very well that goals and actions must be constantly revised in order to achieve high-level objectives (overall purpose) and success, even though this term was not used. He described his approach as 'bold, persistent *experimentation*'. Try something – 'if it fails, admit it frankly and try another...' That tiny phrase 'admit it frankly' in many organisations can be a major barrier to success. What FDR achieved was through pragmatic improvisation in the face of unpredictable circumstances and gravely open-ended problems...[6]

So readers may not leave this work 'knowing' in an utterly straightforward way. In this they will be in good company. As Henry Mintzberg said in a recent work, 'I don't want you to leave this knowing ... but, as I do, imagining, reflecting, questioning...'[7] But I hope readers will be excited too by the examples, particularly if they want to build a business and in the process develop *sufficiently agile* hands to grasp the slippery goal of 'success'.

There is that word again – the logical aim of all organisations – isn't it?

Organisational Journey and Personal Journey: The Same Fuel?

As suggested here, success is a complex brew. With participant organisations it emerges as the journey of the work develops and is linked to the relationship between participant organisations and their respective founders – all of whom are still there. How separable are organisations and their founders? What do they bring? Does having 'successful' people inevitably mean successful organisations – created in their image? Does that make them dependent? How can they be independent, sufficiently agile to counter continually changing circumstances? Do successful leaders have – or need – a secret learning source to counter their natural influence?

---

5   Explored more fully in Chapter 6, The Learning Model, p. 91.
6   John Kay (2010) *Obliquity: Why Our Goals are Best Achieved Indirectly* London, Profile Books.
7   Henry Mintzberg (2009) *Managing* Harlow, FT/Prentice Hall, p. 16.

Or, on the other hand, can those who do *not* consider themselves successful, or where it does not seem important, lead or build successful organisations? How relevant is success at all? Though success can be claimed, it is unlikely to result from a breathy perusal of a Richard Branson primer. Is it more accurately captured in Peter Jones's comment[8] that 'enterprise' is not 'the mechanics of setting up a business but a state of mind, a confidence that you have the knowledge *and the right mindset to be successful?'*

What success means to participant organisations is explored in this work. They were complex and confident without claiming 'success', and revealed my initial assumption of an automatic connection between 'successful' people and 'successful' organisations as lazy and simply wrong. However this emerged on the journey of the work in the organisations as did a 'second' journey, that of the writer/writing itself.[9]

One final point: the innovations mentioned at the start all contained other, hidden innovations. These were in how the organisations involved were managed, how they learned collectively, and how they did business. That is, there were probably innovations in their management, learning and business models. These 'models' are the menu of this book and the inquiry journey, what happened, is the meal.

The Organisations

The five organisations involved are at different stages of development. Three are established, one is a start-up and one is being sold ('grow and go'). They are clearly effective so far, that is, in operational terms, they engage effectively in their markets. They can *be regarded* as successful, though as we shall see, this might not be their term. Their next stage will require a different mindset and greater risk – something the inquiry approach seeks to foster.

---

8   So-called enterprise programmes like 'Dragons Den' (the title gives the purpose away) hide as much as they reveal with the mandatory dependence on the 'dragon' leader, usually the source of growth capital, and the casual dumping of otherwise promising ideas they don't like. More positively, there is the occasional good sense of a 'Dragon': Peter Jones, for instance, stating that 'enterprise is not the mechanics of setting up a business but a state of mind, a confidence that you have the knowledge *and the right mindset to be successful'*. Quoted in *The Times Educational Supplement*, FE Focus, 27 August 2010, and *The Guardian*, 31 August 2010.

9   For further exploration of 'success' see Chapter 8. For the 'second' journey see Chapter 11.

What the organisations have in common is that, as businesses, they have already risked their ideas into their markets: who needs for instance, another t-shirt maker, another charity for the vulnerable homeless, another communications company or another local surgery?

While celebrating the *diversity* of these organisations, the work uses the inquiry tools, the three models, to pose a range of questions including: are the models present implicitly or even explicitly? What strengths of their current approach can they build on? How can they enable a different future and get them to their next stage *faster?*

WHO IS THE BOOK FOR?

This is for *practical visionaries*: anyone anywhere who asks 'how can that customer need be better met?', or, 'are there customers for this idea', or, in any organisation who thinks 'surely we can do better', or, even 'why are we doing this in the first place?' It is for those whose imagination has become engaged by dissatisfaction with current provision and *want to do something about it.* These initial questions, these tin-openers, are the first inkling of new value creation (as defined here).

The book is aimed at entrepreneurs and at those broadly in the business of 'management': practising managers; those responsible for change and improvement in organisations; change leaders, coaches, consultants, scholars and researchers. It is for staff in organisations seeking organisational improvement, those struggling with the limitations of what they know but without (yet) the confidence or fuel to get them beyond this, and those who need external help or prompts to re-recognise where they are now in order to change it. Or those who think the impossible can't be reached. It offers new ideas for old problems for better outcomes – as much for successful organisations and people as those not so.

It will interest managers in all sectors, consultants, HR managers, managers and teachers in further and higher education and in business schools, some of whose assumptions (using my experience of working in one for ten years) it challenges.

For the Reader

This work also seeks to capture the excitement of management innovation, its 'poetry and plumbing' distilled from this journey. And to remind us that in business, as in so many other areas, the first revolution is a new idea, and that new ideas are the natural predator of problems. This work offers the hope that readers experience it in the words of the editor, as 'cost-conscious poetry'!

Finally, it also seeks *more from everybody*: idea-luggers, managers, staff, owners, academics, shopkeepers ... those who produce and consume value, particularly when they might not consider that that is exactly what they are doing. If 'the future is already here – it is just unevenly distributed' how can all organisations get some more of it?

2

The Purpose, the Organisations, the Journey, the Start

For the reader, this section could be called, 'What you're letting yourself in for'.

The purpose is to develop some new ideas which claim to sustainably improve performance and test them. This work is 'applied business research'. It is an inquiry approach using three 'models' based on key principles of 'management', 'business' and 'learning' theories to examine and enable organisational development.

The 'models' are:

- Management model: the choices made about how organisational effort is organised (the *how* of business).

- Business model: the choices made about how organisational value is created, delivered and captured (the *what and why* of business).

- Learning model: the choices made about how organisational thinking is mobilised (the *what best next*).

The Hypothesis

The claim of the work is that reinventing their three 'models' *together* will enable organisations to reach their next stage of development *faster*. This will involve them, *as necessary*, making explicit choices about their three models and also exploring new 'value'. Behind this claim is another one, that the thinking in management, learning and business, their 'theories-in-use', which has got them this far, will be a barrier to future development and through this can be reinvented. It involves them using a radical, value-creating inquiry method to test this out, with free support.

The Journey: Building the Transport System

This may seem fairly obvious: just apply and go! Rinse the organisations in these new ideas and leave them shining! What I had not realised at this stage was that *everything had to be built*: the methods, the relationships, the thinking behind the claim – and had to be maintained. Just as (we assumed) the organisations had growing pains – even that had to be nailed as an issue – so did this work. Two journeys were emerging: the ideas through the organisations and that of the writer. *This is airbrushed with what happened and what we hoped wouldn't.*

What this journey is not is a bloodless imposition of its method on organisational life, or a corralling of defenceless data into what we already know. It's a journey into the less known.

As mentioned in the Preface, it is one I hope the reader experiences as original and *different*.

So much for the certainties: at this stage they seemed few and far between. Here are a few more... tickets to a purpose in various forms of idea-transport.

The Organisations: Generating Interest

The organisations were initially from our professional networks and contacts. However, what I initially envisaged, a mix of one large, one small, one medium, and one from each sector, was not what emerged. For instance, there were also a number of college principals who were very interested but because of restructuring and key contacts moving on, did not continue. The process of approaching organisations and getting feedback on possible interest all took time. Eventually, as the work was becoming 'an experiment over one year', I decided that by a certain date I would start with the organisations with whom I had gained a foothold rather than wait any longer for further 'expressions of interest' to mature. In order to get going at all, you must start with what you have. This is to follow the yet-to-emerge principles of the value-creating method: to start meaningfully rather than perfectly.

We invited interested organisations to test out the claim that to manage *value in organisations sustainably involved using three new models to enable faster development* and included the above outline. We stressed the benefits that the work was time-limited – over one year – and they could draw on free support to enable them to test this out.

Support was provided by the Critical Difference Consultancy (www.criticaldifference.co.uk) and Winning Pathways Coaching (www.winningpathwayscoaching.com).[1]

It is hard to say if this applied business research 'experiment' would have actually occurred without this support or whether it would just have taken much longer. As one manager said, 'It was good it came along when it did as it helped them do *what they should have been doing anyway* ... well supported and for free!'

The organisations do not necessarily connect, other than in facing common problems. They were established and effective, with immense, untapped developmental potential, and facing the question of how – or if – they should harness this. Of the five organisations who did eventually participate we were fortunate in having one at each stage of the business cycle, starting, continuing and finishing.

The Organisations

These consisted of three established, one start-up, and one selling-on.

THE THREE ESTABLISHED ORGANISATIONS

1.   Believe

- Established: 2000 (and operating for five years before that).
- Size: Four full-time staff, many volunteers and around 250 clients (continually expanding).
- Type: Registered charity (private, limited by guarantee).
- Purpose: 'Helping people reconnect with their homeland.'

---

1   Further details of this support are given in Chapter 6, Building the New Models, p. 131.

2. Health House

    – Established: 2004 as part of an overall social enterprise company.
    – Size: Around 20 staff (full and part time), approx. 4,000 patients (stable over five years).
    – Type: Private limited company.
    – Purpose: 'Providing NHS care for patients with some private services.'

3. Philosophy Football Limited

    – Established: 1994.
    – Size: Three full-time, two part-time staff with some highly resourceful, well-connected associates.
    – Type: Private limited company.
    – Purpose: 'Sporting outfitters of intellectual distinction.'

THE START-UP ORGANISATION

4. Social Stock Exchange

    – Established: Will commence trading in 2012.
    – Type: Private limited company.
    – Size: Four to ten full-time staff envisaged.
    – Purpose: 'To contribute to changing the world by funding social mission organisations.'

THE SELLING-ON ORGANISATION

5. Cognac

    – Established: 2005.
    – Type: Private limited company.
    – Size: Four to seven full-time staff (varies).
    – Purpose: 'To communicate anything in ten minutes.'

Other Organisations

Interested organisations, some of whom had gone some way with the research though did not continue, included: London Duck Tours, Zaytoun and ScraperWiki.

Other organisations who helpfully gave their time on issues of 'success', their experience of managing small businesses, and the next stage of development included Printalicious, Hair Designs and Abbey Lofts.

SpecificMedia were also involved in applying, tracking and evaluating the models.

What Next?

All that was needed now was to find a way to get this on the road and start testing what we were about to build – *and* simultaneously..

- Our map: the purpose and our conviction from previous experience that the old models would not suffice.

- Our crash helmets: increasing our rate of learning – with much more of this to come.

Exciting: yes!

The Journey Begins Here

First there are some things to do to establish our case: we have to identify our context, build an appropriate inquiry approach, get evidence of the limitations of current approaches and why a new one is needed, and finally, construct the backbone of the piece, the new models. And then the feasting – applying them.

We would ask the reader to be patient with us in these steps: building our argument is part of the journey too.

3

Context: Collapsonomics, Change Gridlock, More of the Same? Or Just a Bonfire of the Certainties?

Introduction

This section outlines the current business context and its attendant uncertainties, which bring a range of perceptions about change: is 'everything changing' or just some things, while others stay the same, and what are the implications for planning and managing a business? Do organisations respond to 'more for less' with the same thinking and do 'more of the same'? Or is the 'crisis' an opportunity for radical change? Or do they do 'the wrong thing righter'?[1] How should they plan for such uncertainty?

Managing, Coping or Thriving?

> *I think the most important word this year will be reinvention. Be it companies, careers, institutions, public services – you name it, wholesale renewal is required. The dislocation from such a transformation will be uncomfortable for many, but the outcome will prove invigorating. And the alternative of just carrying on as normal will ultimately prove far more painful. In fields as diverse as state education, book publishing, retailing and financial services, brand new ways of doing things must be found. The old models are mostly failing.*[2]

---

1   Russell L. Ackoff and Herbert J. Addison (2007) *Management f-Laws*. Axminster, Triarchy Press Ltd.
2   Luke Johnson, 'Recovery demands a clear-out of the old guard', *The Financial Times*, 17 March 2010.

Doom and gloom, apocalyptical, self-promoting? Note the source, an entrepreneur and private equity company director (such funders were instrumental in creating the current economic problems) but also a highly successful chair of Channel 4.

Now look at this, published on the same day:

> *The current crisis for public services is not just about debt and spending restraint. After years of investment, reform and commitment from our workforce, our public services are failing many of the people who depend on them most. We need an approach that goes 'beyond Beveridge'. His principles which still define the contours of our welfare state, have served us well, but changing times need a new approach. Out interim report (Commission on 2020 Public Services) sets out three building blocks that we think can form the basis of a consensual vision: a shift in culture from social security to social productivity; a shift in power from the centre to citizens; and a shift in finance, reconnecting it with the purposes the services are intended to achieve. Overall our vision is for a new public service settlement that enables citizens to be in control of their own lives and able to take greater responsibility for themselves and others...*[3]

Again, this source has form, its author Sir Andrew Foster having chaired the influential 'Realising the Potential' review[4] which brought significant national focus, resources and resultant improvements to colleges in the Learning and Skills sector. He 'theorised' the policy changes necessary, an important way of expressing change, which this work notes. But is he saying the same thing as Luke Johnson (above) – that we have a choice? Act as normal will mean a slow death or change – radically!

Foster starts his piece saying, 'Cutting public services without paying attention to what kind of society we want to build is like wielding an axe with our eyes closed. The big challenges we face are the elephant in the room ... and we need to articulate the fundamental choices ahead and the risks...'

The message (from these sources anyway) seems to be that fundamental change is needed. What can we learn about the need for change – or not – from other current business practice which are far from unusual, shown below?

---

3   Sir Andrew Foster, 'Bringing Beveridge up to speed' Chair of the Commission on 2020 Public Services, *The Guardian*, 17 March 2010.
4   The (then) Department for Education and Science, 2005.

Business and Change: Old Practices, Old Business?

The Phoenix 4, a group of four experienced businessmen, bought MG Rover from BMW for £10 and managed it till it became bankrupt in April 2005. A September 2009 report by the National Audit Office (NAO) stated that the company pursued to its logical conclusion certain business habits: maximising short-term personal gain; avoiding tax; hiding poor performance in a web of technical complexity; seeking exorbitant remuneration while shedding personal accountability; seeing the main stakeholders as themselves. What did they learn? That this was considered ordinary practice in the business world.[5] If that is so, shouldn't we request that 'return on investment' calculations include the benefits of learning and *the cost of not learning*?

Learning and Change: Web 2.0, Old Learning?

This is an exchange between two consultants working on a change programme with middle and senior managers, in a large private sector company, a minor part of which involved the managers contributing to an easily accessible Web 2.0 forum based on the issues they were jointly experiencing:

C1 (consultant 1): They won't contribute! Web 2.0, social media is too new – I told you this would happen.

C2 (consultant 2): How exactly did you initiate the forum with them?

C1: I told them it was there and available – twice…

C2: Anything more?

C1: No – why should I? They're adults after all and experienced managers!

C2: What learning culture did you seek to develop?

C1: What's that? Anyway, the result is what I said would happen… they can't use IT, even though they seem to be on it all the time.

---

5   'The Phoenix four personified the age of greed' Editorial, *The Observer*, 13 September 2009.

C2: Well – either that or their weak contributing may be the first indicator of their resistance to change.

Experience and Change: Old Habits and the Need for New 'Managing'?

An exchange between a manager and an experienced college teacher, being informed that redundancy was possible due to fewer enrolments on one of his courses:

M (manager): What did you make of trends over the last three years in your course?

T (teacher): I notice students not trends.

M: There were continually decreasing numbers and no improvement in success rates.

T: Trends, success rates… I haven't time for all those or for evaluating round the clock! That's not my job. Anyway, what do you expect with this type of student?

M: More importantly, what do you expect?

T: Anyway what would you know about it – you're just a manager – you've never taught. It was much better in the past when we were left alone to get on with it and used our own judgment.

M: Get on with what?

T: Teaching – what do you think? This management and business-speak is irrelevant.

M: If that's the case – what *business are you in*?

These examples illustrate aspects of ordinary business which are not working, or are working badly, and are evidence of what needs to change. The practices do not lead to greater organisational effectiveness and result in 'failure' at three interlinked, yet distinct levels: management, business and learning. These are:

- In example 1 at the business level, which serves individual interests rather than all stakeholder interests.

- In example 2 at the learning level, where those employed to remedy the problem, the consultants, rehearse an argument about the need to increase *their* own rate of learning, rather than seek comfort in old learning regardless of customer-provided evidence of it not working; there is also the impression that while the consultancy makes claims for 'unique bespoke solutions', the customer, the organisation, gets the same consultancy provision regardless of any different problems they experience,

- In example 3 there is evidence of a dangerous assumption that *experience begets excellence* rather than its opposite; it also begs the question of the kind of management model which enabled this teacher practice for so long. But then, as many education organisations discovered, the quality of a system cannot exceed the quality of its members. The question the manager poses at the end (what business are they in?) is a good starting point for this whole organisation to agree on.

If these are representative, and there are plenty of other examples around, then something needs to be changed. The perspective of this work is that we do need to change: not changing is a far more costly option. However, choices emerging from exhortations to 'change or die' need to be painstakingly created. They require leadership at a level of practice *and* theory. But changes in what exactly?

I suggest that significant change needs to occur in three areas, called 'models' here: the management model, business model and what should be the glue between them, the learning model.

Changing What? Practice *and* Theory

However, be warned: even if the accumulated practices in dominant management, business and learning do not seem to be distinct 'models', they all have powerful influence. They have currency, momentum, are the accumulations of traditional practice and theory, are notoriously slippery, are both more *and* less than what they seem, and should not be taken at face value.

At least one, the management model, has been the 'elephant in the room', having serviced business for over 100 years, and hidden its responsibility in the current state of affairs, which is as much a management crisis as an economic one. However, integrally, and in some cases as much by absence as presence, all three models have been instrumental in the current crisis. This work offers a way to reinvent them all.

But don't *all* new business and management books claim to do this? What is different here is the central argument and claim that change cannot occur without a key recognition that organisations which use the old 'models' unquestioningly condemn their future to the past. In other words, the key management, business and learning ideas that got companies this far have now become barriers to getting them further. These approaches are deeply embedded and are default selections with the economic crisis having accelerated their effects rather than caused them. So if these approaches have not changed, what has and is there always a sting in the tail of 'change'?

The Bonfire of the Certainties?

Even though there is a perception that everything is changing –what has actually? Ideas of leadership and what a business is, let alone a successful one, now seem less reliable and to carry less trust and weight. At the same time, instant gratification, and not just in the form of short-term shareholder value, is demanded of everything:

- *I want it now!*: The impatient tempo of business life is accelerating. Businesses are now shorter lasting. In 1950, the average life of a company (according to S+P) was 47 years and by 2020 will fall to ten; the average tenure of a CEO is less than five years; strategy life cycles are shrinking, industry leadership is changing hands more frequently, and competitive advantage is eroded more rapidly. In the private sector, governance mechanisms and the overwhelming use of shareholder value for measuring purposes have fuelled this intensely. Similarly, in the public sector. The increasing senior manager turnover rate in the Learning and Skills sector suggests that, 'Principals are like football managers – you don't last long if you don't get results.'[6] And to this we should add the turbulent history of small businesses, participants here.

6   Peter Kingston, 'No-win situation?', *Education Guardian*, 5 February 2008.

- *Receding leadership*: The claims for heroic, testosterone-fuelled leadership are challenged increasingly with evidence that characteristics of effective leadership indicate more 'professional humility and personal resolve' and 'servant leadership' in long-term successful companies. Traditional sources of leadership now seem more deficient than ever: for instance, in the financial sector (and elsewhere) claims that this is where 'the best minds go', that they are 'doing God's work' (Goldman Sachs) and are 'slaves of the market' (CEO, RBS) or that Lehman Brothers had 'to be sacrificed so capitalism could survive' are revealed as self-interested, defensive routines used to justify the unjustifiable.

- *What is a business?* Even business *purpose* and *how to do business* are now emerging as far from given. Previously what was assumed as obvious, the single-minded pursuit of stakeholder value, now seems the ultimate business corruption and, according to General Electric's legendary Jack Welch, 'The dumbest idea in the world.'[7] Classically mistaking the score for the game, this measure distracts completely from the need to sustain great products, loyal customers and committed staff. Further, recent research suggests that achieving sustained success while experiencing significant changes comes from a mix of characteristics, the most important of which is continuity – though it seems the opposite – and: 'the reinvention of the company's distinctive business model to fit with prevailing market conditions'.[8] Paywall, anyone? So business models are now not settled once and for all but require sustained thinking from everyone in the organisation developed through 'distributed leadership', not just ascribed 'leaders'.

- *What is a successful business?* Again, this is now not as clear as previously assumed. And who can we trust to tell the tale? Though it was the late 1980s, how many of the best companies from Tom Peters's *In Search of Excellence* (1982) remain? Or more up to date, have those identified as excellent by Jim Collins, in *Good to Great*[9] survived the refutation of his construction in Rosenzweig's *The*

---

7   Andrew Hill, 'Real value looks past quarterly reporting', *The Financial Times*, 19 April 2011, frequently quoted, here as 'its strategic primacy as the dumbest idea in the world' Also *The Observer*, 14 March 2010.
8   Stefan Stern, 'Master the mix of continuity and change', *The Financial Times*, 20 January 2010.
9   Jim Collins (2001) *Good to Great*. London, Random House.

Halo Effect?[10] Or how does 'successful business' square with Collins's own carefully considered monograph aimed at public sector organisations (the social sector in the USA) exhorting that 'business thinking is not the answer'?[11] There is a further emerging conundrum: who actually owns an organisation? In an era of high-speed trading, where 'investors' *own* shares for a nanosecond[12] and where 'latencies', the time taken to complete a trade – are down to *98 microseconds* – as financiers seek competitiveness in even greater speeds, who owns what?[13] What does this do for the long-term purpose of organisations – the reason they should exist? Further, what can they learn from companies like Bose, the high-end music system company where 'patient investing' has kept the company in private hands with longer lasting, more durable performance and incredibly high staff and customer satisfaction rates?

Turmoil *not* Change?

Until recently, anyone who suggested nationalising the banks would have been called a quack. The grip of 'orthodoxy' disqualified the idea and many more without the need to even offer a counter-argument ... And yet when it seems everything should change paradoxically it feels like very little has...'[14] (See also 'Note' at the end of this chapter.)

Of course perception that the 'givens have gone' does not make it so. Change seems to register as 'collapsonomics' (the certainties), change gridlock (everything) or more of the same (it just *seems* so with in reality no change). For the purpose of this work, here are the key elements, causes and effects of change, what has not changed and what should.

More of the Same

Many organisations have responded to the 'more for or less' climate with 'more of the same' by downsizing, getting rid of staff and broadly seeking even more

---

10 Phil Rosenzweig (2007) *The Halo Effect*. New York, Free Press.
11 Jim Collins (2006) *Good to Great and the Social Sectors*. London, Random House Books.
12 Simon Caulkin 'On management: cheques and balances', *The Financial Times*, 6 December 2010.
13 *New York Times*, 23 January 2011 supplement included in *The Observer*, 23 January 2011.
14 Rodrigo Nunes (2009) 'What were you wrong about ten years ago?', *Turbulence: Ideas for Movement*, 5 December, p. 40.

control rather than more trust. If the new 'stable' environment is 'uncertainty', which can seem contradictory and paradoxical, where one moment there is too much information and the next too little, few seemed to have approached it to fundamentally re-examine their purpose and market and develop new skills around how customers give 'attention', or rigorously analyse the data they have already given to explore new opportunities.[15] Some examples of this are staff in participant organisations using customer 'attention' and analytics to (1) actively seek customer engagement to clarify anew their idea of 'value'; and (2) engage loyal customers about their 'unmet needs'; or (3) re-examine 'attribution', the point-of-sale decisions buyers make through advertising and online. But these are broadly exceptions.

Henry Mintzberg[16] talks about 'management' being neither a science nor profession, nor in continuous change, and that we 'risk being mesmerised by the present and biased by stories we know...' This could be applied to the thinking of many organisations caught by having to respond to new uncertainties by doing more of the same, probably more desperately. This is because managers have not interrogated the thinking behind their thinking, the first stage of change, without which the second stage, that of building alternatives, is unlikely to happen.

Identifying, interrogating and reinventing this thinking is a key theme of this work.

Some Givens Going

TRUST IN THE PROFESSIONALS

J.K. Galbraith's comment that economists are 'experts who will know tomorrow that the things they predicted yesterday won't happen today' has considerable traction now. The idea of an 'efficient market' with elegant, complex computer models to deliver its promise, is greeted with well-earned cynicism.

And who now trusts 'business as usual'? For example, banks too big to fail, the best minds go into finance, markets know best, financial innovation is socially useful, managers without a moral compass should be free to self-regulate?

---

15 Cathy Davidson, 'So last century', *Times Higher Education*, 28 April 2011, pp. 30–36.
16 Henry Mintzberg (2009) *Managing*. Harlow, FT/PrenticeHall, p. 13.

Further, given that 'management' was the elephant in the room in the lead up to and during the financial mess, who now trusts 'managers know best'?

The 'cradle to grave' models?

Social work

Social care professionals had been working with families with multiple challenges, over many years at a huge cost to the state, with little effect. Eventually they adopted a new approach, working with a multidisciplinary team (housing, police, NHS, Connexions, children and adult services) which proved far more effective. But to do so they had to reinvent their traditional model and 'quietly ripped up all the rules of conventional social work practice'.[17] This included: moving from the 'professionals know best' and a model of 'rescuing' rather than empowering the families, to one of radically engaging both themselves and the families by putting the families in the driving seat through every stage of the process including having the families 'recruit' the professionals they want to work with. This was fuelled by a new model of working based round a revolutionary idea of 'love' expressed as 'trust, respect, non-judgmentalism and a willingness to share who you are'. This turned upside down the usual conventions of the distant professional making decisions for others. Through this they forged four capabilities with the families. The first thing both families and professionals had to do was *learn faster* and this included unlearning much of their previous thinking.

It is worth stating that not all certainties have 'gone' even though many would prefer they had. Some live on in zombie form, for instance the 'certainty of efficient markets', an expensive, well-constructed, pervasive myth to advantage certain groups revealed as 'reading charts was no better than alchemy'[18] (see also 'Note').

And some certainties are more painful to let go than others. The new approach above led to considerable argument among social workers themselves. It was painful to recognise that their current model had diminishing returns, but it was the first stage of in-building the changes needed to generate greater value in a new one.

Some implications are considered below in 'effects'.

---

17 Madeleine Bunting 'Up close and personal', *The Guardian*, Society, 9 February 2011.
18 James Mackintosh 'The short view' from 'A random walk down Wall Street' by Burton Milkiel, *The Financial Times*, 4 February 2011.

Management

One obvious effect of the current management model is that so many organisations are *less* capable collectively than the people (individually) who work there. As Gary Hamel writes: 'The machinery of modern management gets opinionated, free-spirited human beings to conform to standards and rules but in doing so squanders prodigious quantities of human imagination and initiative … imperils organisational adaptability … and enslaves millions in quasi-feudal top-down organisations.'[19]

Business

Yes, the climate offers great opportunities to develop new business models but this is in great measure because current provision is so poor. For all the investment, resourcing, new ways and channels, business still cannot provide customers what they want, on time, every time. And continual service improvement is still the exception rather than the rule. Paradoxically, poor service can create customer dependence. As a senior manager said to us during a consultancy assignment with a large public sector organisation, 'The system we pay for can't do what we want and slows us down but we are trapped with it', turning what should be 'masters' into 'servants'.

Learning

If learning really is the sole means of competitive advantage, many managers and organisations still consider it irrelevant, or fail to articulate it; for instance in discussions for this work, only one participant used the term, and then extremely well, while in another assignment they used any *term* but 'learning' to describe it. The effect is to make them even more dependent on what they have already learned both in form (how: usually from an expert) and content (what: with an unacknowledged sell by date and also static). As another manager said, 'Why can't things be more certain?' To the reply that the only way to make it more certain was 'faster learning' the response was that this was too hard.

---

19   Gary Hamel (2007) *The Future of Management*. Boston, Harvard Business School Press, p. 8.

Some Effects

MULTIPLYING DEPENDENCE

From the perspective of this work there are two elements which denote a decaying model –perhaps three if we include the inevitable vociferous professional defence which denies the evidence. These elements create a triple dependency, as the decaying models: (1) generate dependence in its customers; and (2) generate dependence in the professionals themselves, who now accept it unthinkingly, so any new thinking – and eventually new models – must be forced in from the outside, as in the social work example above, through a consultancy; and thus (3) create a deeper form of dependence, the conditions of which many organisations unconsciously build.[20]

This can be seen in the anguished comment a senior public sector manager recently made to me: 'They're still here – poor performers – how do we get rid of underperformers?' It's one legacy of 100 years of a traditional management model. A far better question would have been 'How can we build a high performance culture?' But why hadn't he posed that? 'Ah well… too much new thinking, leadership, change – and above all, learning needed.' When I asked about the cost of *not* doing this he replied: 'Too radical to consider.' Trapped in previous thinking and models, he is imprisoned in the triple dependency above without the capacity to address the problems they have created, he will always need external help.

A key challenge of the new models here is that organisations must know not only what their current models are (the thinking behind their thinking) but even if they are going well, how to challenge them 'productively'. (See Chapter 6, 'Building the Models'.)

THE 'LONG FAIL'?

Just to endorse the fact that 'the future isn't what it used to be': without changing these models and increasing learning how can any organisation create opportunities from current continuing changes? Here are a just a random range

---

[20] There is a deeper political dependence when all the old models come together: for example, Government assuming market competition propels improvement and unwilling to promote the idea 'that public sector staff *themselves* can work with citizens and politicians to creatively improve the services…' Jane Dudman 'Choosing words carefully', *The Guardian*, 13 May 2009, quoting from 'Public Sector Reform … But Now as We Know It' by Hilary Wainwright and Mathew Little.

of some possible 'trends': there is a decline in (USA) households owning TV sets; 68 per cent of the FTSE 100 companies have seen a drop in traffic to their own websites – sometimes considerable; and sales of both DVDs and CDs have fallen by 20 per cent or more in the last year.[21]

What's Not Changed... Though Contradictorily, Public Perceptions May Have

THE IMPORTANCE OF PURPOSE IN WORK

We have come a long way since Margaret Thatcher asked a manager working in a nationalised industry why he 'couldn't get a real job'. (As a tease for the reader, just to emphasise how far we seem to have come, who said this: 'I am extremely proud of our country's public services and of the talented people who work in them'? Yes, David Cameron, quoted in Society *Guardian* 25 May 2011)! As well, claims of superior private sector value and an inferior public sector are being challenged; the sense of unifying purpose public sector work provides in serving communities, compared to making money, is now sought by private sector workers: 'Private sector workers are more than twice as likely as their public sector counterparts to think the grass is greener on the other side, according to exclusive research for "Work".'[22]

THE CHANGING NATURE OF WORK

Too many organisations actively endorse a twentieth century world of hierarchy and vertical management which poorly prepares for twenty-first century work where:

(1) Autonomy through earned trust motivates staff; (2) virtual working enables an accountable 'absenteeism' rather than uncommitted presenteeism, or where employees design their own work days and are evaluated solely on results like the Results Only Work Environment;[23] and (3) the internet, the web

---

21 John Naughton 'Are we really about to say goodbye to TV and DVDs?', *The Observer*, 24 April 20011 and Tim Bradshaw 'The fickle value of friendship', *The Financial Times*, 31 March 2011.

22 David Brindle 'See you on the other side', *The Guardian*, Work, 23 January 2010.

23 http://www.fastcompany.com/1724839/what-it-takes-to-be-a-great-employer. Accessed 9 February 2011.

and social media[24] promote a more 'democratic' horizontal, information flow, challenging the vertical flows of previous models and increasing the demand for greater autonomy and trust.

So...

Overall these developments emphasise the need to continuously develop capacity, to enable greater agility, resilience and growth. It also means putting value creation at the core of business; value creation is expressed in this work as the need for all managers to increase their rate of learning *first*! As we later suggest, this is extremely unlikely with current habits. Also the more uncertain climate needs risk, nerve and soft steering hands, and is more akin to surfing than driving.

As Einstein remarked, no problem can be solved with the same level of consciousness that created it. This work gives an opportunity for participant organisations to 'reboot' with the upgraded software of new learning, management, and business approaches.

Note

On the second anniversary of what many commentators called the 'death of market fundamentalism', it now seems that investment bankers are 'back on top'.

> *The 'non-financial economy', that is business and production, which banks are supposed to service, continues to suffer difficulties in gaining necessary credit and 'non-financial' output has not regained pre-crisis levels.*[25]

This is to be expected in a world which to many, remains turned upside down: more money can still be made from betting on failure than investing in organisations seeking sustainable success for all their stakeholders.

---

24 'How Generation Y is Changing Management Work' and 'The Changing Face Of Employee Engagement', in 'How Social Networks Can Improve Interaction, Motivation and Performance'. Presentations by Peter Cheeseman of Accenture and Bruce Rayner, of Choose You at Work, at MLab, London Business School, November 2009.
25 John Kay 'Why we must press on with breaking up banks', *The Financial Times*, 19 September 2010.

So in a world where everything *seems* to be changing, where highly profiled selfish behaviour results in little change, where self-interest and ethics seem elided, and certainties slippery, what endures, what sustains? Which organisations will be brave about purpose, wellbeing for all and mobilising commitment? How can our 'unit of impact', our participants, smaller businesses, grasp the implications quicker? Or build on their current strengths to seize greater opportunities?

What Next?

This is what this work seeks to find out. First, we must build a research method or inquiry approach, as examined in the next chapter.

4

Research Method or Inquiry Approach: A Value-creating Method and the Research Sequence

Methodology is a cruel word for 'how'.[1] But somebody made it cruel. Maybe they thought it would give precision to how we should think about different 'subjects' or fields'. Or be a sturdy fence to separate them. But how do we get into the 'fields'? Is the methodology the door? How easy is it to get from the methodology to the field? And when we get there, knackered with methodology, how worthwhile has the trip been? Or have we two parallel constructions, powerfully ignoring each other, the methodology and the field? And, largely because of this, do we end up with 'ponderous confirmations of the obvious' and a 'weighty investigation of trivia' *about the field*? I'll leave the sources of these quotes to later.

If, as above, 'methodology is a cruel word for 'how' shouldn't we be also asking how to *what*? This is easy: how to produce insights and new thinking about the field. If that is so easy why do we need a methodology at all? Why not march into the field where the animals are at play and observe them – that should give us insights marinated in their lived experience? Hold on. If that is what we want why not carry the method into the field, plant it and let it grow there; the method is itself as much a subject of construction and investigation as what is happening in the field.

So rather than being part of an industry separating practice from theory, the method here seeks to keep them *productively intimate*.

---

1   Donal Carroll (1981) *Don't You Believe It!* London, The Macmillan Press.

Managers are always urged to 'walk the walk' more (put particular theories into practice). How innovative would it be if they 'talked the talk' more, could examine the effectiveness of the theories themselves? And what effect this would have on performance?

I wanted something to restore blood and imagination to 'method' or at the very least express it so managers would be less contemptuous, or afraid of it and give it the respect it requires. After all that's what methodologies are supposed to explain.

Thus, there are three discussions of method overall, tacking the issue from different angles. All, I hope, are mutually reinforcing and give a fuller exploration. The different discussions and their locations are as follows:

1. 'The Research Method: What It Is and What It Is Not' follows immediately below. This chapter ends with 'The Research Sequence', how this method will be employed.

2. 'Giving Method the Shadow: Embracing Ambiguity' describes the writing experience of endless running between theory and practice, the 'reciprocal to-ing and fro-ing necessary to create anew...' This is in a box at the end of this chapter.

1. 'A Musing on Method': This is a discursive conversation in Chapter 11: The Journey, as part of the 'Imaginative Edge for Competitive Edge' final section.

Research Method: What It Is and What It Is Not

Spit on the rhymes and arias and the rose bush and other such mawkishness from the arsenal of the arts... Give us new forms...[2]

What do business books generally offer? How new is their newness – nothing but the same old story? What would a new offer look like? Would business writing improve if it followed the imperative above? What are the current

---

2   Victor Serge (1991) *Year One of the Russian Revolution.* London, Pluto, quoting Mayakovsky in Simon Behrman (2010) *Shostakovich, Socialism, Stalin and Symphonies.* London, Redwords.

'rhymes, arias, rosebush and mawkishness' of business books?[3] What would 'new forms' look like? With a nudge from this unusual source, this work seeks to overcome the predictable rhymes of many business books, offer a new form of applied business research and raise the business imagination. 'New forms' are explored below but apply to the whole work.

To develop the quote above, I would imagine the 'rhymes, arias, and rosebushes' in business writing take the form of sealed comforts of completeness, unruly concepts seemingly handcuffed with definition, trussed traumas, snake-oil, or the supposed easy transplant of 'what works' onto what doesn't without the messy effort of learning and change. On the other hand, some of these things might eventually occur, though not without considerable crafting, that is, *work of the imagination*. This tension between what's known and how to unearth what is not (yet) – is it a 'rhyme' or an insight – informs this whole work and may be the first challenge for a reader, and indeed for the writer.

Identifying the research method, will examine why the old – and current – forms ('the arias, rosebushes' and so on) are incapable of enabling new insights and developments, and how they can be overcome in new – and more risky inquiry forms. These are needed to help organisations understand and thrive in the current business landscape: where 'normal' is uncertainty, a continually shortening timescale, where the smooth running of the routine is wobbling fiercely, and events and problems outpace the capacity of old approaches to solve them: where the greatest risk is probably not taking any. It might also be where future organisations need poets as much as managers and vision as much as resource-muscle.

What Research Method Does This Work Need?

Regardless of what they may be called, *any* method needs to be rigorous and reliable, stand up to critical scrutiny and be credible to all involved – organisations, participants and readers. It needs to 'fit' the issues it seeks to

---

3   It will certainly aim to be the opposite of many business offers: just add your pin number, click, and all the answers to the problems you face in 'your world' rush breathlessly in. One recently chirruped 'I can only imagine how thrilled you are with just him (a Dragon's Den panellist, not UK, but the same idea) and me (the company owner/executive) and not a room full of hundreds and hundreds of attendees'. The expensive 'invitation' went on in full glib-guru mode: 'just wish and it's there'. This is just one example from an increasing range of small business approaches.

address and be sufficiently agile to stay open, to hear and capture emergent thinking.

For participant organisations particularly, it must provide a meaningful challenge, initiate and sustain their interest and do more than abstractly apply new hypotheses to their circumstances. To get to the heartlands of their concerns directly and smartly, and address them anew, it should be inventive, exciting, stimulating and produce benefits. It would be tempting to use, as a recent Harvard Business Review article did, an approach which is 'a combination of anthropology, journalism and empathy'[4] but reinvented, using sociology, politics, observation and provocative empathy. This might still be tempting, even under a different name.

However, for the methods and journey of this work to seek risk, be challenging and adventurous, it must *create value*. This means offering business research in a different way by identifying the limitations of traditional research including how participants perceive these and identifying how these can be tackled. These are addressed in two sections: 'Background issues' and 'Approach'.

Background Issues

CONSIDERING 'APPLIED BUSINESS RESEARCH'

This work is 'applied business research'. However, the dominant perception many organisations have of 'research' is that 'applied' or not, it is 'academic' – too far removed from their practice to matter to them. As one manager said, it already sounds abstract and tends to go down like a French kiss at a family reunion. Another said when, as previously agreed, we turned up to discuss the use of the three models, that today he didn't feel like 'doing theory' as he didn't 'feel like thinking' – though he knew he would have to do it 'sometime'. Another commented that research is usually 'done *to* them – how traditional research occurs'.

There was also a comment that 'research' was an industry separating theory and practice. In our early discussions the issue of theory always occurred: where does theory 'live' – or belong? Isn't it invariably 'hidden' in practice? Do

---

4   Lew McCreary (2010) 'Innovation on the front line', *Harvard Business Review*, September 2010, p. 92.

we need to identify the theory in order to change the practice? Yes. However, theory, though omnipresent should not be seen as omniscient. Thus, our starting point is to enable organisations themselves to identify theories they currently use from actual evidence in their practice, and crucially, to examine their adequacy. Further, the research method needed to convince them that it would produce appropriate benefits.

Traditional Research: What to Avoid

The approach needed to tackle elements of traditional research which could be barriers – if you like, which create 'mawkishness'. Traditional research is commonly informed by the various stages of 'scientific method'[5] which attempts to ensure neutrality and objectivity of research and results – all necessary aspects. However, traditional research can become a form of 'academic purity' with formalised, safety-seeking methods used like a risk-extractor to burn inventive angles of inquiry, or fearful thinking where any minor contradictions get rinsed out, or any half interesting assertion removed if it can't be triangulated for truth-depth. The results deliver far less than is possible, and can determine the finding, *reproduced safety* – what is already known. It is what Charles Handy meant when he talks of 'ponderous confirmation of the obvious' and 'weighty investigation of trivia'.[6] So for this work to generate new insights, we need to retain some strengths of traditional research while risking more to prompt challenge, contradiction, innovation and insight – that is, new thinking.

Method: Master or Servant?

There is a well known put down by one economist of another: 'If you think you don't have a theory you are invariably in thrall to a deeper one.' If theory is everywhere it is important to identify it and the practice it informs, particularly when it works poorly. The premise of this work is that management theories suited to industrial working (the management model from over 100 years ago) not only do not work now, they incur great organisational *debt* and desperately need reinventing. Important as it is for organisations to examine their current theories-in-use, shouldn't they also *choose* them? Thus the research method here

---

5   John Brubacher, Charles Case, Timothy Regan (1994) *Becoming a Reflective Educator*. California, Corwin Press, gives stages to identify and define a problem, forming hypotheses, projecting consequences and testing of hypotheses.

6   Charles Handy (1985) *Understanding Organisations*. London, Penguin Business, p. 13.

must re-present choices to organisations about their management, learning and business models and encourage new choices, as necessary.

In a similar way, the research method should not be the default choice, what is normally done, but should *be in service* – to improve and innovate. For the problems being addressed its role is to be their route to the morgue, not their preservative, the key that fits the lock of the 'problem' – the area of investigation. If the method is wrong the problems endure, presuming the chosen method is applied properly.

'Research': Who Should Do It?

Another issue regarding research for businesses is who should conduct it. Given the perceptions above, there is a need to free business 'research' from its ivory tower otherworldliness and university dominance and also from a key underpinning academic notion, that theory is somehow the highest form of activity.[7] Theory clearly has it place but how theorising seemingly occurs has made for unequal worlds of thinking and doing, creating great distance between them. In this world, advances in thinking appear highly specialised and accessible only with arcane tools. (ibid., p. 31) In academic research, the pursuit of theory and theorising can become an end in itself, leading to, at worst, (implied by the managers above) conceptual narcissism, an abstraction of self-referencing.

This implied 'ownership' of theorising and research can privilege some professionals (academics) while making others (managers) feel they cannot or should not do it. This is even though, as another manager said to us, the word 'manager' is a catchall for 'somebody with problems' and 'research' (or improvement) should be a natural part of their repertoire. The current imbalance lets too many businesses off the hook – the many hostile organisational environments where it is considered 'normal' to batter new ideas because they are 'too theoretical'. The effect is to demean learning, particularly work-focussed learning, a key concern here, and this narrows and inhibits work development

---

7   Gary Thomas 'In search of singular insight', *Times Higher Education*, 9 July 2009, pp. 31–32, quoting Aristotle from 'Nicomachean Ethics', asserting *theoria* as the highest form of activity. This may go some way towards understanding the status given to academic 'researchers' over teachers, where the private secluded world of theorising is so much easier than understanding the mysteries of *learning* which teachers are paid to enable in others. And towards understanding how 400-year-old taxidermist methods – lecturing – have endured aggressively.

and organisational development. There are of course, other factors at work, particularly the management model, which we address later.

To begin to address this we are asking here *who is allowed to theorise* – and research? 'If I am illiterate I am somebody else's shadow' is a famous quote by a previously illiterate farmer in rural Brazil, after Paulo Freire's famous literacy workshops.[8] Could he write? No – not then. Could he think and theorise? Yes.

So part of the purpose here is to 'democratise' research. For many managers, the highest form of work activity is a reflexive *mess* of finding time to think productively – 'theorising' if you like, gaining a balance between maintenance and development thinking, learning, acting and going again. Based on this, we need a research method which replenishes rather than drains managers' ability to construct new theories and actions, and which starts in their own theory-habitat, their practice, *their work*.

Learning at work, regardless of what it is called, is as natural as breathing, but any organisation wanting to use it needs leadership which asserts its *validity*. The integral labour of thinking-at-work has a vital role in refuting the notion that it is of value only if it is trussed up in an academic horse and cart. Of course, there are other problems about learning at work, for instance, that so much of it is learning the wrong thing, or worse, that it doesn't matter. That is why the three new models (or new approaches) here include a new learning model. (See Chapter 6, 'Why a new approach is needed'.)

I want to engage the intelligent thinking going on in organisations where practitioners themselves will do a large part of the telling. If this seems risky and uncertain, it is consistent with the earlier uncertainty of 'knowing'.[9] Longer term, there is a need to find richer ways to release diverse avenues of 'research' where inquiry is an inherent part of work itself, not a separate activity done by somebody else 'to them', so that it is organisations *not* doing their own 'research' that come to be seen as abnormal.

---

8   Paulo Freire (1970) *Education for Critical Consciousness*. London, Penguin Books.
9   Henry Mintzberg (2009) *Managing*. Introduction, p. 3: comment that 'I don't want you to leave this knowing… but, as I do, imagining, reflecting, questioning…'.

Theories, Health and Longevity

The field of 'management' is highly conflictual: seeking status, safety and respectability in claiming to be 'scientific', while increasingly seen as neither science, nor profession but *practice*. Nonetheless, its theories have had a long lasting dominance, with the current management model being over 100 years old. From the evidence of its effects, outlined more fully in Chapter 6, 'Why a new approach is needed', it clearly needs reinventing, or renewing, like the other models. The business model, though around for some time, suffers the opposite timescale, needing to avoid the instant answer, the flash of the fashionable, and with the learning model, the long accepted traditional theories of learning have rarely ensured successful practice. There is a need to recognise that theories which inform the current models can decay over time: today's peacock is tomorrow's feather duster. Thus, we believe that,'A good theory is one that holds together long enough to get you to a better one.'[10]

The key here is the learning model, which enables recognition of when current models are overly mature, decaying or needing of reinvention. Research in Motion's Blackberry is a good example. To counter stagnation, managers had to recognise the need to learn, to strengthen their strategic approach, introduce new improved models, launch an 'Apps store', and enter the tablet market. Doubtless much further learning will be required to continue to reinvent a thriving business model.[11]

The Approach

DEVELOPING AN INNOVATIVE VALUE-CREATING METHOD

Art should be considered a form of production not a mystery; the stage should appear like a factory with the machinery fully exposed.[12]

This, another quote from the arts, looks more suited to a 1960s car plant. It is not to deny that with 'Art', even if the means of production are transparent, the effect can still be mysterious. People's feelings are 'transported'; they can be 'transformed'. We somehow accept the authority 'Art' has to make such claims, even if in many

---

10 Hebb, Donald (1969) 'Hebb on hocus-pocus: A conversation with Elizabeth Hall', *Psychology Today*, 3(6), 20–28, quoted in *Managing* by Henry Mintzberg, p. 43.
11 Partha Mohanran 'How to deal with new competition: adapt the business model constantly', *The Financial Times*, 1 February 2010.
12 Walter Benjamin (1977) *Understanding Brecht*. London, New Left Books.

cases it leaves us in the same state we were in before we experienced it. But, to take another risk: the means of production involved here are transparent – labour-intensive writing, researching and crafting, to create something different. Why not also seek the 'mysterious', some transformative effects?

What is involved? Standard methods can be like the drunk, searching for his car keys beneath a lamppost, who when someone asks why he is looking under the lamppost when he didn't drop them there, replies, because that is where the light is. To tackle emerging issues businesses face in increasingly uncertain circumstances, we need to look in the dark more. We need to get to issues which could be hidden within the organisations, or are unearthed only from sustained prompting, or would 'never be considered' or were basically not planned. This means removing the methodological condom to take more risk for a more nimble inquiry; it means developing a value-creating method which refines the inquiry tools themselves on the journey.

What 'value creating' involves is explained below.

What Is 'Value Creating'?

By this we mean any process which adds something more to an exchange, part or process, so that as a result, it is stronger, better, fitter or more open and is the source of, or contributes to, more 'developmental' choices. It means for whatever issue, as a result of it, *you have more at the end than what you started with*. Value creating is best seen as an *enabler*, a crucial, possibly initial part of any new development without which it would not occur. It opens something previously closed.

Value creating operates at an emotional and rational level, at an entrepreneurial and managing level, is a product of both discipline and wandering, and is probably initially prompted – though this might be denied – at an emotional level.

VALUE CREATING

To put it metaphorically, it bridges rather than barricades, deals rather than denies, links rather than loses, goes again rather than stops, accepts rather than rejects, listens louder, believes rather than blames, takes deep not shallow breaths ... It centres round risk, trust, permission and uncertainty and invariably involves human agency.

You could call it a risk-shoulder, a free-investor, a hip-swiveller, a vulnerability-duvet, a favour-jump, a cold-warmer, a rigour-chill, a direction-illuminator, a me-to-we, an oxygenator, a hope-connector, the creak of a double-door opening...

The ultimate value creation is increasing your rate of learning in a change environment. This means whatever comes your way, in change, there is always a way out, always a way to go again regardless of any apparent slight, fight or loss. And the need for this never goes away.

This can be at a minute or more substantial level, the importance of which may not emerge till much later. Someone prepared to take a risk where previously they were not, saying yes where previously they said no, opening something that has been closed; or more substantially, an organisation making explicit choices about the management, learning or business model which means changing them from a default, 'passive' selection to a chosen one.

In this approach value is created for each element, for each participant and as an outcome.

The Principles of the Value-creating Method

The method (1) uses an approach designed to foster thinking-capacity, growth and depth; and (2) encourages organisations to embrace risk to reach their next stage. This is easier said than done. Many organisations get annoyed with business writing which invariably suggests (even if it is true) they can progress only if their managers 'take more risk'. However, what we ask them we also demand of ourselves. Risk is strongly embedded in the approach here.

(A) The approach is designed to:

1.   Generate independence
     •   It is done with, then by you, not to you. Any method not challenging the 'dependence' of doing research 'to them' cannot serve them well.

2.   Enable organisations 'to improve their own condition'[13]
     •   All participants use the method themselves; through this they develop greater self-managing inquiry experience and when

---

13   Yvon Appleby, Marie Kerwin, Sue McCulloch (2008) 'Making research', *Adults Learning*, May 2008, p. 20.

the inquiry 'ends' they are individually more skilled and organisationally stronger.

3.   Use learning as a bias towards action
   • Reflect on actions and act on reflections reciprocally and iteratively; link thinking and acting – this is the first kind of risk.

4.   Co-create value
   • Participant organisations are active partners in applying the inquiry tools for their improvement; there is also a 'partnership' between the organisations, a continuing social media learning conversation hosted on the Critical Difference website.

5.   Create choices
   • The approach enables the management model to be changed if needed by applying the inquiry tools (the models). It tackles the problem of a 'trapping' management model where 'research' is not wanted though desperately needed, and the new thinking it can prompt. This embraces the intelligent managers, 'the practitioners', which business research is supposed to influence yet rarely reaches.

6.   Be problem rather than 'subject' driven
   • The method recognises that what managers commonly experience is less neatly sealed 'subjects' but problems, which emerge more like 'subjects' in collision with each other in organisational life, for instance 'my staff are not committed' or 'we haven't got time to think' or 'the future is uncertain yet our planning is the same' or 'the same problems occur again and again but we respond by doing what we have always done'.

(B) The approach encourages organisations to:

1.   Be an imagineer: you don't have to be large to be grand
   • Be concerned less about the size of your organisation and more for the size of what you imagine for it. What would

happen if you were tethered only by your dreams? This opens something that is closed – an idea first has to be imagined.

2.   Be reflexive
- The approach seeks to improve the organisations and the inquiry tools themselves by the practitioners. In this it seeks contractive learning between the organisations and this work itself in the form of the inquiry tools.

3.   Be contradictory
- And then figure it out – the lived life is full of contradictions.

4.   Be a thief
- Borrow and steal creatively, encouraging 'that which does not (yet) exist'. The method borrows from scientific method, action research, appreciative inquiry and subjective evidence. Elements include:
  - Assume you can – Intelligent noticing – Curiosity nudging.
  - Crowd wisdom – Crap detecting.
  - Balancing the will, the work and the imagination – *Imagine* it first...
  - Persistent questioning: going again, like a good teacher, and not accepting initial, possibly weak responses.
  - Actionable understanding: new thinking 'completed' only by action.

5.   Be experimental
- Practise rapid piloting and emergence, lubricated by participants encouraged to increase their rate of leaning as their environment changes.

6.   Embrace uncertainty
- Manage uncertainty as an integral part of development: here 'knowing/knowledge' may emerge less as static information and more doubt-infused, driven as much by claimed strategic direction as by the psychological profile of organisation leaders; 'knowledge' is acquired painfully and is highly individually packaged. Take risks beyond 'knowing'.[14]

14   'Not leaving this knowing...', see p. 6 and Henry Mintzberg, *Managing*, Introduction p. 3.

7. Stay open: its fuel
   - If we are to address new business problems, which are increasingly more open-ended and emergent, then we must have a more open-ended approach ourselves to even perceive them. Otherwise, we miss the 'new eyes' needed to see new possibilities.

8. Seek deliverable impact
   - There will be a struggle to find 'deliverable impact' if participants behave like 'academics who continue to take their questions from their peers and not from perplexed mankind … or if they sacrifice the humanising potential of cultural study to theoretical frisson'[15] Soft strategic handling also requires soft metrics.

9. Begin with the questions we do not know the answers to
   - Will the three new models enable development faster? Will organisations make new choices about their three models? What resistance will current models produce? How can they be transformed?

10. Start less than perfectly
    - 'We are really good at getting to the starting line of change…' said a senior manager from a badly underperforming organisation to the author during a consultancy assignment some years ago. That organisation has since been merged. The approach here is a starting point only. 'Getting to the starting line' is crucial but it needs to be explicit to all involved that it is not a landing pad, that is, they cannot be here (at this point) again. It is more important to start meaningfully than start 'perfectly' – with a strong sense of direction, knowing who you are, want to be and where you want to go.[16]

11. Finally: the form informs the content
    - By 'form' we mean using the three models as inquiry tools. In too much research, as mentioned above, the form, the method

15 Mark Ogden re-reviewing *Sincerity and Authenticity* by Lionel Trilling, *Times Higher Education*, 7 October 2010.
16 M. B. McCaskey (1988) 'Coping creatively with messes' in L. R. Pondy, R. J. Boland, H. Thomas, *Managing Ambiguity and Change*. New York, Wiley, pp. 2–11.

– the scaffolding – obscures the building, what's inside. It is as if form 'is most manifest only in those who have not mastered it'.[17] This work 'masters form' by ensuring it serves the purpose of generating new insights, tapping emergent thinking and taking risks, to unearth hidden value rather than drawing attention to itself. It also forges new links between practice and theory, starting with current 'theories-in-use', or even what has been claimed as 'theory-less' practice, and working back to theory.

The Research Sequence

The purpose is to test the claim that organisations can get to their next stage of 'development' *faster* using the three new learning, business and management models.

It involved the organisations in:

- using the new models to assess where they are now and want to be two years on;

- identifying their current and future challenges;

- identifying their current three models, however implicit, and their adequacy to meet these challenges;

- identifying their 'theories-in-use', those underpinning their current models;

- identifying their future challenges and the adequacy of their current models to meet them;

- where necessary, making explicit choices about new models and testing their validity and usefulness;

- identifying the next stage of their development and integrating this into new business plans;

---

17 Leon Trotsky (1968) *Literature and Revolution*. Ann Arbor, Michigan, The University of Michigan Press.

- applying the new models to activate this stage (identify, inform and develop);

This also involves:

- testing out 'new value';

- overall, using the value-creating inquiry method.

What Next?

Having established a context and built an appropriate research or inquiry method, it is now necessary to show evidence of the limitations of current approaches – or models – why new models are needed and then apply them using the method above.

GIVING METHOD 'THE SHADOW': EMBRACING AMBIGUITY[a]

Speak, but don't split off no from yes. Give your say this meaning too: give it the shadow.

This applied business research investigates a seemingly simple proposition: that if organisations used the three models together (interdependently) they would develop *faster*. The overall approach suggests the need to innovate management itself, something I thought would somehow inevitably fall out of the process – an assumption which needed testing. When initially attempting to identify an inquiry approach I considered many of the headings discussed above including perceptions of 'research'; where should theory live; is research an industry separating theory and practice; how to 'democratise' theorising and how to start less than perfectly. As a result of considering these issues – a new method emerged.

There were key issues around 'theory and practice' such as if theory is everywhere why is it so hard to identify it? And the contradictions of theory: entrapment or liberator? The former offering safety from practice, or the latter, shouldn't managers theorise more and better, on the basis that if you can't theorise you'll be its victim? As well, if theory was to a liberator it would need to prove itself in new practice.

---

a Neil Astley and Pamela Robertson-Bruce (2007) *Soul Food: Nourishing Poems for Starved Minds*. Northumberland, Bloodaxe Books. 'A zero-circle' is by Rumi with translation from Persian by John Moyne and Coleman Barks, p. 64. 'Speak you too' is by Paul Celan translated from the German by John Fekstiner, p. 63.

But also which comes first the theory or the practice? Just because I'm doing it in practice and don't know the theory does not mean there isn't a theory. And just because there is a theory how does the right practice follow – or if it's not working is it the wrong practice, or was the theory wrong in the first place?

Though eventually a new method was identified, it still seemed to read in a predictable, plodding way – much heavy lifting and not a song to be sung. Even with a different name, how similar was it to other 'applied business research'? More dry rot of hardworking statements – legitimate doubts before *enacting* it?

But there was also something else: as a result a more contradictory feeling emerged of an endless running between theory and practice. They seemed less set entities and more fractious antagonists, continually crossing each others' borders. Which is parent, which is child?

For the method to be appropriate it must do what all research needs and *explain* contradictions but in this journey it must also *embody* them, and capture this ambiguity of theory made practicable, practice en-theorised. To illustrate this sense of looking both ways at once, which is somehow hidden, consider this example of quite ordinary business writing:

> '... *most venture capitalists believe that ideas are a dime a dozen: only execution skills count.*'[b]

This initially feels transparent – and seemingly obvious. But look again: does it illustrate hidden contradictions and assumptions, the likes of which the method chosen here will make explicit? Let us start with what exactly is being *executed*? Which are dime ideas and which are dollar ones? How would we know? Aren't dollars made up of dimes? Don't 'execution skills' involve evaluating *all* the ideas? Why '*only*' execution skills? Why not skills needed for generating ideas? Wasn't the eventual 'execution' idea made up of bits of the dime ones? Can there be one without the other? Is there a too easy assumption that ideas = theory, and execution = practice? Is this condemning theory in a rush for practice? Or evidence of their inseparability? Or evidence of the inevitable reciprocal toing and froing necessary to create anew? Note how virtually every reader goes along with the embedded assumptions of the writing – it makes sense, it is obvious.

The implications for the method then are that while it clearly must test the proposed ideas (the three models) in a meaningful way, it also needs to be set on a much more tentative footing – less either/or and more either/and; both driving *and* surfing. Generating new discoveries might require 'old' problems as drivers,

---

b   William A. Sahlman (2008) *How to Write a Great Business Plan*. Boston, Harvard Business Review Classics, Harvard Business School Publishing Corporation, originally published in *Harvard Business Review*, July 1997, p. 11.

but new methods and new risks also, and a recognition that it is both light and dark, a product of contradictions and unravellings.

The poem 'Speak You Too' by Paul Celan, captures this sense of both ways at once:

'Speak – but don't split off NO from Yes
Give your say this meaning too:
Give it the shadow'

As does another poem 'A Zero-Circle' by Rumi:

'Be helpless, dumbfounded,
unable to say yes or no...
We are too dull-eyed to see the beauty.
If we say *Yes we can*, we'll be lying.
If we say *No, we don't see it*,
that *No* will behead us
and shut tight our windows into spirit.
So let us rather not be sure of anything
Beside ourselves, and only that, so
Miraculous beings come running to help...'

The research method also captures this contradictory flavour.

PART II

The Old and New Approaches

5

The Old Approach

This chapter consists of:

- The current mould: Four case studies.

- Some implications of current management, learning and business approaches.

The Current Mould: Four Case Studies

Do we need yet another management tool? Aren't there enough already to help organisations assess the effectiveness of how they manage? Do they use them? And how appropriate are they for the current climate: that is, do they enable organisations to *seed greater thinking power*, look forward, challenge the clichés of '*everything* is changing/uncertain', pose and begin to address radical questions (that is, rarely posed) without which they will remain as they are? Or more fundamentally, are many current tools based on old theories, which got organisations into their current problems in the first place, and are in need of reinventing to enable sustainable effectiveness?

The three new 'models' this work is concerned with – a management model, learning model and business model – were formed over an extended period of time while I was working in various organisations – and only partly consciously. They are based on my experience of working for over 14 years as a consultant with over 100 organisations across all sectors, mainly in improvement and change; over ten years teaching on the Open University Business School MBA unit in 'Creativity, Innovation and Change'; and over many years as head of teacher training for adults in a college, gaining invaluable experience of how adults learn – and don't. During this whole period, the continuing, stretching challenges I faced, meant I needed to learn effectively *myself*. However obvious this may seem, it proved an irregular, uneven pathway, where I had to absorb things not going as planned but where barriers could be anticipated, and where 'failure' was not incompleteness or imperfection, but giving up. This learning was incomplete without action, the next intelligent move, where new ideas were continuously tested, where they were '*learned*' into practice.

I also realised the importance of getting a balance between theory and practice. This is particularly true of learning; whatever the learning theory, it did not ensure its effective production in practice. Further, much of what was called learning was learning-lite requiring little more than reception–transmission. In my experience, 'real' learning (whatever that was) was more likely to emerge from unpromising circumstances and the mess its need created.

Through a slow cyclical trail, and with the luxury of having sustained time with individual learners, organisations and a number of patient colleagues, I began to build a learning culture for individual learners which was designed to develop independent, critical, creative learners, *and* for collective (organisational) learning, designed (you guessed it) to produce independent, critical, creative organisations.[1] And though it took longer to articulate it, a key element for learning 'success' also emerged – how to *increase the rate of learning* in circumstances of change. None of these approaches or frameworks are substitutes for other kinds of planning, strategic and business, which are also needed. However, as I hope to demonstrate, these learning approaches are the most effective foundation.

The reason for highlighting learning approaches is their importance in addressing problems at an individual and organisational level. Most organisational problems – regardless of how difficult the organisations themselves *claim* they are – are solvable. So why don't they solve them? In my experience as a consultant (and in previous roles) it is because in many organisations *they don't want to*. However, the form this 'don't want to' takes is usually indirect, implied, deliberately foggy and contradictory. Nonetheless, the effect is that the desire *not* to solve the problem is at least as strong as the desire to solve it. Conventional organisational inertia does the rest. At this point, it is not even necessary to do the critical mass sums.

Working as a consultant is like serving a permanent 'apprenticeship-in-change'. For the author, this apprenticeship was crafted in many organisations where the predominant currency was habits, where individually and

---

1   Donal Carroll (2008) *Know Learning, Know Change: Developing an Organisational Learning Culture for Sustained Higher Performance*. Critical Difference, available from the author.

organisationally, minds *had stopped* thinking. The challenge for everyone was to find new ways to get it started again to forge appetite and energy without which new action was unlikely or would simply compound the initial 'problem'. And where also crucially, the consultants themselves had to increase their rate of learning and explicitly model this.

What follows are examples of consultancy work, where all the change issues emerge in a 'mess'. They are from a range of organisations, in all sectors, where the initial brief was to 'facilitate change'. For the vast majority of consultancy work, whatever the presenting issues some form of change in invariably involved. In the end assignments can resemble lift music: they all sound the same without ever *quite* repeating themselves. However, for the purposes of this work, what makes these examples 'common' is that what was learned, along with the eventual outcomes – usually negotiated and agreed – was not what was intended. But to identify this, it was necessary to 'chase' how what should have been learned became different from what was actually learned. Whereas many consultancies are quite content to live with this kind of 'different' outcome we believed that it contains crucial 'value' if we could capture it. In my experience because they are representative, these examples have immense implications for effective change and crucially for the development and structure of the three new models.

In the case studies, from our experience as consultants, it is important to say that they were all significantly challenging and though we made our fair share of mistakes none diminished our commitment to enabling sustainable improvement; further, we met many staff also committed to the same, though in actual practice, these were *never* the majority of staff.

The four case studies of organisational 'problems' give an outline of how they were tackled using the organisations' traditional management, learning and business thinking, which had reached its limits; and how they can be addressed effectively only by reinventing their management, learning and business thinking or 'models'.

Case Study 1: Coasting College

THE ORGANISATION

A general further education college in West England.

THE GROUP

The whole organisation was involved in this work, starting with the senior management team (SMT).

THE CONTEXT

Performance management was the initial problem 'frame'. However, on inquiry it emerged there was a perfectly adequate performance system in place but no one seemed to take much notice of it. The organisation was always in preparation for 'yet another inspection' by some external body, creating a paranoid 'if only they'd leave us alone' climate. It had a new, head-hunted chief executive and many long serving staff. The more performance did not improve, the longer the SMT spent in meetings, a decision-making process many attending characterised as 'management by mood'. Meanwhile staff awaited their resultant exhortations, largely to ignore or disparage them. Through the organisation there was a truculent, 'independence' stand off by the two key groups of managers and staff, as if they didn't need each other. The SMT consisted of nine experienced managers. After one meeting I attended, where the chief executive spent 80 per cent of the time talking at other members, one manager said that this was a 'better' meeting, probably because an external person was present. Normally the chief executive talked 'almost all the time'.

PERFORMANCE

Over three years organisational performance had slowly worsened in terms of student success rates, various improvement strategies had made little impact and according to Inspection reports there was 'considerable room for improvement'.

OVERHEARDS

> By managers: 'The more senior the manager the higher the degree – in undermining.' 'A challenge is seen as insubordination.'
>
> By staff: 'I'll deliver excellence when I'm paid an excellent salary.'

THE PROPOSAL

Traditional training had been tried with little change or improvement so an innovative approach was negotiated. This aimed to clarify and redefine purpose, get everyone aligned with it, and on a continuing improvement journey towards 'excellence'. It involved getting some ordinary staff, those most committed to improvement, to lead 'learning conversations' around 'issues that matter'; these would initially be with their peers and once confidence and change momentum were built up, they would invite a senior manager to attend. The ground rules were that all staff were equal and contributions must be solution-focussed. This was a risk, a key trust-gesture, and a reversal; in traditional change initiatives, precisely these staff now leading it, would have been in receipt of it. At the same time, the SMT who had also already received 'significant training' in team working, would themselves have a facilitated learning conversation on how an 'excellent' organisation could only come about with an excellent SMT. A key part of the senior managers' conversation was each identifying one key strength of the SMT and one 'brutal fact' they faced. Most did not identify any strengths beyond 'working hard'.

PROMISING BEGINNINGS

As her 'one brutal fact' the chief executive stated that that her own management style was the biggest barrier to the development of the organisation. Though the rest of the team expressed relief at this 'admission' they could not muster the *collective* nerve needed to build on it and make it sustainable, as part of a renewed, larger organisational purpose.

THE OUTCOME

After a few more meetings – and no improvement in performance, for which they increasingly offloaded responsibility – they were back to the same habits. Despite much bottom-up work, the committed staff leading this also got demoralised and the college entered another cycle of coming to life to take its performance more seriously mainly by responding to external quality controls and inspection. Of course, the worse it performed the more these were required – a trapping, vicious cycle. New thinking needed.

A NEW APPROACH TO THIS PROBLEM

To attempt to tackle this 'problem' more effectively, a new approach is developed here using three interlinked headings: management, learning and business. This first identifies the current approach –and its limitations, and then develops a new one using the same headings. *However, this new approach should be seen as highly ambitious, to recognise the deep-seated nature of the 'problems', the thinking which produced them, and how previous attempts have largely strengthened them.* The new approach is further developed in Chapter 6, The Three Models: Facing the Future.

THE CURRENT APPROACH

Management:

- consists of command and control where control is a zero-sum game – one group can have it only at the expense of others. The practice is straight from the theories of FW Taylor;[2]

- substitutes followership for leadership;

- results in 'trust is bust' with little consideration given to repairing it;

- shows little awareness that 'if you want only control you're going too slow'.

Learning involves:

- confirming only what is already known, a sort of learning-for-combat ('proves I'm right!') to sustain 'comfortable enmity'. Worse, the *rate* of learning is subtractive.

Business:

- follows from the current management and learning approaches;

- results in a *'customers can come later'* culture, where 'satisfactory' is sufficient;

---

2   Frederick Winslow Taylor (1911) *The Principles of Scientific Management.* New York: Harpers, 1912

- systems and performance metrics have become ends in themselves rather than tools which improve the service.

IN A NEW APPROACH FOR SUSTAINABLE CHANGE

Management needs to:

- recognise the current approach is based on traditional, hierarchical, challenging *down*;

- challenge *up* far more, starting with challenging self, then challenging collectively, to agree *and contract* the role of management as a means to an end in generating commitment to a common purpose.

Learning needs to:

- recognise that the current approach stems directly from the management approach and that a new one – and not just because it is core business here – should lead the management approach with learning as the first source of *value creation* (as opposed to value subtraction);

- start with committed staff at any level acknowledging and asking that if they are learning the wrong things, what are the right things? And posing the challenging question 'how can we learn our way out of this?' in such a way that the issue does not go away.

Business needs to:

- create an explicit business model as a crucial part of a clarified organisational purpose and a means of balancing more effectively different stakeholder needs;

- 'democratise' control more so that those involved in administering systems and processes should also be involved in building them;

- listen louder across the organisation: one staff-led learning conversation posed a key leadership question: why not base organisational behaviour and performance on best practices with its customers, that is, engagement, trust, high expectations, and make this mandatory for all staff, as an agreed employment contract.

Thus, in terms of this work, change was needed in all three approaches or 'models', with change in management not feasible without equivalent changes in the others and led by the learning model. The broader implications of this are developed at the end of the following case studies.

Case Study 2: Primary Care Trust (PCT/NHS)

THE ORGANISATION

Two primary care trusts (this concentrates on PCT1, the second joining much later).

THE GROUP

Experienced senior and middle managers in a NHS Primary Care Trust.

THE CONTEXT

The initial 'problem' frame was the need to develop greater 'business readiness' in preparation for a major Government initiative separating providers from commissioners, to ensure better health, care and value[3] and also widen the market for providers. Participants were also encouraged to 'use the space the assignment provided to reflect on the challenging demands' of this new environment with an unstated assumption that they could leave the organisation.

The staff were all long-serving, experienced managers who claimed that everything was in continuous change, yet the practice of block contracting had created a 'more of the same' culture rather than an explicit improvement one. All were ex-clinicians and those still part-practising regarded 'managing' negatively. Among other aspects the leading policy document 'World Class Commissioning' asked PCTs to 'engage with patients and public' and 'stimulate the market' to 'manage knowledge and needs' and 'promote improvement and innovation'. This called for greater manager skills in leading, managing in an uncertain environment and evidencing and marketing the improving quality of their provision.

---

3   World Class Commissioning Department of Health, December 2007.

PERFORMANCE

Though performance was perceived by staff as 'satisfactory' there were difficulties against a demanding range of national priorities designed to improve health in the community and in evidencing improvements in patient care against local claims.

One example of current team performance: team meetings consisted of individual managers soapboxing their interests; a toxic litany of what *they* (senior managers) did to us; a dim focus on improvement; no challenges to divisive inputs; and at the next meeting, attempts to overturn previous decisions by those who felt they had 'lost'.

THE CLIMATE

This was 'fearful'. What fuels fear? If we consider organisational fear as a sociological phenomenon then we can address how it occurs, is reproduced and who benefits. In this PCT the chief executive saw her job as *inflictive*, equating punishment with improved performance. This led to a range of contradictions.

The managers colluded with it being 'fearful' and by *choosing* to not challenge it while deeply resenting it; psychologically internalising it by telling themselves their future was out of their hands and to expect little from themselves; welcoming this programme, yet showing themselves unwilling to use it to tackle these (and other emerging) issues.

The result: they had become comfortable in their discomfort; performance was adequate, though not improving; they were *concerned* though not leading relevant action; they were doing the best they could *considering*. The 'adult-to-adult' behaviour[4] routinely found in high-performing organisations was completely absent.

OVERHEARDS

> *'I love change' – an experienced manager who would not contribute to a new Web 2.0 forum designed to promote new (to this manager anyway) ways of communicating within the NHS and which could be used for hard-to-reach communities.*

---

4   Lynda Gratton (2004) *The Democratic Enterprise*. London, Pearson Education Limited, p. 35. Adult-to-adult behaviour is one of the 'six tenets of a democratic enterprise'.

'We don't need to learn marketing?' – a senior manager's view, the exact opposite of her manager's view in commissioning the programme.

'Don't bully me' – an experienced manager's response to a legitimate challenging of 'I didn't have time' as a repeated response to not producing agreed work.

THE PROPOSAL

This consisted of one-to-one coaching to identify and tackle barriers to greater 'business readiness'; while at a collective level, developing better orientation to new business problems and ways to tackle them through a series of negotiated workshops. These led up to a final 'showcase' workshop, titled 'Evidencing Agile Providers' using new ideas of leadership, environmental scanning, marketing, branding, influencing and anticipating futures – all discussed in previous workshops.

PROMISING BEGINNINGS

The one-to-one sessions were extremely valuable with all participants saying they had benefited from them. For most, this was their first experience of coaching and many previously 'hidden' personal issues emerged, with new pathways to action.

Collectively, the initial workshops sessions looking at their old problems through new lens, for instance, building innovation into ordinary working, and more creative, riskier practice by some PCTs using digital methods to access hard-to-reach communities, were very enthusiastically greeted.

THE OUTCOME: THE CONTRADICTIONS CONTINUE

As work progressed less work was done, with repeated claims for busyness, meetings and an assumed powerlessness of 'what do you expect here anyway?'

The programme was designed to culminate with participants presenting their services as part of a business case to a 'commissioning' panel. However, in the meeting to prepare for this, once it became clear that they were expected to honour what they had agreed, a row broke out between participants about the 'relevance' of the programme – not raised before – with some, including the most senior manager refusing to complete it. This group then sought the support of *their* managers (the initial commissioners) in ending it – the final classic contradiction.

Thus the cycle of running away from challenge, using collective intellect to ensure they stay where they are, and a later final defensive offshoot, attempting to professionally 'rubbish' those who dared to disagree.

In all change projects a 'breaking point' emerges, when participants move from passive to active engagement, or in this case, to active resistance. At this point the commissioners had a choice: back change or back down. Here they backed down.

A NEW APPROACH TO THIS PROBLEM

As with the previous case study, to attempt to tackle the 'problems' more effectively, a new approach is developed here, using the three interlinked headings of management, learning and business. The narrative first identifies the current approach and its limitations, then the new one, using the same headings. Again, we want to emphasise that this new approach is highly ambitious. The new approach is further developed in Chapter 6, 'The Three Models: Facing the Future'.

THE CURRENT APPROACH

Management consists of:

- a claimed 'co-operative' style with the effect of diluting challenges;

- a 'Today' focus with all energy expended on daily operations at the expense of 'Tomorrow';

- operant conditioning as the mould of local behaviour, for example, claims that the chief executive sees her job as making her managers tremble and cry 'to prove her status'.

Learning consists of:

- an assumption of learning-limits, where intelligence is finite rather than infinite, underpinned by 'there's no need to learn new things', a 'no-coated' way as one manager said, of dispensing 'growth-killers'.

Business consists of:

- an overly producer-led approach; insufficient patient feedback;

- struggling to contact hard-to-reach communities;

- sclerotic decision-making via 'death by diary' meetings with hard questioning discouraged, resulting in 'reversible' decision-making;

- the immediate driving out the important where tomorrow becomes simply more of today.

IN A NEW APPROACH FOR SUSTAINABLE CHANGE

Management needs to:

- transform the agenda from escaping challenges to engaging with them;

- be provoked (1) and use some techniques to enable this beginning with: *confront and consequence*: this where managers confront an image of themselves facing a wall with writing saying: 'We can't go on like this.' They are asked to make a collective commitment to breaking it down – the rational part. This presents a choice and a consequence: active choices are invited here including taking responsibility for them;

- be provoked (2) and use another technique, *Imagineering* in the form of '*What if*': this is where managers are asked to imagine an open, empowered, entrusted organisation where staff feel committed and ready for any challenge – what would that look and feel like and what would staff be doing? This represents the emotional part of work which they claim is 'deficient';

- address key adult questions posed for them *as a collective*, for example, how can we be more than the sum of our parts, and to what purpose? What choices do we have in organising organisational effort? And to explicitly insert 'tomorrow', what will tomorrow look like if we continue as we are?

- observe a high-performing team in action and ask what's stopping us being them, and answer the question!

Learning needs to:

- start with the *self* (individual manager) to look inwards and challenge the self through hard questions: What have I learned here in the last year? Is this the best I can do? What do I stand for? What do I want for my own future? What exactly would my best friend say to me? What genuine 1 per cent of my growth could I celebrate? How can I get to 2 per cent?

- confront a probably unrecognised feature, that,'You lose the muscle in your head by refusing challenge – the easy life leads to fewer options.'[5] Unless managers commit to accepting the new challenges, they cannot stay;

- observe a high-performing manager, discuss her approach and steal three of her techniques.

Business needs to:

- cost the effects of current business decision-making;

- ask collectively: Is this the best we can do for our patients and communities now and in the future?

- examine 'value' and how it can be used to re-animate organisational purpose as part of new business model(s).

Again, from the perspective of this book, change was needed in all three approaches or 'models', with change in management not feasible without equivalent changes in the others. The broader implications are developed at the end of the following case studies.

---

5   Carmel McConnell (2001) *Change Activist*. Harlow, Pearson Education, p. 106.

Case Study 3: Digital Inc.

THE ORGANISATION

A small, highly successful media advertising company, seeking to establish a stronger identity as part of continuing growth, prior to a likely, though not explicitly confirmed, Initial Public Offering (IPO). American owned, it has a strong, expanding London presence, is also present in European capitals, and increasingly world-wide.

THE GROUP

The commissioners were the chief executive and vice president. The 'task' of 'developing organisational values' involved consulting all staff including the SMT and included an initial 'guiding coalition' group to advocate and propagate the initiative.

THE CONTEXT

The task was to identify and agree organisational values and enact them to develop organisational excellence and agility, and a stronger identity, using methods to engage staff across the company.

We negotiated a project specification including what would be delivered, and crucially, how the eventual values would be embedded. The project was initially introduced to all staff at a large teleconference; its first tangible impact was to form a guiding coalition of staff (mainly non-managers) who would initially build up interest and then increasingly advocate it through peers and the organisation as a whole. These were invited Human Resources (HR). The company was around four years old and exhibited a youthful exuberant energy though with strongly demarcated sections and seven management layers. Though some were merely titles, this contradicted the claimed 'flat' structure. The firm prided itself on delivering explosive growth. However it was just one company in an expanding sector with many participants, moving from traditional to online advertising. In 2010 online spending overtook traditional advertising spending for the first time.

Why should they bother with values was a question we put to them in the initial meeting. The idea of values had emerged from a previous staff meeting in which employees said they wanted to feel part of a unified team, to belong to a larger family, sharing common purpose. This initiative was management's way of ensuring staff had been listened to.

We then asked if this could not be met by other means, and what was the overall purpose now? The responses left some gaps but there was overall agreement that the values 'initiative' was not an end in itself but a means of improvement – that is, fuel for excellence, where more staff thinking would contribute towards a more agile organisation. We also set up a Web 2.0[6]-type forum dedicated solely to the values initiative, a publicising vehicle and a democratic means to record whole company discussion and argument on values in a sustained way – something that had not happened before. This included a section on questions only. The single ground rule: say anything but in a direction that builds.

The CEO spent considerable time travelling in the US and setting up more world-wide offices. His main concern was 'Can you do it by 30 June', three months away, when a whole company meeting, including US employees, would take place in London.

We then agreed a means to engage all European staff and how this would relate to the American side, which we were told, had given the project 'carte blanche'.

PERFORMANCE

Organisational performance was impressive though manifested largely through a single lens, a Key Performance Indicator of revenue (income) with the spoils richly diversified in targets and bonuses, making very high salaries for quite young staff in sales. Lots of time and energy was spent by HR each month on individualising bonuses. There had also been sector-leading customer satisfaction rates for a number of years, though competitors were catching up fast while, over time, their high rates were dropping.

---

6   There is now evidence of use of social media in high-performing organisations. Broadly Web 1.0 is learning as one-way transmission and dissemination, Web 2.0 *at its best but not always* is more 'We participate therefore we are': interactive, socially constructed understanding, pooling collective intelligence to harness the spirit of 'none of us is as smart as all of us'. See also Chapter 8, More 'Value': Some Ideas for Other Organisations in Using This Approach – 15: Embrace Social Media p. 206.

OVERHEARDS

'We have so many brilliant, intelligent individuals here' (a manager mantra).

'We don't use the term 'learning' to prove our success – look at our record in revenue, salaries and bonuses' (experienced manager).

'We will push branded entertainment aggressively' (CEO, on another acquisition).

'Eat the also-rans' (senior manager).

THE PROPOSAL

This consisted of identifying, agreeing and enacting organisational values to develop excellence and greater engagement across the company particularly bottom up, to create a more agile organisation. Also, to consult with all European staff across ten countries to generate draft values; to develop a forum to sustain a learning conversation on the issue; to issue a draft version with further discussion and feedback from all staff before crafting a final version. It was a continuing journey engaging all staff all the way.

PROMISING BEGINNINGS

There were very lively staff meetings with London and European-based teams welcoming the initiative with an 'about time' mentality. European teams were particularly engaged. There was also impressive discussion and disagreements, and early feedback on the conviction of the 'advocates'.

THE OUTCOME

As the initial identifying of draft values and behaviour was completed and the advocates group was evaluating them for the next stage, a circulation of drafts with a timeframe for further feedback, we were suddenly informed that these quite initial drafts 'was sufficient' and the initiative was ending.

A NEW APPROACH TO THIS PROBLEM

As with the previous case studies, to attempt to tackle the 'problems' more effectively, a new approach is developed, using three interlinked headings of management, learning and business. The narrative first identifies the current approach and its limitations, then the new one, using the same headings. Again, we want to emphasise the ambitious nature of this new approach which is further developed in Chapter 6, The Three Models: Facing the Future.

A DIFFERENT ANGLE – EVALUATING THE CONSULTANTS

In this case study we will apply the old and new approach to the *consultants themselves*. This is to get beyond approaches which the consultants themselves might claim when evaluating an assignment but which could limit their learning when making familiar criticisms such as the 'skilled incompetence' of senior managers or their reluctance to raise difficult issues. This different angle tests the idea that real[7] proactiveness comes from seeing how we contribute to our own problems. The consultants were key contributors to the initiative, and as joint leaders they should be *joint learning leaders too*, able to change the course of events in the light of feedback from the environment. So as consultants producing 'poor results' we should look in the mirror before looking out of the window. Our reflective practice should begin by using ourselves as data.[8] Also as the 'new approach' is developed later as the basis of the new three models, it is a good opportunity to test its feasibility and potential effectiveness.

THE CURRENT APPROACH

Management consists of:

- conforming with the current transactional human relations theory in the form of a mutually respectful 'hands-off' in which HR functions as an administrator when what is needed is for it to be more than a servant of strategy, however implicit this strategy is;

- concentrating on maintaining a smart assignment pace by keeping to agreed planned activities, however radical the gap that emerges between what 'they' understand and what the plan says;

- 'bar of soap' leadership which is fumbled, dropped and eventually left to the consultants to pick up;

---

7 Peter Senge (1990) *The Fifth Discipline*. London, Century Business Books, p. 21.
8 Mike Pedler, John Burgoyne, Tom Boydell (2004) *A Manager's Guide to Leadership*. Maidenhead, Berkshire, McGraw-Hill Professional, p. 39. This work makes other 'leadership development' seem pedestrian.

- running on assumptions that lead the consultants to mistake their default leadership for staff compliance. They do not address the question of whether an organisation with a sole leader can obstruct distributed leadership yet thrive.

Learning consists of:

- keeping their key doubts to themselves;

- sleeping on indicator questions: for instance, why didn't Shevla on reception, a key company 'nudger', contribute to the staff forum specifically designed to capture staff thinking on this initiative?

- ignoring many warning signs for instance: (1) a CEO comment on the issues of sustainability as a value, that there was *generally* a 'gap between what staff claimed they wanted and their actions'; (2) feedback from other committed staff about the effects of the advocates group whose agreed role was to influence and create momentum for the initiative: 'What are they doing?'; (3) the revealing comment of the HR director on a parallel innovation initiative where an informal group was established (very willing volunteers) to capture 'good thinking' and tackle frustrating, enduring problems: 'We have a committee for that'; (4) changing behaviours within the advocate group towards the consultants, from respectful to less so; (5) staff who would have developed most through the initiative – given a key aim was to encourage distributed leadership – were allowed by HR to opt out;

- noticing these signs but only in soft focus because the driving consultant focus was on the *product*: achieving the numbers, consulting all staff in every country rather than being vigilant about the *process* and getting feedback from the environment to ascertain the quality and purpose of the journey.

Business consists of:

- an apparent growth strategy of mergers and acquisitions where stakeholder value could feature as a crucial element. If this was to occur then consultants should require this to be made explicit; also if, for instance, 'cashcow' products had matured or key innovative products were in decline the implications for the selection of organisational values needed addressing.

IN A NEW APPROACH FOR SUSTAINABLE CHANGE

Management needs to:

- move to transformative mode with HR and the commissioners. This is where co-created collective wisdom can emerge so that proper foundations can be built; but also the key arguments needed identifying, posing and winning for the initiative to be effective for instance, who is the initiative for (internal or external)?

- rectify early mistakes *early* if they lead to holes below the waterline: for instance with no 'entry test' for project 'advocates' as they were selected by HR, we could not select more effective leaders who emerged through the workshops. We also needed to find ways to make advocate accountability more creative;

- not mistake pace for effectiveness;

- *manage* their leadership (see below);

- not take yes for an answer – rather take their agreed actions. *Contract in* what happens if people don't do what they agreed, for instance, when leaders, that is, advocates, 'subtract' value remove them or use *peer bruising;*[9]

- recognise a key transformation: less control means greater trust. This starts with the consultants giving the customer the right to success or 'failure';

- take more risks: for example, identifying successful uplifting examples of values such as the 'Life is for sharing' T-Mobile ad – an assured example, begging to be shared without being asked; also experiment by enacting some draft new values in current forums to get a sense of their power, for instance, 'accountability'.

---

9   *Peer bruising*: a change technique. See Chapter 12, Techniques – 12 'Peer Bruising', p. 259.

Learning needs to:

- chase learning down: the richest dividends come from the most unpromising circumstances. Where necessary pose key questions upwards to generate clarity – or indeed closure (of the whole project) as 'doubt ascending speeds wisdom from above'.[10] Secure answers to key questions (however obvious) – what is the degree of change envisaged by the initiative, how does it currently 'fit', what improvements are sought, what Return on Investment (ROI) measures are used and with what customer involvement. Also track why answers may not occur as key to consultant learning and leadership without which the exercise is taking place in an echo chamber;

- put it more provocatively: to avoid an own goal go back to *the* goal;

- *learn to not lead* if this means taking foundational problems away from their rightful owners; learn to use (or generate) leadership *within*, to 'define reality' through setting direction, fuelling purpose, clarifying what is and is not negotiable; practice what you preach by internalising leadership as a continuing experiment where risk is not an option but gold dust, the very ground of learning;[11]

- mix its metaphors better: organisational development requires leaving something behind (or cutting the umbilical): this initiative was the organisation's first explicit piece of *collective development* where the whole needs to be greater than the sum of its parts, where individuals need to sacrifice the 'I for the we', where peers weed out self-interested performance, and 'managers' replace 'friends'; where leading is in the foreground and the organisation moves from parenting to managing;

- take heed of a healthy warning: who pays the wages of learning? Reflections like this are post-event and a luxury, so it is necessary to 'increase the rate of learning' within and throughout any initiative.

---

10   Mike Pedler, John Burgoyne, Tom Boydell (2004) *A Manager's Guide to Leadership.* Maidenhead, Berkshire, McGraw-Hill Professional, p. 131.
11   Ibid., p. 85.

Business needs to:

- use different value-scenarios so senior managers can identify (1) uncertainties in their strategy; (2) how the strategy can be made explicit to all staff there; and (3) what they want to reveal and why;

- as a consultancy, complete a risk discovery and acknowledgement[12] exercise and recognise that optimism and claimed rapid action learning are not enough;

- make clear to the organisation that in challenging situations, conflict is normal, including self-conflict; indeed, it is a precursor to reaching the next stage of development. Identify the key business arguments which leaders must 'win' for the initiative to be successful;

- not mirror 'accepted behaviour': for instance, a behaviour attached to a possible value of 'engagement and accountability' was 'never walk past a problem': despite all their experience, they did.

Case Study 4: The South Organisation

THE ORGANISATION

A general further education college in South East England

THE GROUP

Whole organisation group consisting of a majority of experienced teaching staff, with some middle and senior managers, including the chief executive, all committed to change.

THE CONTEXT

The organisation was located on a sprawling campus in a sleepy rural area surrounded by fields. It had more than 8,000 students. A typical longstanding warning sign had been ignored in that external agencies (inspection and regulation) had made judgements on performance completely at odds with

---

12 Ibid, pp. 76–77.

their own, far more generous internal assessments. The organisation had a long-established SMT with also many long-staying staff.

The comfortable, old fashioned feel was reflected in the built environment – old farmhouses renovated for administration purposes connected by grass walkways with occasional warehouse-style buildings dotted among them. Though planning permission had been made to renew most buildings, the only new one so far was the management block. This had a reverential feel – entry was difficult – it was quiet, spacious and some way removed from the teaching rooms, the locus of the college's main business. The clustered management team met regularly but decision-making was sclerotic, ineffectual and increasingly shrill. The SMT spent more time approving its own decisions than on convincing its subordinates.

The language staff used gave an indication of deep-seated feelings: 'sheepwalking' was their term for managers who did not challenge *their* managers, nor poor performance and 'glittering compliance' was their reward. Many management posts went uncontested as suitable staff expressed a lack of faith in the appointment process, claiming that only compliant staff who would not raise 'difficult questions' would be selected. None of these managers came to the change initiative when consultants were asked in.

PERFORMANCE

Performance had been declining for some time. The most recent inspection report, based on college evidence, noted that a high proportion of courses and programmes were producing less than 50 per cent student success rates, leading to the judgement that the institution was a 'failing college' – although with, of course, immense capacity for improvement. Support was being given for improvement which included this consultancy.

OVERHEARDS

'We don't know how liberating it would be if we were all on the same side...' (marketing director).

'Leap and the net will find you – take a risk' (member of change team).

'Effective leadership should create more innovation: here we demoralise ourselves by repeatedly doing what has failed and rejecting new ideas' (experienced teacher).

THE PROPOSAL

This consisted of a longer-term (one year) consultancy intervention to develop an organisational learning culture based on agreed values to enable sustainable improvement. This took the form of a 'Change Team' consisting of staff with some authority committed to improvement, and some senior managers including the CEO. The ground rules were 'democratic' – all team members were equal regardless of status and could say 'what they think' to build improvement, with one jointly negotiated provision: that all must convey the same message to the outside. Over the period, the team would identify challenges, priorities and how to address them, and identify organisational values and associated behaviour to enable longer-term sustained improvement.

Once the meetings got going, the team worked hard to get an appropriate adult-to-adult tone, with a degree of respect and confidence that the initiative could develop them. Then some unpalatable views emerged, particularly for the long-standing SMT: it was evident that they did not have the respect, trust or faith of staff and what little remained was dwindling by the day. When asked what it would take to make the college a high-performing organisation, a long-serving respected teacher replied that it would happen when the institutional power of managers was based on the value they brought to it. There was an immense, uncomfortable, productive silence after that.

PROMISING BEGINNINGS

The Change Team contributed some startling energy and insights – such that someone asked why, if this commitment was already present, they were in such a poor position and how could it now be harnessed? This was the first time they had met *together* (an intention of the initiative) in any meaningful improvement forum. There was also an acknowledgement that though professionally they provided learning, as collective learners, they were deficient; if 'collective learning' (as such) had been inspected they would have been given the lowest grade.

OUTCOME

The entire SMT resigned, meaning that the staff would now have to lead in some new and ambiguous ways. Top managers had learned that they could not stay. Other pressures had also been brought to bear by the inspectorate and funding bodies.

A NEW APPROACH TO THIS PROBLEM

As with the previous case studies, to attempt to tackle the 'problems' more effectively, a new approach is developed, using three interlinked headings of management, learning and business. The narrative first identifies the current approach and its limitations, then the new one, using the same headings. Again, we want to emphasise the ambitious nature of this new approach, which is further developed in Chapter 6, The Three Models: Facing the Future.

THE CURRENT APPROACH

Imagine a disjointed, jagged-edged triptych a la Francis Bacon made up of:

1. Management: male faces at a meeting in a darkened room, the sun shining splendidly outside, staring forward together blankly, in different directions.

2. Learning: the same group looking uneasy, dishevelled and not looking at one another with the sun stronger giving an impression of dehydration, with plenty of water jugs on the table marked 'learning' but untouched.

3. Business: a barely recognisable shape in the form of a question mark like a sword, hanging above the heads of a now smaller group.

A NEW APPROACH

Again, a triptych seamlessly joined up, consisting of:

1. Management: a throng of customers receiving awards, smiling while in the background, a large convoy of trucks marked 'quality police' are leaving.

2.   Learning: computer-generated menu with kaleidoscopes of terms
      including learning, collective, improvement, trust, autonomy,
      engagement, success.

3.   Business: customers advocating, eagerly urging their friends and
      others to come to the college.

Key issues arising from the old approach are discussed in the next section.

Some Implications of Current Management, Learning and Business Approaches

What do these case studies tell us? We can see the limitations of current
thinking, what these approaches are called in the organisations even if they
are not recognised as such, and the implications for a new approach, to enable
sustainable development.

In brief, the key weaknesses in the case studies are:

Case Study 1: A learning model, where learning is not based on,
nor understood as collective *action* and in addition is buttressed by
a management model which is subtractive and rapidly accruing
organisational debt.

Case Study 2: A learning model in which what is learned reassembles
the past in order to stay there, and a business model lacking strong
organisational purpose to inform the business.

Case Study 3: (Consultancy approach) The learning model adopts
a parenting rather than a managing approach which mirrors both the
prevailing organisational model and the management model of not
challenging upwards, to ascertain 'fit' of key strategic intentions with the
values initiative.

Case Study 4: A paradoxical learning model yielding both failure and success: the old model of isolated learning, both individual *and* group, led to the current performance failure. The new one, successful collective learning, which got the organisation to a new learning point resulted in senior managers leaving, and initiated a new, different learning journey for the organisation.

Moving from Old to New: Some Initial Implications for a New Approach

THE TRADITIONAL THEORIES APPLY

The theories-in-use in the case studies broadly are: in management, classical command and control thinking to plan, co-ordinate and organise, and when this does not work, do it more forcefully. Learning theories are traditionally subject-based and didactic in method with little *return on investment* evaluation. In business, there is a dim focus on the customer – they seem to come *later* – even if things are currently going well (Case Study 3).

THE OLD THEORIES TAKE US ONLY SO FAR BUT THEY HAVE A POWERFUL LEGACY

Traditional thinking in management, learning and business which led to the current problems *and* how they were tackled, is now a barrier to development however implied these are, as in Case Study 4, with the old management approach constantly offered as the future or as one teacher said, 'They kept doing what had previously failed.' Though some creditable risks were taken by commissioners, in each case accepting a new 'proposal', their temptation where change was needed was to initially do more of the same then seek external assistance (for example, consultancy) as in Case Study 2, but to lose their nerve at a key stage where inevitable resistance occurs, similar to that experienced before. Management then has no choice: to back down – more evidence of the enduring power of the old management model – or back change, which is less likely.

THE STRESS POINTS OF CHANGE ARE LIKELY TO ILLUSTRATE 'FAILURE'

In Case Studies 1, 2 and 3 'failure' occurred at a particular point, as is the case with many such interventions where changed behaviour was sought. So a new model needs to make explicit and integrate both the ingredients of effective change and their *effects*, that is, how they work or if they do not, what exactly is involved. This means building in commitment, trust, risk and leadership and 'forcing in' the idea of 'Tomorrow' rather than leaving unchallenged the assumption that it will come as if by *automagic* means from Today's efforts: the less thinking about Tomorrow the more of Today.

AT WORK WE DON'T JUST *NOT* LEARN, WE LEARN THE WRONG THINGS

It is impossible not to learn at work – so people often learn the wrong things (Case Studies 1 and 4). Too little consideration is given to the cost of the *unlearning* which is needed to transform behaviour. The more the wrong things have been learned, the higher the cost. Hence, a new learning approach needs to be an experiment in sense-making, with the capacity to transform perceived 'reality'. To overcome many managers' own low expectations of effective change, it should be designed to make problems pay.

LEARNING STARTS WITH THE INDIVIDUAL BUT COLLECTIVE LEARNING IS THE MOST POWERFUL CHANGER

From the case studies, though new learning starts with the individual, the biggest challenge is invariably at a collective level, where the biggest failures usually are and where the biggest leaps and gains can be made. Case Study 4 is an example, though the change came too late to save the SMT. A new learning model must address collective learning as at least as important as, if not taking priority over, individual learning, *and* include the language of the learning model.

IT TAKES MORE THAN A CHANGE IN THE MANAGEMENT MODEL TO CHANGE THE MANAGEMENT MODEL

The models are interrelated, provoking interdependent changes. The case studies illustrate that much traditional learning is based on a traditional managing; that is, the learning approach follows the management one. Unfortunately, as can be seen, it doesn't work. The traditional management approach, where managers exert power functions in this way: the less it is accepted the more it is reinforced, while the object of the effort, the staff, predictably, react by withdrawing consent, becoming more truculent, being at best negatively compliant, thus triggering the need for even more managers, and worse performance. The new learning approach must *lead* the management *and* business approach, as business focus should be on customers who can get 'lost' in the internal melee.

IT MUST EMBRACE SOCIAL MEDIA

In three of the case studies social media was used with the aim of enabling the contribution of all staff involved, in an open and equal way. The overall benefits of these forums included: creating learning conversations for discussion and argument; useful exploring by an inhibited group who rarely met and which over time, became a record of their changing perceptions of the value of the work; and finally, creating a democratic record of tasks and actions across ten countries where selection of organisational values were justified.

However, effective use of social media requires 'offline energy' and an open management approach to build an effective learning culture – just as with any productive learning – the fact that it is online doesn't make this need go away.

In Chapter 3 we looked at how the internet and social media promote a more 'democratic' horizontal, information flow, challenging the vertical flows of previous models. Its attraction is that above all it confers freedom, and for the purposes of this work should be seen against the predominant academic way of learning which is tightly controlled as to how, where, and what 'learners' can contribute. With social media people are self-determining, do not need permission and learning is anytime, anyplace. Web 1.0 is: 'I think therefore I am': learning as a one-way transmission and dissemination from 'experts'; by contrast Web 2.0 is 'We participate therefore we are': interactive and participatory, where understanding is socially constructed, enabling a pooling of collective intelligence, harnessing the spirit of 'none of us is as smart as all of us' *at its best but not always.*

There is now plenty of evidence of the potent use of social media learning in high-performing organisations.[13]

---

13 Jane Hart (2010) '10 steps for working smarter with social media', Centre for Learning and Performance Technologies (http://c4lpt.co.uk/articles/10steps.html) and Jacques Bughin and Michael Chui 'The rise of the networked enterprise: Web 2.0 finds its payday' McKinsey Global Institute, December 2010 (http://www.mckinseyquarterly.com/Organization/Strategic_Organization/The_rise_of_the_networked_enterprise_Web_20_finds_its_payday_2716) accessed 3 July 2011.

CHANGE OR INNOVATION DOES NOT NEED NEW THEORIES

Being 'innovative' where previous practice has failed doesn't need a theory to justify itself. It needs commitment, energy and a recognition, in the spirit of the value-creating method of this work, that even though theory 'isn't needed' it is always present!

Two further key aspects need addressing for sustainable improvement. These are briefly outlined below and are developed more fully in Chapter 6, Interdependence and Learning as a Midwife.

1. *The starting point for change is always learning.*
    Learning kick-starts the improvement journey by opening something that is currently closed. Questions such as, how can we get a better system, modify our management styles, or deal better with customers are necessary but not sufficient. They are simply not powerful enough, and can let specific non-learning issues and holders, off the hook. The learning model of this work claims that 'real learning' is produced from mess; it involves risk and a degree of self-leading, and is always new for the protagonists. Only a changed learning model can break the value-subtracting cycle in which senior managers ignore or limit their staff, who in turn, ignore or limit their customers, resulting in continuing performance decline. 'Significant learning' is needed.[14]

2. *A more connected, interdependent model is needed.*
    A new model needs to bring together the artificially separated 'areas' of management, learning and business and connect them in a more holistic and systemic way as key enablers of effectiveness. As can be seen from the case studies, necessary changes are interdependent; changing part of one model, or 'productive tinkering' can lead to improvement though begging that the question that if it was relatively easy, why wasn't it done in the first place?

The new models also need to embrace the implications of two key contradictions which arise in many providers in the Learning and Skills sector but also apply to other sectors: (1) though providing learning, they are poor organisational (that is, collective) learners themselves; and (2) though their staff are typical 'knowledge workers', they are managed by methods more suitable to industrial

---

14 See 'The Three Models: Facing the Future' in Chapter 6, p. 83.

mass production of 100 years ago, and with now one in seven as a manager, little sign of this changing. Staff response of 'learned helplessness', however much a legacy, is a form of collusion with this.

What Next?

The three new models are now developed and explored in Chapter 6, The New Approach.

6

The New Approach

This chapter consists of:

- The Three Models: Facing the Future.

- Exploring Customer Need and Value and Facing up to Facebook.

- The New Models: Interdependence and Learning as a Midwife.

- Building the New Models.

The Three Models: Facing the Future

This section examines the background thinking in the current three models – management, learning and business, their limitations, how they need to be reinvented and what new models should be based on.

We examine the current theories that inform each of them and argue that in practice, having become barriers to further development, they all now need reinventing. None has consistently delivered their purpose in terms of, for instance: the management model to enable commitment, the learning model to enable staff (learner) independence, and the business model to enable increasingly satisfied customers. The section argues that their legacy has been a *form of dispossession*: in management, *engagement dispossession*, in learning, *independence–dispossession*, and in business *customer dispossession* – reliably 'getting what I want'. 'Customer Need and Value' p. 114 also analyses the Facebook business model and customer 'need and value' and the implications for participant organisations.

The work concentrates on how these approaches occur mainly in '*collectives at work*'. However, the new models recognise that part of the 'management' problem is that for too long, 'managers' rather than 'organisations'[1] have been the unit by which effort is organised. This attention needs to shift to *collectives* in pursuit of *purpose*.

The Management Model

A recent advertisement for Jack Daniels played with the question: How many people work here? The answer: about half! However, to make the joke more meaningful, we need to ask are most *engaged*? If so, they are in a *positive* minority, compared with most organisations. While the effects of capitalism's recent nervous breakdown make noisy headlines, they mask an enduring legacy of the current management model: disengagement at work and the resultant high cost of low trust, which is getting worse.

Pointedly, while most people can readily provide an example of a 'good teacher' and probably of disengagement (however expressed) they frequently struggle for an example of a 'good manager'. Maybe that is the point.

A pilot in a recent British Airways dispute remarked: 'I can raise your costs faster than you can cut my wages', while recently I witnessed a middle manager in a college saying to other managers: '*I work here in spite of you.*' What is discouraging yet inevitable about these comments is that they are *ordinary* instances of disengagement at work, an effect which has become automatic and acceptable. In another organisation where we worked as consultants, there was a prominently displayed sign: 'Be the most admired person in your organisation – leave!' It was not seen as a joke and remained in place even though every member of staff walked past it every day.

'Ordinary' the examples may be but it is possible that they are getting uglier, more deeply embedded and more costly both financially and emotionally: witness the recent extensive adverts for 'British Airways' for instance; or a recent comment by an experienced teacher in a college, even before the current cuts, that relations between teachers and managers 'was a relationship in search of a precipice'; or the CIPD report that many workplaces were 'the *exact* opposite of productive'.[2]

---

1   Martin Parker (2008) 'If only business schools wouldn't teach business', *The Observer* 'Management' column, 30 November 2008.
2   The Chartered Institute of Personnel Development (CIPD) (2010) 'Building productive public sector workplaces', p. 3.

What exactly then, is disengagement and why is it so rife? Disengagement is where staff are present, but *absent*[3] in a far more powerful way, with low trust, low performance and probably, more managers. At its worst, the nature of the work is brought into question with 'knowledge workers' claiming that getting to work is more challenging than being there.

On the other hand, the higher the engagement the higher the performance. Engagement procures discretionary staff effort that is used to continuously improve and leads to higher output and positive side effects such as easier recruitment. High-performing organisations usually need less 'management' because there is more self-managing.

ORGANISATIONAL DEBT

A legacy of the traditional management approach is that it creates neither goodwill nor commitment but accrues what is best understood as a colossal organisational debt. Over time, staff without official power (though the phenomenon can be found at every level) find unofficial ways to reclaim it; a 'forced' pay back in the form of 'creative non-compliance' where minimised effort and satisficing runs deep in organisational memory and infects every exchange. It commonly results in 'learned helplessness', where employees collude with the idea that 'nothing can be done'. A sustained legacy in the Learning and Skills sector though it also applies elsewhere, is 'split ends',[4] in which staff pursue aims which contradict those that the organisation proclaims. However, internalising resentment and 'professional withdrawing' is a form of arrested development, which will not create the 'adult-to-adult'[5] behaviour of high performance.

THE HIGH COST OF LOW TRUST

Arguably alienation and disengagement have been around since capitalism itself but evidence suggests it is increasing: 80 per cent of UK staff lack any

---

3   *'Being within yet without*: where staff "withdraw" from their organisations so that in *organisational development* terms, a crucial part of its intellect – the evaluative aspect – goes missing'. Donal Carroll (2004) 'My part of the ship is afloat' Issue 20, 'How colleges don't learn', Issue 19, 'Is that the best we can do?' Issue 18. All available from *Post-16 Educator*, 221 Firth Park Road, Sheffield S5 6WW.

4   Donal Carroll (2009) *Shovelling Mercury with a Pitchfork*. London, Critical Difference, available from the author.

5   Lynda Gratton (2004) *The Democratic Enterprise*, 'Adult to adult behaviour is one of the "six tenets of a democratic enterprise"'. London, Pearson Education Limited, p. 35.

real engagement with their work;[6] 73 per cent are disengaged and 19 per cent would happily sabotage it.[7] Just 21 per cent are positively engaged.[8] The economic benefits of reducing the worst disengagement was estimated at £54bn in 2001[9] – it may be higher now. At the same time, to counter this, the number of 'managers' is rising, one in seven is now a manager.[10] The high cost of low trust can also be seen in the quality and auditing frameworks which many public sector bodies experience as a form of very expensive distrust.[11] The high cost has prompted moves towards self-regulation. However, the use of quality frameworks which add cost rather than quality is common in all sectors because their culture is based on old management models.

Two well-known sources among many, who are committed to transforming these models, are Gary Hamel[12] (*The Future of Management*, 2007) mentioned later, and Henry Stewart, CEO of 'Happy Computers', a company that has won a string of 'best workplace' awards, over the last decade.[13] One of Stewart's tweets provides a link to Business in the Community (BITC) with evidence that only 14 per cent of staff are 'actively engaged' and the colossal cost of this.[14]

'HEARTS STARVE AS WELL AS BODIES'

Everybody has to work: it involves a search for daily meaning as well as bread. Work and where it occurs, is a complex mix of power, orders, tasks and relations which involve the rational and the emotional, and choices people make as result of how they feel they are treated. All people who work for organisations make a form of psychological contract with them, which has a crucial effect on performance. There is a kind of 'relationship agreement' between a worker and organisation and 'the richer the web of reciprocal promises and obligations

6   Richard Scase 'Why we're so clockwise', *The Observer*, 26 August 2001.
7   Proudfoot Consultancy (2005) quoted in Simon Caulkin, *The Observer*, 23 October 2005.
8   Tower Perrins Global Survey (2008) quoted in 'The hidden cost of overbearing bosses' by Gary Hamel in MLab Labnotes, Issue 14, December 2009 (London Business School).
9   Richard Scase 'Why we're so clockwise', *The Observer*, 26 August 2001.
10 Simon Caulkin 'The age of the Euro-customer' Management, *The Observer*, 26 June 2005, quoting the late Sumantra Ghoshal.
11 *Times Higher Education*, 4 March 2010. Though the dates are spread over a number of years the trend is relentlessly downward.
12 Gary Hamel, http://www.managementlab.org/blog/2009/hidden-costs-overbearing-bosses. Accessed 4 February 2011.
13 Henry Stewart, Cathy Busani, James Moran (2009) *Relax: A Happy Business Story*. London, Happy Publications.
14 http://www.bitc.org.uk/workplace/health_and_wellbeing/about_our_campaign.html. Accessed 12 February 2011.

the greater the job satisfaction and performance...'[15] Of course, as mentioned above, there are also 'unofficial contracts' which can be more important than the official one.[16]

Scase[17] describes three types of contract – embellished here by the author:

1. *Resentful compliance*: where typical behaviour is a 'grudging performance', the management response 'heavy policing' and performance fails half its customers. Features are low trust, low productivity, poor quality, high production costs, expectation of disengagement, and high manager numbers to 'police' the effects they have created themselves.

2. *Instrumental compliance summed up by*: 'is it in my job description? If not I won't do it' and the management response is typically 'support policing' while performance continues to trundle along the low road. 'Learned helplessness' fits here as well as 'within yet without'. The 'contract' is self-interest, a materialistic approach based on classical economic theory. It involves a series of warcries: from staff 'I get what I can' and managers, 'they need to be told'.

3. *Internalised commitment is*, where behaviour is informed by high trust with higher responsibility and accountability, that is, self-managing, giving the organisation sustained competitive advantage. Staff say things like 'My brain – and soul – are on board'. High trust engenders high performance and lower 'management' costs.

Readers are invited to apply these headings to their own organisations. Do at least 50 per cent of employees subscribe to the third form of 'contract'? What are the implications – whatever the 'result'?

Unfortunately, even *expressed commitment* – though clearly plenty of committed staff exist – may not be what it seems. As Peter Senge has claimed,

---

15 Simon Caulkin (2002) 'Performance through people: the new people management' CIPD 2002, quoted in Donal Carroll (2008) *Know Learning, Know Change*. Available from the author.
16 LSDA (Learning and Skills Development Agency) (2002) *Pride or Prejudice*. London, LSDA.
17 Richard Scase (2002) *Living in the Corporate Zoo: Life and Work in 2010*. Oxford, Capstone Publishing Limited, pp. 39–41.

'Real commitment is rare in todays' organisations. It is our experience that 90 per cent of the time what passes for commitment is compliance.'[18]

TRANSFORMING 'MANAGEMENT'

Evidencing and costing disengagement isn't new. Even though many organisations do not reflect it in their behaviour, the cost of disengagement is always greater than that of engagement. There is also evidence of organisations transforming the management model based on the understanding that if it is only as good as its people, how well it engages with them can be the difference between success and failure.

It is not just that staff should be treated better but that they need to be treated as well as organisations claim they treat their customers. It is not either/or, it is both. That is why some high-performing companies work to create organisations where people *want to work*. Two that have overcome the limitations of the current model and thus provide pointers for the new management model in this work are: HCL Technologies and Happy Computers. At IT firm HCL, CEO Vineet Nayar, used employee engagement to transform the company into one of the most prominent and sustainably successful in India. His book *Employees First, Customers Second* describes how he accomplished the change by 'creating trust through transparency'.[19] Stewart built Happy Computers specifically as a place 'people would want to come to'. It is no accident that these companies are both top performers and have long waiting lists of potential staff.

Other organisations include Groupon, the dotcom specialising in group discounts and deals, which specifically set out not only to treat customers well, but as founder Andrew Mason noted, 'to correct all the mistakes we perceived in all the big companies where they had previously worked'.[20]

The John Lewis Partnership is another example of a radically different management model in which 'partners' are expected to be proactive and take responsibility. The formula is summed up in a new staffer's comment that she is expected to 'show that I am willing to be interested'. Evidence that staff-owned businesses do better has persuaded Blackwell, the famous book store

---

18 Peter Senge (1990) *The Fifth Discipline: The Art and Practice of the Learning Organisation*. New York, Doubleday.
19 Vineet Nayar (2010) 'Employees first, customers second' quoted in 'Give more power to your people', Ravi Mattu, *The Financial Times*, 7 October 2010.
20 Jonathan Birchall (2011) 'Best deal on the block' in Boldness in Business, *The Financial Times*, 17 March 2011, pp. 36–39.

and publisher in Oxford, to follow the John Lewis model and hand over the business to its staff.

This occurs not just in the private sector. In the Learning and Skills sector, to achieve outstanding results, Warwickshire College[21] has built a high trust, high commitment culture 'rooted in core values' where customer and staff satisfaction is high and staff and learner engagement is continually used to develop the organisation. They also have a track record of successful management of mergers (the private sector would do well to note). Key to its success is the development of independent learners.

Incidentally, the Nayar book *sounds* heretical only because of the powerful legacy of the old management model. On reading the title you can practically hear many managers sigh, 'How can you trust them!?'

These are small, but increasing examples and the approaches behind them, consistent with this approach, is well within the grasp of other organisations if they want it.

'MANAGEMENT': A CRISIS OF IDENTITY?

If the most visible aspect of the traditional management model is declining staff commitment, rising disengagement and its cost, the bigger effect is more systemic.

As Gary Hamel writes:

> ... *modern management has been incredibly successful* ... *Yet these successes have come at a heavy price* ... *and while modern management has helped to make businesses more efficient there is little evidence that it has made them more ethical.*

Modern management had given much but it has taken much in return, and continues to take. Perhaps it is time to renegotiate the bargain. We must learn how to co-ordinate the efforts of thousands without creating a burdensome hierarchy of overseers; to keep a tight rein on costs without strangling human imagination; and to build organisations where discipline and freedom aren't mutually exclusive. In this new century we must strive to transcend

---

21 OFSTED (2008) Warwickshire College Inspection Report.

the seemingly unavoidable trade-offs that have been a legacy of modern management.[22]

Ironically, the model we use today celebrates its 100th anniversary this year: 'The Principles of Scientific Management' by Frederick Winslow Taylor. The design flaw is in the model itself not the people. The effect, felt over many years, is a form of dispossession which generates compliance not commitment, a scandalous waste of human capacity[23] where organisations end up being 'less capable than the people who work there'.

However, some claim that 'management' is changing, the influence of the conventional model remains stubbornly negative. We have previously quoted Henry Mintzberg[24] view that management is neither science, nor profession, nor much in change. The work we have to do is to reinvent it.

THE IMPLICATIONS FOR A NEW MANAGEMENT MODEL

The new model management model proposed here aims to enable organisations to make choices about how organisational effort is organised (*the how of business*). It needs to:

- *move from control to trust*: recognising that in the changing landscape, the only way to retain control is to give it away;

- align with purpose and direction *first* through greater use of collective wisdom and emergent thinking;

- balance more effectively concern for 'Tomorrow' with concern for 'Today' as part of (along with both above) seeking overall greater 'Agility';

- link to changes in the other two models, for instance, using the business model to re-energise purpose and seek new 'value'.

---

22 Gary Hamel (2007) *The Future of Management*. Boston, Harvard Business School Press, p. 9.
23 Simon Caulkin (2010) *The Observer*, 23 August 2010.
24 Henry Mintzberg (2009) 'Context Bonfire' in *Managing*. Harlow, FT/PrenticeHall.

The Learning Model

In a sense this section should be called 'learning through work'. '*Learning is work*' said Studs Terkel, the legendary oral historian of working people, in the appropriately named *Working*.[25] I think he means that thinking is labour and that work is thinking, as a key source of learning. According to Terkel, everyone can do it, not just bosses, managers or graduates, but ordinary workers too. We agree. However, the question posed here is, exactly what kind of learning does occur at work – does it ensnare or liberate? If it is so automatic how come so many workers seem not to learn? Further, if we ask most people what is the purpose of 'learning at work' they will likely reply say 'to improve the service, to do your job better'. But is that what happens? When in a recent exchange I asked some police personnel what they learned at work: they said obvious things about dealing with ordinary and complex issues but they added that they also learned 'wrong things' that somehow 'got approved' – shortcuts, cutting corners, getting away with it, satisficing… The danger, they commented, was that new recruits would learn that the 'unofficial curriculum' was how to get on.

To address what learning-at-work should be and how its potential can be released, we need to examine how the current learning approach (or model) is commonly a key limitation to effectiveness at an individual and organisational level and contrast it with what a new model would consist of.

Our assumption here is that work is an immense *potential* source of learning and that it is not possible to *not* learn at work. But also though learning is assumed to be positive, the exact opposite may be what happens in practice.

Here are two examples of learning at work in action. The organisations involved were high profile but the theory and practice of learning they illustrate is common, ordinary and applies to many other organisations.

1.　A member of the 'insolvency team' dealing with the effects of the bankruptcy of Lehman Brothers investment bank and its role in the financial crisis, while 'clearing up' reflected, two years on: 'The biggest learning point for me is that there is a real difference between advising your clients and actually taking responsibility for the consequences of that advice.'[26]

25　Studs Terkel (1974 reissued 2009) *Working*. New York, Pantheon Books. A graphic/comic illustration of the work history of ordinary people.
26　Jennifer Hughes 'Tasked with tidying up Lehman: The financial fall, 2 years on', *The Financial Times*, 14 September 2010.

2.   Staff in the children and families services at Haringey were 'beleaguered and battered' ... The 'quality of the service *of the basics* (my italics) of delivering a high-quality safe front door into social care' for children was weak, with 'initial assessments having little or no information and then passed on' ... an 'office atmosphere that was loud, frenetic and disorganised, and with long hours, high caseloads and little or no supervision' ... 'no thresholds were in place and there was a high level of distrust across agencies which impacted negatively on the quality of work' ... 'staff felt isolated disconnected and disempowered'.[27]

How exactly did the learning work in these cases and what were the theories underpinning them?

Both organisations provide professional services, which at an individual level, involves professional behaviour: their learning approach would certainly involve subject expertise, and an 'assumed professionalism' with protocols for doing the best for clients. So, for instance, 'taking responsibility for advice' should be what normally occurs. This practice would be informed by the underlying learning theory – the traditionally accepted body of knowledge which has stood the test of time. However, over time, this can increasingly be perceived as *where the thinking has already been done* and professionalism is now used to defend, not to renew it ('what's wrong with what we have always done?') The learning approach then becomes passive, backward looking and disconnected from what is being currently experienced; it becomes collective *unlearning*, or learning the wrong things, for instance, that we don't *really* need to learn or that challenges are 'disrespectful'.

It is worth identifying what exactly *was* being learned – work independent of others, align work with individual rewards, *assume* the overall purpose?[28]

The learning model in use was determined not organically, by feedback from the environment and client needs (or *enough* responsibility), but *by the*

---

27 Eleanor Brazil (Interim Deputy Director of Children and Family Services at the London Borough of Haringey) 'Pieced together', *Guardian Society*, 24 February 2010.

28 Significantly, JP Morgan Chase was one of the least affected players in the financial crisis precisely because part of its approach to risk management, was 'personalisation' – giving responsibility for evaluating and making judgements on risk to those making the decisions and requiring them to live with the consequences of those decisions. For the purpose of *this* work, this involved them in 'increasing their rate of learning'. Julian Birkinshaw and Huw Jenkins (2009) *Risk Management Gets Personal*. London: AIM Research (London Business School).

management model which it is intended to service: it is as much a model of control as of learning designed to enable predominant forms of learning around turnover, numbers, profits and targets, an armed flotilla of apparent purpose, with outriders to *align* awkward questions, and where the immediate does drive out the important ('because it's not unless we say so'). In some cases, staff become highly trained pessimists, throwing weed killer on peer-carriers with different or new ideas.

There is also a sense in the second case (and by implication in the first) of learning being disconnected, or of it not being used to *connect*, and of staff being at best passive consumers of traditional learning when what was needed (as in the new model) was them to be its *producers*. It is worth wondering what disempowerment prevents staff from doing *'the basics'* well? Is this how staff and organisations get trapped in a shrivelling web of vice-versa? This is not to be unsympathetic; it is to recognise that the sheer weight of daily operations can create disengagement but not without, on its way, generating many learning opportunities. Among these is the chance to ask: 'Is what we are doing creating greater customer value and improving the service?' We say, rather generously, 'learning opportunities' because they are unpromising and challenging, to say the least. They do however bring into focus what exactly the organisational purpose is, whether it is enacted or deflected, and crucially, what should be done about it.

What is being said here is in itself hardly new but the assertion in this work is: that with an effective learning model, what happened with both these organisations could have been avoided. A new learning model would go far beyond subject-based and individual expertise, with staff as consumers of learning, and would be built on key features apparently absent here such as: staff seeking connection, producing learning, where purpose is always in question – for example, a vertebrate 'why am I doing this?', and as collective learners. Above all it would ensure 'productive interference'[29] between individual learning and the organisation's practices *and systems*, so the organisation changes, *and has the thinking capacity to*, as its environment does.

Of course all this would depend on a changed management model. So to investigate how this would occur we need to recognise that though failure occurred in all three current models, it begins with the learning model: 'failure' in the management model involves 'working predictably', that is, not being disloyal

---

29 A key principle in the learning model here – see learning model grid in Chapter 6, Building the New Models, p. 141.

to management purpose; in the business model where value is subtracted for the customer; and in the learning model where learning is superficial, satisfied with the first returns (auto-learning, learning-lite). But the first point of failure, however strongly determined by the management model, is at the learning level: too much assuming 'what I do is enough', not doing the hard thinking and extracting learning from immediate experience, and acquiescing in an unlearning mentality.

Value development is not automatic and is unlikely without deploying uncomfortable questions, which is how learning engages. In the cases here the reciprocal learning and management models become both effect and cause: the most valued behaviour is doing what you are told. The result: dependence. The corporate cost and outcome: immense loss.

The claim made here is that any change has to begin with learning and to build a learning model which starts by asking what we can learn from the effects of our current management model.

THE MYTH OF EASY LEARNING

There are common assumptions about the importance of learning that 'we all need to learn more in this time of change', that 'people learn all the time' or that 'it is more difficult not to learn'. But is that what actually happens? Here are some everyday examples which challenge these assumptions and position learning as more demanding, which is why it is frequently resisted.

In one organisation we worked in, a senior manager told us about a coaching programme he had been referred to. To the coach's question what challenges he faced, he mentioned a string of operational issues. The coaching proceeded for four sessions at which stage the manager decided to end them. When asked why, he replied that he wasn't getting enough from them. The coach naturally asked him what he had learned. This began a much more demanding conversation around the issues for coaching that the manager had chosen –why these issues rather than the more challenging ones he now faced? Once these issues were surfaced and brought into the sessions by the manager, he got much more from them. At the end, when he was asked what he had learned, the response was not to be afraid of what learning brings – if it's *learning*, it has to be heard.

Another example is where people in a new job say they experience a 'steep learning curve'. The kind of learning this usually involves is fact-dominated, procedure rich, not disputed, and essentially unchanging. But isn't learning much more than this: '...more an evolutionary sense-making, experiential process of development than a process of simple acquisition'.[30] We would claim that the real learning begins only after this 'learning' ends (as in the new job example) when new decisions have to be made, when opinions or positions have to be taken *through others*, and particularly groups, where information is incomplete and new status is 'neutralised'. This moves from surface to deeper learning where things *must* change, when problems come dancing through whatever defences have been erected.

In both of these cases, clearly learning does take place initially but it is little more than comforting assurance around the already known, a form of learning-lite. It poorly prepares us for the messy, resistant and strangely-shaped issues we will inevitably face where, to benefit, our first response needs to be that we don't know, and only by recognising this can we can begin down the path to deeper learning.

LEARNING: THE FECUND CONTRADICTION?

The world of learning has always had a contradictory and slightly defensive feel at an individual level, (as when a manager says resignedly of his staff, 'Why don't they ever learn?' as if it was easy) but more so at a collective level. A senior manager at a failing organisation remarked to me recently, 'It's more natural for managers here not to learn...'. Note that from the perspective of this work, how even her framing is wrong: she would be well advised to tackle how the managers can confidently express that they *learned* the wrong thing, that is, that 'it was natural to not learn'. And at a collective, organisational level the 'learning organisation', such a necessary and confident idea, bristling with promise, seems dogged with ambivalence and fear.[31] To put it another way, Simon Caulkin, the radical management commentator, characterised the learning organisation as 'the Loch Ness monster – frequently sighted but never captured'. Yes 'learning organisations' are meant to be visionary and elusive and are, thus by nature, difficult to find. Why? And what does that make other ordinary organisations that presumably are less elusive and visionary. Are they 'non-learning'? And if so why is this acceptable? As another manager said to us about learning, 'It is hard to sympathise with or understand why

---

30   Alan Rogers (2003) *What is the Difference? A New Critique of Adult Learning and Teaching.*
     Leicester, NIACE, quoting Brown International Encyclopedia of Education (1990) p. 16.
31   Organisations and People (2010) 'In search of organisations that learn', *The Journal of the Association of Management Education and Development,* May (Spring) 2010.

this (learning) should make such a difference.' The comment was fuelled by enduring issues he faced to which he took a steadfastly symptomatic approach, with continually unsustainable results because 'doing anything else was so difficult'. He was caught in a trap in which the comforts of learning-lite can make organisations appear happy – for a limited period. Eventually, 'we lose the muscle in our head by refusing challenges – the easy life will inevitably lead to fewer options'.[32]

OLD LEARNING WON'T DO

The challenge 'learning' offers is commonly refuted in a range of ways, that it has already been learned, or its need offloaded, or responsibility for generating it dumped on others, and is evident in these common examples:

1. Jeremy Taylor, chair of National Voices (NV) (the patients and carer's coalition), commented on the reaction he experienced when offering some 'much needed thought leadership' about resource-allocation in the NHS. The NV evidence suggested that many hospitals do not provide optimal care. For instance, 'dementia patients left in hospitals get worse, too many are admitted as emergencies, for example, diabetics and asthmatics because their care has not been managed properly in the community, and hi-tech and drugs can now treat many conditions at doctors surgeries or at home'. Therefore he says, 'in the future we will need less hospital beds'. In the furious reaction he encountered, he argued that the 'save our hospitals is the line of least resistance and not always the right one'. He did go further, claiming that those elected on a 'save our hospital ticket' can 'be guilty of political hypocrisy'.[a]

2. 'Cut out consultants': a news item condemning the use of consultants when staff are being made redundant, submitted as a motion to the TUC, demanding that colleges cut spending on consultants to protect the pay and jobs of staff.[b]

This ignores the reason consultants are used in the first place, commonly because both something is not working in an organisation *and* the capacity (skills and approaches) to tackle it have not been built. Unfortunately this thinking can be part of the problem, possibly from those whose job is to manage it, a self-interested denial.

a   Randeep Ramesh 'Sense of Closure' interviewing Jeremy Taylor, *The Guardian*, 19 May 2010.
b   *Times Education Supplement*, FE Focus, 20 August 2010.

32   Carmel McConnell (2001) *Change Activist*. London, Pearson Education.

General Stanislaw Maczek, commander of the 10th Polish brigade during the German invasion of Poland wrote a report on the German blitzkrieg tactics to the French General Command. It was found unopened by the Germans when they invaded France soon after. What was the cost of not learning from it?

CURRENT LEARNING APPROACH LIMITATIONS

In identifying the new learning model we considered the strengths and limitations of current thinking which affects how organisations do or do not learn and consequently do or do not develop. They include:

1. Their common learning approach or model is a default one (or an implicit version) informed by a traditional academic approach which has crucial limitations at three levels:
   - *Content*: knowledge is set, finite and 'expert-driven' as opposed to fluid and indeterminate and developed by others as well as 'experts' (used as an occasional resource rather than for a complete learning approach); an effect of this approach is to make ordinary employees consumers rather than producers of learning.
   - *Method*: we call this the 400–year-old 'taxidermy legacy', based on a teaching model rather than a learning one, more concerned with control than use and, crucially, generating learner dependence. It also separates information into separated segments.[33] These 'hidden' limitations may go some way towards explaining the *contributory* attraction and success of social media.[34]
   - *Action* or purpose: it dilutes or obstructs what the purpose of learning should be, some kind of action. Commonly input is seen as enough, somehow an end in itself. It discourages ordinary employees from using and testing their own learning and risking new actions as a next step in tackling problems or issues to *generate new learning*. By contrast, the

---

33 Alan Rogers (2003) *What is the Difference? A New Critique of Adult Learning and Teaching.* Leicester, NIACE. These are based on the arbitrary construction of 'subjects'.

34 For instance: http://c4lpt.co.uk/articles/10steps.html. Freed of the controlling aspect, people want to contribute, for free, in a more 'democratic' way, rejecting hierarchy and vertical management for a more horizontal, open learning flow. Social media, part of Web 2.0 enables *at best, though not always,* interactive, socially constructed understanding, a pooling of collective intelligence. Accessed 1 February 2010.

new learning model here always seeks the 'what best next' stage.

3.   It privileges individual learning when, most of the time, organisations require us to work and learn together, where new learning needs to be manoeuvred through complex agendas and groups, to emerge stronger and *different* from its starting point.

4.   It contaminates informal learning and learning through work.

The default model is a legacy of formalised learning, again academic, and a sociological and Western construct.[35] 'There is no God-given formalisation of learning, simply frequently-agreed ways of breaking up learning matter...'

It is invariably theoretical, which is obviously important, but learning also needs a route into application, to be trundled into practice to tackle emergent unbounded issues *and change and strengthen in the light of its journey* (see Chapter 4: Research Method or Inquiry Approach). Also the status of formal learning expressed at its clearest in 'education systems' is higher than 'informal learning' though informal learning can be the only route for many at work and of more value. Every time an adult experiences a problem, they can't, or shouldn't, have to go on 'a course'. Much formal learning weakly prepares us not only for life changes but also for work-problems where invariably we are not the only ones facing them and have not created them. Hence the importance of the collective, and of collective learning.

THE OVERALL LEGACY

There remain other overhanging influences: 'The partitioned thinking which has flowed from the white collar versus blue collar, mental versus manual, grammar versus technical, and most manifest in the assumption of downward mobility of those working with their hands...'[36] For managers and organisations it can seem that 'learning through work', the richest source of learning, somehow doesn't count; it might if it was an academic thesis, being *done to* rather than *done by* them.[37] The effect of the often implicit model is that

---

35 Alan Rogers (2003) *What is the Difference?* Leicester, NIACE, p. 24.
36 Simon Jenkins 'Keyboard and mouse are outdated. Let's hear it for the chisel and oil can', *The Guardian*, 8 October 2010, quoting from Richard Sennett on 'Craftsmanship', *The Craftsman*. New Haven, Yale University Press 2008.
37 Hence the importance of the 'value-creating method' in Chapter 4: Research Method or Inquiry Approach.

learning capacity (like intelligence) seems fixed and finite – 'some people can't learn' so why invest in them – rather than infinite.

Above all, the effect of all three models is to create *dependence*. Thus the need to reinvent them all by ensuring key ingredients must embrace uncertainty and enable flexibility, agility and independence.

DEFINITION AND THEORIES

This work is not a detailed evaluation of all learning theories effectively carried out elsewhere, rather a new model based on particular learning theories, at the same time recognising that having a learning theory in itself does not ensure learning. Also, our concern, collective learning in practice in organisations, has with notable exceptions, received sparse attention compared with individual learning.[38] So given the undervalued nature of learning, it is important that managers in participant organisations identify their current theories-in-use of learning, and the new ones, so they are aware of what exactly is happening to them as they learn.

We agree with the claim by Alan Rogers that 'the search for a single, all embracing theory of learning would seem to be a fool's paradise'.[39] Some avenues seem attractive such as ways of learning that 'function as an instrument to support the logic of the present system' or as 'the practice of freedom'.[40] However, while both are needed, in current models 'present system' needs overwhelm 'freedom-practices'. And, as suggested previously, too many organisations generate 'disabling learning'. So the new learning model will contain principles which are explicit in leading to 'disabling' or 'enabling' learning,[41] the difference being that managers (and all users) can now make explicit choices about their model. It is worth emphasising that though many approaches to learning can contribute something, 'in the final analysis, (they) are based on certain fundamental assumptions that cannot be proven in any scientific sense...'[42] Much, it could be said, like 'management'.

---

38 For instance Peter Senge (1990) *The Fifth Discipline*. London, Century Business Books and also Peter Senge (1999) *The Fifth Discipline Fieldbook*. London, Nicholas Brealey.

39 Alan Rogers (2003) *What is the Difference?* Leicester, NIACE, p. 13.

40 Alan Rogers (2003) *What is the Difference?* Leicester, NIACE, p. 14.

41 Donal Carroll (2009) *Shovelling Mercury with a Pitchfork: Leaders, Led, Hearing and How to Organise What is Worth Learning at Work*. London, Critical Difference. Available from the author.

42 Knud Illeris (2004) *The Three Dimensions of Learning*. Gylling, Denmark, Roskilde University Press, p. 27.

This approach then takes some elements of learning to use them for new purposes. It borrows from cognitive theory (learning as active, meaning-making) and humanist theory (meeting emotional needs) where learners are encouraged to take responsibility for their own learning and to self-assess it.[43] The approach also recognises that learning in organisations needs to be less a store or library, and more a pump for use stimulated by the need for new *actions*, previous ones having failed or resulted in stalemate. Learning through work happens when 'practice is not the measure of learning it is its medium'.[44] And, it must be designed to produce 'learning-conscious learners'.[45]

This requires 'significant learning',[46] which involves 'the cognitive, the emotional and the social ... a change in the organisation of the self and turbulence within the individual and the system...'.

SIGNIFICANT LEARNING

'Any significant learning involves a certain amount of pain, either pain connected with the learning itself, or distress connected with giving up certain previous learning ... learning which involves a change in self-organisation – in the perception of oneself ... is threatening and tends to be resisted ... all significant learning is to some degree painful and involves turbulence within the individual and within the system'.[c]

c   Knud Illeris (2004) *The Three Dimensions of Learning*. Gylling, Denmark, Roskilde University Press, p. 36.

Given that in many cases, learning is *not* the default position, significant learning also requires some self-leading by individuals so that an individual in problematic circumstances says, 'I need what (new) learning will produce and a potential blockage can be my own disposition, or how I frame my need. But I accept the challenge' (see 'Individual Learning' case study below).

The models also recognises how *more* significant learning can occur when individual learning is developed in groups to become 'collective learning', which changes both individual and collective learning. This requires individual learners to bring their learning into a collective environment – which work in

43   Geoffrey Petty (1998) *Teaching Today*. Cheltenham, Stanley Thornes Ltd, p. 9.
44   Donal Carroll (2009) *Shovelling Mercury*, quoting John Seeley Brown, available from the author.
45   Alan Rogers (2003) *What is The Difference?* Leicester, NIACE, p. 27.
46   Knud Illeris (2004) *The Three Dimensions of Learning*. Gylling, Denmark, Roskilde University Press, pp. 35–36 using Carl Rogers's idea (1969) *Freedom to Learn*. Columbus, OH, Charles E. Merrill.

an organisation entails, where the strongest learners in this sense, carry along the weakest (see Case Study 4 in Chapter 5).

The alternative is the Varney example[47] where learning remains 'unconscious'. In this new model, individuals who have not gone through the 'what I need is learning' process are developed in a collective context through others who have, hence the overall strength of collective learning. It is the equivalent of the effective business model where customers 'pull' rather than organisation 'push'. The peer 'pull' in this instance, the direction, is to enhance organisational purpose.

HOW DOES NEW LEARNING WORK IN PRACTICE?

Here are two examples which exemplify how the new learning model seeks to generate greater effectiveness at: (1) individual and (2) collective level.

(1) Individual learning

One participant manager had based business planning for his new venture on a range of potential customers, carefully scoped. However, the initial assumption that they would apply for an IPO did not materialise. In practice, this emerged only well into the project timeframe, where customers were still not confirmed. What was he to do? He could keep to his initial plan and pursue other IPO-seeking customers. However this would be to ignore the incoming messages from his environment, and potential learning. So, over time, he reframed his plan. He recognised he would need to go right back to the initial purpose of his business: *what new value was he providing for customers?* It was no longer making them IPO-ready but 'offering them more effective, reliable, convenient or affordable solving of their problem(s) or satisfying a job-to-be-done',[48] a formulation which emerged from the present exercise. This means in practice offering them something better than their current providers. He constructed this thinking in a highly ambiguous environment, where little was certain and proportionate risk was crucial. Over time, he was successful in getting a range of new customers. This meant strengthening his offer to ensure it was of greater value to customers than competitor offers. He achieved this by not running from new messages, not repeating his original offer more forcefully or more seductively (for example, offering greater discounts) or refusing the invitation

---

47 See Chapter 6, The New Models – Interdependence and Learning as a Midwife, p. 122.
48 See 'Customer Value Proposition (CVP)' in Chapter 6, The New Approach – Capturing Value: the New Business Model, p. 110.

to think harder, but *by increasing his rate of learning*. This was 'significant learning'.

The customer 'need' he was presented with brought together the cognitive (*what* knowledge?) the emotional (what if I fail?) and the social (what particular environment?) and merged an internal acquisition process and an external interactive one[49] from what was initially an unpromising mess. This he transformed. To be effective meant recognising his choices: he could reject it, blame the customer, or accept it and change something *about himself*. That is why we say that learning in these 'real' circumstances, when things go deeply 'wrong', starts with self-leading, a form of self-correcting leadership.[50]

(2) Collective learning

In Case Study 4[51] the group consisted of a majority of experienced staff with some middle and senior managers, including the chief executive, all committed to change.

The issue was how to transform a 'failing organisation' but just as important, how to learn from the resultant 'mess'. The 'failure' was a collective production in that all had contributed, though clearly, the senior management team (SMT) had a more explicit duty and responsibility. To enable collective learning, we established a favourable environment where meaningful exchanges were possible for the first time. Unlike the Lehman Brothers example above, each member (particularly those with less formal power) soon learned to take responsibility for their contributions in an adult-to-adult way. For instance, any disclaiming or blaming led immediately to a challenge by another team member along the lines of: 'How long have you been here and what was your contribution?'

Senior managers became 'de-isolated' (the opposite of their default state) and ideas which seemed 'impossible' now seemed far more likely. Learning as a collective meant 'productive interference' between themselves. Opinions were challenged for evidence, perceptions for power, with 'democratic access' to worries, fears and organisational data, whether triangulated or not. It was pointed out that while we all of us may have at one stage or another some self-limiting beliefs, for senior managers to have them about the ability of their

---

49 Knud Illeris (2004) *The Three Dimensions of Learning*. Gylling, Denmark, Roskilde University Press, p. 9.
50 See examples in Chapter 5, The Current Mould: Four Case Studies.
51 See Chapter 5, Case Study 4: The South Organisation.

organisation to journey towards 'excellence' had immense implications for how staff performed and for overall performance.

In the sessions, the whole became greater than the sum of its parts – exactly what an effective organisation would require, though ironically, not now applicable here since through collectively *increasing their rate of learning*, they were able to 'agree' that their relationship had ended and the entire SMT resigned.

This was a good example of learning-conscious-learning which took immense courage, and was led by the more committed, non-manager, Change Team members.

From the examples above it can be seen that learning involves:

At an individual level:

- *Starting* at a personal level with a significant change in self-concept;[52] growing risk anew through self-leading; being transformative, with the capacity to transform that reality and become easy with it particularly at its initial, unsettling stage; and recognising that it is less what they learn but how they hurry it into action when they need to as a result of significant changes in their strategic environment.

- Having or developing, a learning orientation.

- Responding *earlier* to disruption; having an initial inbuilt resilience in tackling traditional defensive routines which are a key part of why a 'job isn't getting done' – but starting with these with the self and finding an easier route to and from practice.

THE IMPLICATIONS FOR A NEW LEARNING MODEL

The new learning model always seeks the *'what best next'* stage and recognises that learning can be highly emergent, and in flow. It recognises:

- learning is invariably embedded in 'other' activities and is prompted by 'need' which can get immensely displaced;

---

52 Knud Illeris (2004) *The Three Dimensions of Learning*. Gylling, Denmark, Roskilde University Press, p. 36.

- it starts with the individual or the 'self' and involves self-leading by asking, 'What can we learn from this?' This 'bridges the development gap' between now and what we want in future with colleagues, who can be transformed on the journey. In this it acts as a 'zone of proximal development';[53]

- it enables sense-making regardless of subject, theme or complexity by posing, 'What can I/we learn from this?' or as[54] Petty notes, at an individual level, successful learning 'is a process of personal hypothesis-making';

- it must seek collective learning where individual learning is sharpened, strengthened or transformed;

- it has the capacity to transform the 'incoming' reality;

- it's messy, invariably unfinished but crucially, leads to actionable understanding and it does not need to be perfect to grasp it;

- it is always in transit;

- it is usually stimulated by unpromising circumstance where previous change-attempts not only 'fail' but solidify the 'problem' so new thinking is needed at a more fundamental level to reinvent the old model;

- it doesn't end: one participant organisation worked by selling on what had been learned, that is 'selling smarts'; this is the inevitable journey of a committed entrepreneur whose learning is always seeking 'the next stage';

- it links to and informs changes in both management and business models;

- social media can enhance it – though this need 'constituting' to ensure a democratic learning culture.

---

53 Knud Illeris (2004) *The Three Dimensions of Learning*. Gylling, Denmark, Roskilde University Press, p. 50.
54 Geoffrey Petty (1998) *Teaching Today*. Cheltenham, Stanley Thornes Ltd, p. 5.

THE NEW MODEL

In summary, the new model recognises that everybody has the capacity to learn; that learning is the best toolkit for futuring; that it is 'problem-solving-productive'; and that effective learners are 'sense-makers' and 'learning-conscious'.

It is captured in the Arie De Guis comment that, 'Organisations need to be better at fast learning than forward planning.'[55] Clearly, so do its individuals.

Finally, in *Future Shock*[56] Alvin Toffler said that in dealing with the future it is more important to be imaginative and insightful than to be 100 per cent right. We add to this, that only learning can ensure it. This learning model is designed to enable it.

The Business Model

ENTERTAINING THE BUSINESS MODEL

What is your image of the 18–24 age group: lazy, apolitical, no ideals?

What is your image of a 'progressive' organisation running a business – hectoring, inefficient, business-begrudging, unsustainable?

Read on.

Here is an organisation which said to a whole range of people:

Do you want to get to a famous music festival – for free?

Do you want to get to a famous music festival for free and contribute to your own cause or campaigning organisation, for example, MAP, WaterAid, War on Want?

However, this isn't any old festival. It is now the most sought after, with its entire 150,000 tickets selling out the day they are issued. So to ask people if they want to attend for free with a virtually guaranteed place, must involve something unusual. This is the basis of the business model Workers Beer Company has employed for around 15 years, generating over £10 million for various causes. WBC supplies bars to

---

55 Organisations and People (2010) 'In search of organisations that learn', *The Journal of the Association of Management Education and Development*, May.
56 Alvin Toffler (1970) *Future Shock*. London, Bantam Books.

festivals manned by volunteers who donate their 'earnings' to approved causes and campaigns. They can attend any of the events free. The 'customer value proposition' is 'generating funds for meaningful causes' and the business model of (something like) a seamless way to attend high profile festivals, generate funds for meaningful causes and make a difference in an enjoyable and committed way. Who said that business models were dull and boring? Would you like to go to Glastonbury?

IF THIS WAS A RAP IT WOULD BE CALLED: THIEVING-DELETION, PROSECUTION-ABSOLVING!

'Three quarters of music tracks are downloaded illegally'[d]

In what circumstances would you admit stealing? In 2010 Carphone Warehouse launched a 'groundbreaking mobile music service' that allows music lovers to access their entire music collection on their phone (iPhone or Blackberry). At £30 per year the service undercut a range of competitors. But what happens if they have illegal downloads? To deal with prosecution dangers, the service does not distinguish between pirated and bought tracks and all artists get paid as with current radio play.

Because of this aspect, the venture is endorsed by all the record labels, the BPI and the rights collecting society, PRS for Music. However, note the comment of the Carphone Chief Executive: 'This is a real turning point for the music industry and will help to reduce piracy ... it is so simple, easy and cheap that it is an encouragement for pirates not to bother stealing ... it has the potential to transform the music industry because it also provides a new source of revenue ...'[e]

Amongst the minor miracles being performed are the continuing emergence of new technology and the neat cleansing of guilt (with payment to the respective artists). But is this just another incremental improvement for users, just a new source of revenue or a new business model (which is the perspective of this work)? It seems to overturn the traditional music industry business model of product push rather than the customer pull (hence the success of iTunes). And it is an opportunity to meet customer needs in new ways, or the jobs they want done ... even those they might not have thought they have ... As a new business model it contains a key new Customer Value Proposition[f] washing away any guilt. The moral legitimacy of its proposition simply adds to its (company) value.

---

d   James Robinson 'Three quarters of music tracks "downloaded illegally"', *The Guardian*, 20 December 2010.

e   *The Guardian*, 3 August 2010.

f   Mark W. Johnson (2010) *Seizing the White Space: Business Model Innovation for Growth and Renewal*. Boston, MA, Harvard Business Press. Customer Value proposition: 'An offering that helps customers more effectively, reliably, conveniently or affordably, solve an important problem or satisfy a job-to-be-done) at a given price' p. 25. See below for development of this.

ANYTHING BUT *BUSINESS*!

This section, again like the management and learning models, is not an exhaustive analysis of business, finance or financial planning. It builds on some key ideas to develop a new business approach which can be used creatively to understand, develop and decide what to do next in business and to encourage risk and provide the 'new eyes' in business terms. It will suggest that when linked to the new management and learning approaches here it can be used interdependently to explore and exploit new business opportunities.

First, what do these have in common: The Grateful Dead and the German national football team (or more accurately, its source, the Bundesliga)? Answer: They have revolutionised business models.

The Grateful Dead from 1965 to 1995 played around 200 live concerts each year in the United States.[57] The band encouraged fans to make, distribute and exchange recordings at concerts, the opposite of traditional record company practice. They turned the music sector's business model on its head by sharing music, freely creating an authenticity fans loved, with their shows more of a pilgrimage than the formulaic 'experience' many current venues – and groups – mechanically reproduce.

At a more general level, business models emerged as a probable crucial ingredient in the recent World Cup when Germany beat England.[58] The only European countries whose premier leagues do not make a loss are reported to be, yes Germany and France. It could be argued that a key contributing factor to the success of the German side was a business model learned from the German poor performance in the 2002 World Cup when the team failed to progress beyond the group stages. The business learning was based on fundamental changes requiring all Bundesliga clubs to invest in academies, and have at half or more of their players qualified to play for Germany. Roughly half the national team came from these sources. Even more sobering – and in the longer term potentially more effective – was an agreed plan for all clubs to be majority-owned by a democratic supporters association.

---

57 David Meerman Scott and Brian Halligan (2010) *Marketing Lessons from the Grateful Dead: What Every Business Can Learn from the Most Iconic Band in History*. New Jersey, John Wiley.

58 David Conn (2010) 'Community champions', *The Guardian*, 18 August 2010.

CAPTURING VALUE: THE NEW BUSINESS MODEL

Everyone talks about business models these days so it seems like the new business Viagra but it has always been in existence, in one form or another. Whatever its different interpretations there is no disagreement about its significance:

- '... to cope with crises and big strategic change without being driven off course ... a combination of four characteristics seems to be crucial including continuity ... which involves reinventing a distinctive business model to fit with prevailing market conditions...'[59]

- '... which revenue streams flow and which don't ... what does (customer) engagement mean? How to start to rebuild business models ... because measuring what works and what doesn't is where every new model begins...'[60]

There are also concerns about the dangers of some business models – or strictly speaking how they are used. In 2009 the then Chancellor[61] suggested that the Financial Services Authority should be responsible not just for regulating individual banks but ensuring the impact of their business model did not endanger the overall system. Nonetheless business models have gained astonishing ascendancy in business thinking.

'Strategy has been the primary building block of competitiveness ... but in the future, the quest for sustainable advantage may well begin with the business model ... forces such as deregulation, technological change, globalisation and sustainability have rekindled interest in the business model today. Since 2006, the IBM Institute for Business Value's biannual Global CEO study has reported that senior executives across industries regard developing innovative business models as a major priority. A 2009 follow-up study reveals that seven out of ten companies are engaging in business model innovation and an incredible 98 per cent are modifying their business models to some extent. Business model innovation is undoubtedly here to stay.'[62]

---

59 Stefan Stern (2010) 'Master the mix of continuity and change' quoting research by the Advanced Institute of Management Research (AIMS), *The Financial Times*, 20 January 2010.
60 Peter Preston, *The Observer*, 21 March 2010.
61 *The Financial Times*, 26 June 2009.
62 Ramon Casadesus-Masanelli and Joan Ricart (2011) 'How to design a winning business model', *Harvard Business Review*, January–February, p. 101.

The business model should be the *playmaker* of a business – what a business is built on. However it is not always easy to identify – a business Salome in hiding, yet at the same time necessarily drawing attention to what it must reveal. Even the customers of a successful business may have to guess what its business model is. Try this: what is the business model of your dry cleaners, your favourite bar, or the company you most frequently receive service from? Should customers – or organisations be able to identify it? What are the implications if they can, or can't?

Customers don't have to be explicitly aware of the business model if their *experience* of the underlying value-creating engine of the business[63] is good. This issue is taken up in the principles (Implicit/Explicit) in the new model here.

The term – and what it means in practice – has gone through a range of expressions from the initial dot-com revolution of the late 1990s ('dotgones') excited and resurfaced it, to its current assertion of how an organisation makes money or monetises its mission; as Seth Godin more dramatically proposes, 'What compelling reason exists for a person to give you money?'[64]

By a 'business model' we mean, in some sense, all of these, but with a greater emphasis on the continuing challenge of 'value': *the choices made about how organisational value is created, delivered and captured* (the what and why of business).[65]

A crucial aspect of this, and one with immense potential, is the Customer Value Proposition (CVP) – broadly: 'An offering that helps customers more effectively, reliably, conveniently or affordably, solve an important problem (*or satisfy a job-to-be-done*) at a given price'.[66] 'Value' in this sense, can be quantitative or qualitative and can include price, speed, design, cost or risk reduction, customer experience, newness, performance customisation, brand/status, accessibility, convenience/usability.[67] See Figure 6.1, the Customer Value Proposition Model.

---

63 Mark W. Johnson (2010) *Seizing the White Space: Business Model Innovation for Growth and Renewal*. Boston, MA, Harvard Business Press, p. 109.
64 Seth Godin (2009) *Meatball Sundae*. Chatham, Little, Brown Book Group.
65 Alexander Osterwalder and Yves Pigneur (2010) *Business Model Generation*. New Jersey, John Wiley, p. 14.
66 Mark W. Johnson (2010) *Seizing the White Space: Business Model Innovation for Growth and Renewal*. Boston, MA, Harvard Business Press, pp. 25–27.
67 Alexander Osterwalder and Yves Pigneur (2010) *Business Model Generation*. New Jersey, John Wiley, pp. 23–25.

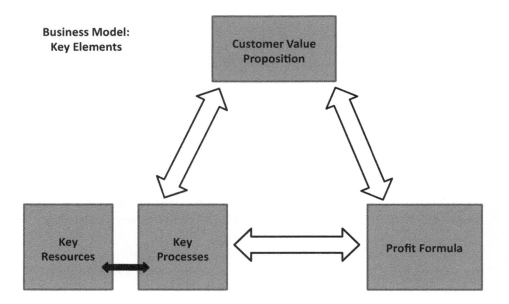

Figure 6.1   Customer Value Proposition Model

A business model[68] is a representation of how a business creates, delivers and captures value for both customer and company. The clearer this is the more effective it is in trying circumstances, or in pursuit of new growth.

THE BUSINESS MODEL: WHY IS IT SO IMPORTANT NOW?

A business model is *nominally* about how a company makes money – but significantly more than this and more than conventional business thinking rebottled. It is best used as a method of inquiry to help understand, develop and decide what to do next. Further, testing and iteration[69] are crucial elements. However important a business model is, the business is actually more than this.

Peter Drucker implicitly defined it as 'a theory of business' to include the customer experience. Typically, Drucker also said that though every organisation has one, such theories do not last forever, 'indeed today they rarely last for long at all. Eventually they become obsolete and invalid.' A business model will always need new thinking to optimise it. This includes

---

68   Mark W. Johnson (2010) *Seizing the White Space: Business Model Innovation for Growth and Renewal*. Boston, MA, Harvard Business Press, p. 22.
69   Alexander Osterwalder and Yves Pigneur (2010) *Business Model Generation*. New Jersey, John Wiley, p. 260.

how it fits with (however imprecisely or implicitly) the new management and learning models.

Many organisations claim to deliver 'value' but rarely articulate how they do it with sufficient clarity.

'Too often there is insufficient focus on the elements in a business system central to the creation and delivery of value. Most leaders don't sufficiently understand their existing model, the premise behind its development, its natural interdependencies, or its strength and weaknesses ... Value remains curiously implicit as if some guiding presence hovering beneath the surface of the enterprise.'[70]

In today's changing business world, with proliferating internet channels and greater customer choice, selecting an appropriate business model offers immense business opportunities, and the clearer organisations are about theirs the more effective they will be.

Here are brief examples of how five organisations successfully developed a new business model with the CVP as a core aspect, for competitive advantage. I describe their actual 'business models', as 'something like' as they can be difficult to pin down without reducing their distinctiveness. Developing an effective business model is an exercise in iteration and approximation. Also, it is important not to *confuse the overture for the opera*: what companies start with may not be where they end up.

THE BIG ISSUE

The Big Issue is a registered charity set up to provide homeless and vulnerably housed people with an opportunity to earn a legitimate income. Big Issue vendors are given training, sign a code of conduct, can be identified, and are given support to tackle the issues which led to them becoming homeless. They buy the magazine for half its cover price and keep the difference.

CVP: Contributing to tackling the social problem of homelessness.

Business model: Something like *Giving a handup not a handout* – supporting vendors as budding entrepreneurs (this is *seamless* – see iTunes example below).

70 Mark W. Johnson (2010) *Seizing the White Space: Business Model Innovation for Growth and Renewal*. Boston, MA, Harvard Business Press, p. 22.

RADIOHEAD

To retain copyright of their music, the group left EMI. They then gave their music away as 'free' internet download, fans paying what they liked, and developed a new business model[71] to recognise the change, sometimes referred to as moving from 'a star is born' (group-centric) to 'winning a fan' (customer-centric).

CVP: Free music, loyalty, with likely purchase of other, associated merchandise

Business model: Something like 'Fremium' which blends free basic services with paid premium services. It is self-managing and cuts out the middle man in order to deal directly with the customer.

ZOPA

The first online peer-to-peer social lending marketplace, having lent over £100 million and secured 1 per cent of the personal loan market. The default rate of 0.7 per cent is far better than that of banks.

CVP: Contribute to ethical, sustainable (and gain cheaper) financing

Business model: 'Everybody wins except the fat cats' (from their website).[72]

HEXAYURT

Builds simplified disaster relief shelter designs, freely available on the internet. These use common building materials including insulation boards which cost a third as much as a tent so poorer people can afford them.[73]

CVP: Low-cost shelter and utilities solutions in emergency relief.

Business model: Open source: similar open source 'products' are Wikipedia, while software includes the Firefox browser and Linux operating systems.

---

71 Ludovic Hunter-Tiley 'Off the record', *The Financial Times Magazine*, 11/12 September 2010.
72 Zopa, http://uk.zopa.com/ZopaWeb/public/about-zopa/about-zopa-home.html, accessed 30 May 2011.
73 Hexayurt, http://hexayurt.com, accessed 30 May 2011.

IPOD/ITUNES

Arguably the blockbuster business model: while devices from other companies were technically as good, Apple linked hardware (the iPod), software (iTunes) and digital music (online music store) into one user-friendly package, *seamlessly*. Customers could now populate their personal music players according to their own taste and preference instead those of the music industry. This became a $10 billion product and a key element of Apple's stellar growth, accounting for almost 50 per cent of its revenue and rising market capitalisation.

CVP: A seamless music experience.

Business model: Something like enabling customer *pull* (they choose) rather than music provider *push*.

THE IMPLICATIONS FOR A NEW BUSINESS MODEL

(Including lessons from Facebook, further developed in the section on 'Customer Need and Value').

The new business model is to enable organisations to make choices about how organisational value is created, delivered and captured. What follows are some lessons from the examples above followed by more inspired success of Facebook. Lessons include:

- *Value creation is at its heart*: in a new model this must drive the process for creating, capturing and delivering value though all four elements (Figure 6.1 above) need to have the same rigour to ensure growth.

- *The more explicit the better*: the clearer the business model is to both employees and customers the more likely it is to be successful, for example, Zopa. Crucially, even if users can't define the model, they must *experience* it – feel what it is.

- *Value subtraction needs to be identified*: a new model needs to recognise the need to tackle customer dissatisfaction by, for instance, greater robust customer engagement.

- *Dissatisfaction is a rich source of new business models*: as reflected in Zopa, the new bank Metro,[74] and the reinvented music industry in particular.

- *It can embrace diversity*: there can be alternative kinds of business model – doing things for the common good for nothing because somebody *should*, for example, Hexayurt.

- *Providing a 'seamless' customer experience*: for example, through the internet-enabled iTunes. The 'Big Issue' also provides this directly to customers.

- *It can have radical purchase* in re-engaging staff with organisational purpose and customer value and in tackling disengagement caused by barriers in the other models (for example, the management model) which also need addressing.

- *It can combat short-term* thinking in terms of say, shareholder value[75] since the business model is the generic value chain underlying all businesses, which clearly includes the customer experience.

- *Better business models* create 'stickiness, loyalty, with high barriers to entry'.[76]

- *However trendy some models appear*, it is worth remembering that they do not last forever and continually need reinventing.

- *Developing an effective business model* means spending as much time on the business as in it.

- It will need to link to the learning and new management models outlined here

Customer Need and Value – and Facing up to Facebook

See Appendix 1: Don't Do This at Home!

---

74 See Chapter 12, Techniques – Cross-border Raiding.
75 Roger Martin (2010) 'The age of customer capitalism', *Harvard Business Review*, January–February 2010, pp. 59–65.
76 Rita Gunther McGrath (2011) 'When your business model is in trouble', *Harvard Business Review*, January–February 2011, pp. 96–99.

FACING UP TO FACEBOOK

This section continues the implications for a new business model.

For organisations examining business models, Facebook seems infectious, sprinkled with excitement and possibility-stardust. But perhaps it is *uniquely* successful because of its circumstances, sector and mission. So some guarded lessons are drawn here from its business journey. In just five years, Facebook, now big enough to behave like a utility, has 10 per cent of the planet as users, is the equivalent of the 'third biggest country in the world'[77] and its name is established as an active verb ('Facebook me'). However, if it was in any sector other than social networking, it is doubtful if it would have lasted this long without demonstrating convincing evidence of covering its costs. Facebook faced a unique set of circumstances, some inherited, some self-created, which emerged organically as its business developed to which it adjusted and began to control, *so far*. These included the changing role of the internet and more broadly:

- *The two-way mirror – seeing but being seen*: in terms of *access* more of the world is using the internet and in terms of *usage* there is a 'maturing' of social networking. This has involved moving from the essentially narcissistic, 'masked ball' phase attracting self- publicists, a playful, anonymity stage, to a more pragmatic, professionalised business-embedded use. Facebook hosts around 1 million transactions every minute.

- *Emergence needs nerve*: for successful business models to *emerge* from persistent probing market-trysts requires risk and nerve and above all the ability to increase the rate of learning (as in the learning model here) as the environment changes.

- *Eventual effective business models can seem contradictory*: Facebook's business is now 'advertising' but initially it was 'anything but'. The founders capitalised on what emerged – more data than many countries had on their citizens – and developed analytics to format it. Their data, individual preferences expressed interactively, was in a form marketers regarded as the Holy Grail, for which they would pay handsomely. However, while its current success may seem to be advertising it is *not in the form it would have been* if used when it began.

---

77 'Person of the Year', *Time Magazine*, 3 December/January 2011.

- *New business models keep the revolution going*: crucial to success was another emerging concept, the intuitively-grasped mission to 'socialise everything' fundamentally reshaping the online experience and driving ways to meet changing business needs. Facebook is now 'the new company website',[78] having been both a cause *and* effect in the decline in web traffic to many major company websites and in shifting their presence to Facebook (and other social media) pages. This is 'advertising' revolutionised, used in ways not possible in the framework of the company's starting and implicit business model *even if* it does use more traditional advertising. To grasp the scale of Facebook's business journey, recall that its initial implicit business model was something like dating. Success with the current business model requires testing, iteration and the same innovative energy which animated its first market sorties.

- *'Value' and need are (advantageously) slippery*: customers know what they want – *or do they*? Facebook's privacy paradox meant customers framed their 'need' in a self-advantageous way, *acceptably trading* it. Their 'job to be done' was to connect with their chosen others. Thus need was exchangeable, with *value* produced as a result of an exchange with the provider, a 'product' mutually created between producer and customer. In this way 'need' is a new commodity. The lesson for other organisations: *customer needs are of infinite variety, immensely negotiable and adjustable.*[79]

- *In my own image?*: even more than with other businesses, there is a moulding influence between Facebook's founder and the organisation itself, including: for the 'Face' in Facebook read chutzpah – a key part of its founder; however implicit, it involves being much more than *just a face*: facing up, facing down, being a face, facing-off, having face; its real business *identity* again, is chutzpah. This is impossible without scalable confidence. Arguably, at least in the initial stages, Facebook brought together the founder's and the users' chutzpah: it tapped the narcissism of the first digital generation who sought 'chutzpah-value'.

---

78 Tim Bradshaw 'The fickle value of friendship', *The Financial Times*, 31 March 2011.
79 See section below 'Customer Need and Value'.

So a new business model will have to examine seriously, and *anew*, the whole area of 'customer need' and how this has changed with the internet giving greater customer choice, feedback and power, and how value is constituted.

CUSTOMER NEED AND VALUE

The common business mantra is that customer value is how an organisation meets customer needs. Aren't needs obvious and simple – one click and you're there? Today, how an organisation makes choices about how organisational value is created, delivered and captured, that is, its business model, is hugely important. Further, the simple one-off transaction in which a customer 'buys something and is done' might now be the least effective one while the more effective models 'create stickiness or loyalty or barriers to entry'.[80] To capitalise on business models, organisations must explore both value and need.

However, this is also to recognise that how 'need' is constituted and met is complex. Too often human need is confused with market need[81] – in the sense of 'we'll tell you what you want'.

TRADITIONAL VALUE – SUBTRACTING VALUE?

Whatever 'value' is, it is sought by companies to gain competitive advantage. It is often traditionally expressed as economic value, which clearly, every organisation must address. However, if this is the sole meaning it can have negative consequences and limited sustainability.

VALUE-SUBTRACTING VALUE?

An example of what we claim is 'value-subtracting value' is a recent book on 'value' which, to be fair concentrated particularly on financial value. It identifies four cornerstones of corporate finance. The first is 'the core of value', where companies create value by investing capital to generate future cash flows at a higher rate of return than the cost. The three other cornerstones continue the theme, including 'conserving value', generating higher cash flows and inevitably, driving the company's stock price, *as well as* its actual performance. Put baldly, some of this is necessary, but put uncritically, it is in danger of leading right back to the debacle of *shareholder value*. This narrows the purpose of a company to

---

80 Rita Gunther McGrath (2011) 'When your business model is in trouble', *Harvard Business Review*, January–February 2011, pp. 96–99.
81 Primyamvada Gopal 'University's mustn't again be the rich's hereditary domain', *The Guardian*, 20 August 2010.

maximising shareholder value and has resulted in reductive, short-term thinking. It has, of course, a theory to underpin it in the shape of agency theory, which is designed to align the interests of senior managers with those of shareholders through incentives such as stock options or other forms of 'stock-based compensation'. This has dominated most business thinking and continues to do so with dire effects that we have seen in the financial sector.

The claim that maximising shareholder value benefits both shareholder and society is increasingly questioned. As mentioned above, Jack Welch, former CEO of General Electric, previously a strong champion, recently dismissed its strategic primacy as 'the dumbest idea in the world'.[82] The extraction of shareholder value was a key issue in the Southern Cross care-home debacle, whose poor quality of care for elders was highlighted by the BBC's 'Panorama'[83] programme. It brings us right back to the issue of what the purpose of an organisation is, and how important customers are. However, opposed to the shareholder value approach, there is also evidence that shareholders do better when firms put *customers* first.[84] This aligns with Peter Drucker's assertion that the purpose of a business is to acquire and keep customers.

There is also increasing evidence from high-performing organisations that managing for value not cost is more effective:

> *Managing cost drives cost up. Cost reduction is a by-product of focusingon value. Most managers assume that improving service pushes costs up.*
>
> *But that is ... a faulty definition of service ... driving out failure demand, working to deliver the service that people need in the shortest possible time with the minimum effort releases capacity and reduces overall cost.'[85]*

---

82 Andrew Hill (2011) 'Real value looks past quarterly reporting', *The Financial Times*, 19 April 2011.

83 Heather Stewart 'Lansley has a Southern Cross to bear', *The Observer*, June 2011. Their original 'alert' in May 2009, suggested that 'short-term shareholder value through financial engineering, used by many private equity firms sits uneasily with providing care'.

84 Roger Martin (2010) 'The age of customer capitalism', *Harvard Business Review*, January–February 2010, pp. 59–65.

85 Simon Caulkin (2011) '7 counterintuitive truths for managers' Vanguard Leaders' Summit, December 2010. The title itself indicates the degree of anti-mythic struggle needed.

This summary of the experience of nine effective organisations, suggests that if value is built and managed meaningfully the rest will automatically follow.

WHAT IS 'CUSTOMER NEED'?

Customer need seems straightforward: customer buys a car = need settled. But why did he or she buy *that* car? Apart from obvious factors like price, what other factors were came into play? The seller's attitude, care or carelessness, the whole customer experience – this is where the action of buying something is a construction of need and offer. There is expectation, choice, what the customer has previously experienced and knows, and of course what she needs it for. When Henry Ford asked customers what they wanted from his first cars, they replied: a faster horse. As Apple's Steve Jobs put it, 'A lot of the time, people don't know what they want until you show it to them.' Or again, Peter Drucker's, 'The customer rarely buys what the company thinks it is selling to him.' (sic)[86]

How 'need' is constituted and met is complex. We found this with one participant organisation as it became clear that (their) customer value was significantly more than 'supplying a t-shirt'. When explored, this 'more' ranged from the fashionable to the fundamental: to be cool, nice colours, part of a movement, identity, alignment with a broad aim, for political reasons, even, 'It says who I am.'

However, this work suggests a new source of value: the CVP, 'An offering that helps customers more effectively, reliably, conveniently or affordably, solve an important problem – *or satisfy a job to be done* at a given price.' This moves an organisation from asking,[87] 'What do you need?' to 'What job are you trying to get done…?' The second question has radical potential for opening up every aspect of the business to creating greater value. It also links the three models: the management model to manage value not cost; the learning model without which none of this can occur and the business model with the CVP as the keystone of a successful business model.

HOW NEED MEETS VALUE: A CUSTOMER FRIENDLY CONTRADICTION

To clarify this idea of 'value' here is an example of the complex relationship between customer need and value and their implications for organisations today.

---

86 Peter Drucker (1993) *Managing for Results*. New York, Collins, p. 94.
87 Mark W. Johnson (2010) *Seizing the White Space: Business Model Innovation for Growth and Renewal*. Boston, MA, Harvard Business Press, p. 116.

'Accomplishment'

Take the most obvious customer 'need' when attending college – to obtain a qualification. However, this is only the beginning of the journey for the holder. It should lead somewhere – to another higher qualification, or a job. And the marketplace is crowded with many such qualifications. Further, the learning culture developed at this college continually asks students to make decisions, to take responsibility for what exactly they want which includes something they may not have bargained for: becoming an independent learner. The latter, students slowly realise, is what will distinguish them from others with the same piece of paper. It is much more demanding. But when the rewards are examined, more employers and gatekeepers seem to prefer it. It confers advantage. The student 'need' after constructive dialogue with the provider paid to meet it, might have included things students did not initially want. Had they known this beforehand, they might have taken their custom elsewhere. Nonetheless, it is a hallmark of success. The 'job to be done' for the student is thus not just getting the qualification. It is getting to, and past, the next gatekeeper, the next employer, a higher course.

With 'learning' and other customer requirements, 'needs' can be defined too broadly or thought of only in relation to existing products and services, rather than as with the CVP, 'what job do they want to get done'. So paradoxically, needs can produce an initial resistance or defensiveness, and the tackling of this is a key part of why the 'job isn't getting done'.

This 'constructed value' and how it is not necessarily straightforward is evident in the following instances:

- When the founder of one participant organisation says 'I never think about customer needs' – that is fine as long as it generates perceived value and (as we note above), as long as they *experience* it.

- Having identified the initial customer need, Serco, the FTSE 100 service company regularly redefines and renegotiates it to create greater value.

- Some larger consultancies, particularly when working with companies like banks, have what might be called an 'inserted need' where regardless of actual client need, they insert their own so that the ultimate negotiated offer is designed to meet their interests as well as those of clients.

It is interesting to note that even the notoriously quixotic marketing industry, in its choice of 'superbrands',[88] while claiming such brands are based on 'quality, reliability and distinction' also recognises the unconscious filtering decisions customers make every day which have a phenomenal impact on the balance sheets of the world's biggest companies. Though they don't say so explicitly this is customer need at work.

In the 'accomplishment' example above, customer need is a complex negotiation, which builds 'endurance' beyond the immediate 'need' and is a key source of potential value for all involved. Thus value, constructed between producer and customer, is of infinite variety and immensely negotiable.

This work offers, as part of a business model, the exploration of new 'value'. But it can be seen that this inherently involves learning and managing for both organisations and, to some degree, customers. To take customers through to actual 'value' in the case above involves a learning process which organisations probably have to initiate.

To capitalise on 'value' they will need to tackle their internal barriers to 'value creation'. These can appear in the form of *value subtraction*: this is broadly where 'inside-out' – what the producer has, dominates 'outside-in' what the customer 'needs' and appears in a range of ways such as: staff working in disconnected ways; delays and arguments are routine; where 'rules are rules' with rigid planning and improvement ideas ignored; with little attempt to explore potential customer value through unmet needs; and where staff say, 'Why should we know what "value" is?'[89] It is ultimately, where compliance is the greatest value.

Using these new models, the learning model creates value through improvement ideas of staff; the management model enables trust to oil this by opening 'discretionary effort'; and the business model's potential source of value, and organisational wealth, is robust customer engagement, so their unmet or unsatisfied needs, or 'job to be done' becomes explicit. For all organisations today, the challenge is to create value from need.

---

88 'Superbrands', an Independent supplement distributed by *The Guardian* on behalf of Superbrands (UK), 5 March 2011.
89 See Chapter 6, Building the New Models – The Business Model, p. 144 from which all these instances are taken.

A recognition of how 'value' and 'need' can be advantageously slippery, and how 'need' can be a new commodity, of infinite variety, infinitely negotiable, and infinitely adjustable, needs to be included in the new business model.

See also the lessons from Facebook more fully explored in the Appendix 1: Don't Try This at Home!

The New Models – Interdependence and Learning as a Midwife

THE ROLE OF LEARNING AS A MIDWIFE TO THE OTHER MODELS

In this section we continue to develop the models which participant organisations will use and note two key, emerging features, starting with the role of the learning model as midwife, or lubricant for the others, management and business.

As can be seen from the case studies, it is not easy for any organisation to decide if their management model needs amending or complete reinvention. We considered that by first identifying their challenges then their practice, using the new models would enable them to decide the *scale* of change needed in each model. Organisations generally find endless reasons to ignore or make excuses for the effects of their management model. However, the longer they stand off tackling problems their management model creates, the more muscular and expensive they become. But there is another key reason, illustrated in the case studies above, which is only vaguely recognised, *that it takes more than a change in the management model itself to change the management model.*

This is because not only are the models interdependent, with effects in one felt in them all, but the initial starting point for change is not via the management model but *through 'learning' or the learning model.*

'LEARNING': THE NEW SWEARWORD

'Learning' may be 'loved' but it has many fairweather supporters and many blockages, which are explored below. As one manager said to us 'learning' is an anagram for 'difficulty' as if even using the term meant having to wear gloves! So where learning is concerned, the first difficulty is even recognising its need, illustrated in these two representative examples:

- David Varney, CEO ex-O2, Essex Hospital said:

'One of the things I discovered is that you need three ingredients to be really unsuccessful. You need to be blind; you need to be blind to the fact that you're blind and then you need to make it undiscussable...'[90]

- Dan Ariely describes helping a company having trouble – ironically – getting its bonus system right. He asked why the company didn't test out some ideas, do some experiments or carry out a survey. The HR department replied no, it was a miserable time there, saying:

'We don't want to cause trouble messing about with people's bonuses merely for the sake of learning.'

Ariely made the point that the employees were already unhappy ...[91]

How should these blockages to 'development' be tackled? Courses, qualifications, training events, where it is assumed or hoped the particular issue is tackled? The 'old' ways? We propose that the way to tackle them is through 'learning' – though not the comfortable sit-down-unchallenged-event learning can become. As the barriers are all psychological they will need to be tackled anyway. And to do so, the protagonists can't be *unconscious* of learning! So the learning needs to be of a particular kind, *learning-conscious learning*,[92] which actually draws attention to itself, particularly when used anew, and enables actionable understanding through experimenting in action. Further, the claim here is that 'real learning' (begging another question!) occurs in unpromising circumstances – where weight is firmly against it.

The blockages include:

Admitting its need

Effective learning means in the first place, someone admitting that something is wrong, or even feels wrong, however difficult and uncomfortable. This could just as easily be about systems or processes or cash flow which worked effectively for years.

However, once we start using terms like recognition, feelings, admitting or discomfort, we are less in the field of management, systems theory or finance

90 Jane Dudman 'Tough Call' interview with Sir David Varney, *Society Guardian*, 14 July 2010.
91 Dan Ariely 'Why businesses don't experiment', *Harvard Business Review*, April 2010, p. 34.
92 Alan Rogers (2003) *What is the Difference?* Leicester, NIACE.

and more firmly in the field of psychology, where everybody's behaviour inflicts on everybody else, in large or small measure, because that is what *organisational life* entails. We call this 'learning'. And this will need to be deeper learning if those with the initial feelings, possibly managers themselves, are also part of the problem.

Though acknowledging a problem is frequently cited as the first evidence of *letting learning in*, it need not necessarily be so – defensiveness may still have a strong hand. As well, if not acknowledged, it can take considerable confidence for someone to raise not just the problem, however much its presence nags, but that it can be addressed through 'learning'. That is why there needs to be an explicit learning model specifically included to challenge the management model.

Consider briefly the Varney example noted above: the assumption of a management world where everything is illuminated by the sunlight of rational discourse conveniently ignores the world of company culture and how power presents itself in relationships, feelings and the self. In other words, the political sphere, usually disdainfully dismissed as if everybody was above it, 'Oh please, can't we get above the politics?' Considerable learning is needed to admit it is present everywhere and in the Varney case, to approach him with a belief that learning can improve him. Unpromising circumstances indeed, though with immense potential rewards. For such enduring problems, *learning is the new politics* – but it demands *a* more democratic currency.

The power and influence of habit

A key reason learning organisations are of interest is that it is claimed they can unlock potential at a collective level. We are saying that clearly learning can do this starting at an *individual* level – a claim hardly above a cliché – but *recognising the unpromising difficulties*. Why is it that so many managers, or people generally, who describe themselves as good learners shy away from what seems to others obviously needed change? This is because such issues, need *learning energy, risk and interference*. If something doesn't work, something different, that is, new, needs to be thought up and urged into practice. This has to be inserted into the ordinary mess of everyday operations, *of practice*, precisely at the point of 'how we've always done it' with its immense power, its well-rehearsed rhythm, routines and hierarchies, where thinking and acting intertwine in an apparently seamless single endeavour. And because previous learning has worked this can become an attractive form of arrested development. In such circumstances, change is unlikely at the first, or probably the second attempt unless the change-agent can *in the first place* increase their rate of learning. This means ensuring their learning is at least as fast as the rate of change in the environment they seek to influence. Thus the need for learning-conscious learning.[93] Consider the exponential rate of liberating change in the Varney instance if someone made 'blindness' discussable – how other improvements would begin to flow.

What did you say it was called?

Many organisations not only blame those needing learning for not having it ('It's up to them isn't it') but use any term but learning to describe the need, for example, 'problems, issues, HR's bag...' And once over the defensive repertoire[94] of denial and blame, they then use traditional means to eliminate it as quickly as possible. This is usually through set inputs, formal training with an assumption that attendance is enough and staff as consumers. Learning, in the sense we mean here, does not have a leading role.

'What has *learning* got to do with it?' a senior manager said to me recently, ironically in a change initiative, followed by the admission that 'learning is not my best suit'. When I asked what his 'best suit' was, his answer was, 'Telling people what they don't know – that is, they need to learn!' This is just the same defensiveness in duller clothing. Claiming learning as the starting point more confidently, might not completely delete blame but it should begin to turn round the habit-tanker to focus on 'what next'. The solution has more sustainable fuel if one of those involved can ask, 'What can we learn from this?' This is a key value-creating activity and change-lubricant. Without this, symptom-dealing or in Rosabeth Moss Kanter's phrase, putting 'lipstick on the bulldog' are likely to occur, which leaves the initial 'problem' not merely untouched ('at least we tried') but *strengthens* it, making it even more difficult to tackle next time. Think porcupine.

Further, though some organisations may recognise the need for individual 'learning' they rarely do at a collective level. In change circumstances, this is their Achilles heel. They learn poorly, if they learn at all, learn the wrong things, or worse, consider learning irrelevant.

---

93 See the Learning Model in Chapter 6, The Three Models: Facing the Future.
94 Chris Argyris (1994) 'Good communication that blocks learning', *Harvard Business Review*, July/ August 1994.

Reacting with the old models

When 'real' problems emerge many organisations react with the old or default models: in learning, according those with most power far greater listening-depth, making it very difficult for ordinary staff ideas to be heard; with management, controlling-out healthy challenges; and in business, requiring organisational purpose to be constantly restated as inertia puts customers second. Fatally, they are unconnected whereas the new models emphasise their interdependence: for instance, *learning* to listen and share also means *managing* to accept necessary challenges, and in *business*, striving to retain customer-focussed vigilance. Nonetheless, the starting point is in the psychology of learning: who can lead, who has the confidence, how can the unsayable be said, productively? So a *consequence of raising the need for learning* must also be considered, no easy feat.

The kind of learning needed

To grow in such terrain learning needs to be transformative and 'significant', that is, 'to some degree involving turbulence within the individual and the system'[95] and, as identified earlier.

As can be seen in the case of one organisation, at an individual level, it also requires endurance beyond the immediate, which it can build.[96]

Learning is a key source of value; it is a key component of every change task but is too easily missed as a starting point, or in how people grasp an issue. At an individual and organisational level it is a hidden hub, where anxieties *and* solutions live, an intersection and crossover platform, where the first transformative response needed is to reconfigure it as learning. In the learning model we envisage learning is not just a heading but the *headlights* for the future.

The importance of learning cannot be overstated: not only should it be 'democratically accessible'; its denial should be seen as an organisational crime. This is why many managers in non-improving organisations, their role having invested them with the power to grant access to learning, instead,

---

95 Knud Illeris (2004) *The Three Dimensions of Learning*. Gylling, Denmark, Roskilde University Press, p. 36. Also as identified more fully in Chapter 6, The Three Models: Facing the Future.
96 See 'Individual learning' example in Chapter 6, The Three Models: Facing the Future – the Learning Model.

make their staff dependent on *their* learning. To reverse this so they can learn means changing the management model, moving from control to trust, where organisations choose the principles and practice designed to set their staff free as learners. In this way the three models can harness problems far beyond symptom-dealing by always seeking the 'what's best next?' stage. In the new learning model, it is always in demand as a multiplier of 'value'. This is why we claim that the learning model is midwife to problems and to changes needed which are prompted by the other two models.

'Management' has always sought respectability by attempting to imitate the physical sciences. For learning purposes, a useful model is the 'law of requisite variety' in quantum physics where 'that part of the system with most flexibility ends up controlling the system'.[97] We are suggesting here that this 'most flexible element' is learning, with its capacity to transform; having dominated management by its frequent absence it now does so through its powerful presence.

HIDDEN CONNECTIONS: HOW THE THREE MODELS ARE INTERCONNECTED

To demonstrate how the three models are interconnected, here is an illustration of their inseparability in practice.

For more than ten years, I have been attending a large NHS hospital in London as an eye patient. Over that period, I have seen the reduction of staff and at least a doubling of patients. The eye clinic has had various makeovers. This particular hospital is notorious for losing patient records though the IT system does now seem to work. It has tried different forms of management models, beginning with the 'because I can', where nurses take out their passive empowerment on patients with a bellowing crowd management approach which moves them round the room for no effective purpose. Next was silent management, with administrative staff being left to explain why patients cannot be seen and finally, modern management where three different services connect only at the end when a consultant pronounces on the information gathered from the other services. All the different systems 'work' but in a disconnected way, creating a fraction of the value they could – a key concept in this work. Only consultants can make 'knowledge judgements' even though

97 Steve McDermott (2002) *How to be a Complete and Utter Failure in Life, Work and Everything: 39 ½ Steps to Lasting Underachievement.* Harlow, Prentice Hall Business.

staff at each service are quite capable of explaining the meaning of the various test results and are regularly asked by patients to do so.

Here are some typical exchanges in each of related services (or systems):

Eye testing: Have you taken your drops? Yes. What are they called? XYZ. When did you take them? 9am. Pause. I ask if there isn't another question she should ask me. No. Well, I say, you could ask are they having any effect? That's not my job, she says ending the exchange.

Field testing: I say to the nurse that I notice this test seems to take much longer. It took eight minutes she says. I ask is that longer thant before? Yes, she replies, looking at my previous records. What does that mean, I ask – a deterioration? The consultant will tell you, she says. Are there more gaps, I ask, pointing at the printout she has? The next patient is coming in and needs to be seated, she says, ending the exchange.

The consultant: I ask why the other service staff cannot give details and results of the tests they supervise and what it means. I do that he says. But couldn't they keep the patient informed and enable them to better self-manage? Maybe, he says, cautiously, but that assumes some things… remember the best minds do not come into the NHS! With his concluding diagnosis – little improvement and more of the same treatment – I ask him where the 'best minds' do go and shouldn't this hospital be developing them?

In this instance, improving patient service requires amending or, more likely, completely reinventing the three models:

- *Management model*: organising effort better – this needs to move from 'not my job' to how silly it is if it is not, and how much more efficient it would be if I was allowed to impart standard information to the patient.

- *Business model*: creating greater patient value – this needs to centre on how to get patients through more quickly, and with better information, while at the same time giving the practitioner the incentive to contribute to the improvement of the service. This means aligning the practitioner with an active organisational purpose of 'doing the best for the patient' which the organisation's current models obstruct.

- *Learning model*: how organisational thinking is mobilised – the *what best next*. The individual learning – what the nurse gleaned from the test *and* how the patient responds to her conveying the results, is fed back into the system and 'interferes' for better, faster, more informed patient management. But the crucial point is the three new models must start here with learning. And the first point of learning is: '*doing my job isn't my job – it's interconnecting with other jobs, to get the patient's job (CVP) done!*' These approaches *together*, ensure organisational purpose and learning to work better interdependently *for greater value*. This should provide value-based self-managing for staff *and* patients.

When I brought these issues up the standard response was the provider's need to be aware of possible litigation and risk – for instance, staff could give the wrong information. I asked what if the three elements of the service together were creating no patient improvement over ten years? Ah the consultant replied, but the condition hasn't got worse has it? I left thinking that consultants rehearse their lines in a kindergarten.

From the perspective of this work, each stage with these current (old) models continually interrupts value and, at worst, subtracts it. They also create dependence whereas in the new models each stage creates greater value. To begin the new models, all that is needed is for someone to think 'surely we can do better than this', and then lead, in order to enable patients to do the same. Interconnections will inevitably follow. The new models are certainly not *less* challenging.

GETTING BEYOND TRAPPED THINKING

As mentioned earlier, the new three models are based on the radical claim that the old ones are a key part of current problems. One key way in which the old models work is to limit us to what we already are. I once observed a manager in an organisation urgently needing improvement having had her carefully laid out plans for improvement casually rejected by her (senior) manager saying: 'So you're saying what we should do is get back in our boxes and sweat more'. It takes such little energy to fall back on the old models. They reinforce established notions that, for instance, we can learn only in certain ways ('You haven't got a degree, or the necessary theory') or that excellence equals length of service ('You can make suggestions when you've been here as long as I have') or that predictable plodding-planning works ('That half-baked idea has never not been proved') or that we've always pulled through ('The customers will find us').

Yet, at the same time we don't need a theory of learning to ask, 'What can we learn?' or a theory of innovation to innovate – yes, there is a theory even for that – or seniority to have good ideas. We don't need to know every 'discipline' or be a specialist in it to improve it: because we can't do everything we can't do *something*.

The old approach (or theories in use) in separating problem headings as in the case studies also has the effect of keeping solutions under separate headings. Thus for instance, even when the need for change across boundaries is recognised common organisational responses are:

- with learning, to invest even further in *individual* learning – the old model – when the need is for far greater collective learning;

- for 'better' business, to imitate competitors or employ tough 'producer push' – the old model – without confidently investigating what customers need, 'customer-pull';

- in management, to complaints of there being an authoritarian management style, bringing in a suggestion scheme which trails right back to the manager whose style was the source of the complaints – the old model – rather than building a climate for productive self-managing.

Not only are these responses quick-fixes that tackle only low-hanging fruit, they are insufficient to sustain change, and are *unconnected*.

The design of the new models recognises that in practice what managers experience are problems rather than comfortably sealed 'subjects' or 'disciplines'. Regardless of the boxes they emerge in, 'managing', 'financing', 'producing' or indeed 'development' problems travel across boundaries, arise from and have an impact on management, learning and ultimately, business. Most 'problems' will embrace human agency. For each one, *somebody experiences it*, be they problem holders, posers, solvers or deniers, and the problems cannot be tackled till their human source is addressed too.

The new models – though they can be seen as conceptually separate – are three parts of a single approach and are (as this work will assert) 'interdisciplinary'. They also act as heuristics.

The work gives organisations the opportunity to make explicit choices about key structural *enablers* in their businesses, their management, learning and business models *and* to connect them.

SUMMARY: THE JOURNEY OF THE NEW MODELS

The models[98] act as change-enablers and supply direction under a range of principles which inform practice. The journey of the new ideas begins with organisations outlining their current key challenges and then using the three models to assess both where they are now and where they want to be two years on to meet those challenges. This involves judging the adequacy of their current models to get them to their next stage of development by asking if the thinking and models which got them this far can get them further. If, as anticipated, they need to reinvent their models, this will mean in practice, interconnecting the new thinking, rather than separating – the old thinking – the three models. And, however hidden, starting with learning.

Building the New Models

This section consists of an explanation and analysis of each model. Also, the end of the chapter has a brief reminder of the research sequence using the value-creating inquiry approach, and 'getting into practice', the support offered to each organisation.

The three 'models' comprise an inquiry approach based on key principles of 'management', 'business' and 'learning' theories used to examine and enable organisational development. The claim of this work is that using the three models together will enable organisations to reach their next stage of development *faster*. Their use will also involve organisations, as necessary, in making explicit choices about their three models and explore new 'value'.

Behind the above claim is another radical one, that the thinking – in management, learning and business – their 'theories-in-use', which has got the

---

98 See Chapter 6, Building the New Models for details of each.

organisations this far will be a barrier to future development and will need reinventing.

The three models are:

Management Model: the choices made about how organisational effort is organised (the *how* of business).

Business Model: the choices made about how organisational value is created, delivered and captured (the *what and why* of business).

Learning Model: the choices made about how organisational thinking is mobilised (the *what best next*).

Each model consists of the following (see Figure 6.2):

- Three 'dimensions' or key activities (of management, learning or business) which consists of not every aspect of each but those most important and relevant to this approach.

- Three sets of 'principles' which are expressed along a continuum: 'principles' are an underlying belief which informs work in practice, that is, how staff enact and experience it in action.

- Three sets of 'effects', located at the bottom of the list of principles, to capture the consequences of using particular principles in practice.

- An 'explanation of terms' which includes typical 'sayings' associated with each principle to illustrate them in practice.

- The models and explanations were used as guidance for participants for their initial assessment. In the assessment each organisation identified where it was now and where it wanted to be in two years time. A complete version of all the models is included in Chapter 12, Techniques.

It is may be useful to think of the models as 'expansive metaphor'[99] or, as one manager, commented during the work, 'as heuristics' as much as theories.

---

99 Gillian Tett, The very model of a modern major market influence, reviewing '*Metaphors, models and theories*' by Emanuel Derman, *The Financial Times*, 24 December 2010. See also Chapter 4, Research Method or Inquiry Approach.

Dimension or Key Activity	Principles or Underlying Beliefs	Continuum	Principles or Underlying Beliefs
Managing direction	**Hierarchy**	⬅➡	**Collective wisdom**
Managing means	**Bureaucracy**	⬅➡	**Emergence**
Managing capacity	**Today**	⬅➡	**Tomorrow**
Effect	**Static**	⬅➡	**Agile**

Today | 2 years on

Explanation of Terms

Hierarchy	Collective wisdom
Goals and direction are set through authority of managers; leaders are ascribed	In certain conditions, collective expertise of large numbers can produce better decisions and forecasts than a small number of experts; once confident, oblique principles are adopted (goals pursued indirectly); leaders emerge
Saying: *The boss/manager knows best*	**Saying**: *More open sourcing will accelerate 'wisdom' – or learning*
Bureaucracy Work is structured through formal rules ensuring consistency, maintaining tradition	**Emergence** Purposive self-organising occurs with actors working more independently, taking responsibility for co-ordinating their work
Saying: *Use the sign-off procedure – or else*	**Saying:** *Let's self-organise to get there faster*
Today Concern for control; little staff discretion; most energy consumed in daily operations; works predictably; 'permission culture'; 'development' is more of the same; extrinsic motivation	**Tomorrow** Concern for trust; staff autonomy; high improvement and innovation rate; freedom in how work is done; 'forgiveness culture'; stretching rather than striving; challenging climate; intrinsic motivation
Saying: *Limits are limits*	**Saying:** *The more challenging the goal (purpose) the more other goals will be reached*
Static Has a fading respect; traditional; inflexible; 'job for life'; comfortable; long-staying staff	**Agile** Flexible, seeks continual successful market adjustment; potentially stressful; high trust leading to sustained high performance; long list of people who want to work there
Saying: *Tomorrow is more of today*	**Saying**: *With engagement, tomorrow begins today*

Figure 6.2   Management Model*

* See Acknowledgement (below) to Julian Birkinshaw's model in *Reinventing Management* (2010)
San Francisco, Jossey-Bass.

THE BACKGROUND TO THE MODELS

The models are based on, amongst other considerations, what has been learned from 'failed change' as occurred in the case studies.[100] They include the current thinking which contributed to 'failed change'. In the new models, there is a deliberate attempt to draw attention to the 'Effects' of whatever balance of principles each organisation uses. The language used in the 'effects' in each model, 'Static/Agile', 'Asphyxiation and Resilience', and 'Stagnation/Decline or Growth and Renewal' is designed to provoke and *dramatise* the powerful effects of using particular principles and, as was often the case, particular ones used in tandem. This gets the models beyond the purely theoretical (though obviously based on theory), with the inevitable outcomes of using particular ones clearly identified. There would have been little point in attempting to measure each principle and then not measuring the effects.

Another reason for selecting this language was that many organisations have default thinking (or models) where managers may have left behind urgency, improvement energy, or an eye for innovation, for a life of comfortable challenges – that is, more of the known. Some management commentators use milder terms than these in identifying similar results – 'chugging' was the term used by the late Sumantra Ghoshal.[101] And while it might be more acceptable than say, 'Static', *for those experiencing it*, it is just as dangerous but may seem easier to ignore as it is so soothingly expressed. This default thinking, once acknowledged, needs 'renewing'. Similarly the 'Today/Tomorrow' continuum is designed to explicitly identify and 'force in' thinking about the future, rather than collude with assumptions that it would emerge *automagically* from efforts concentrated almost solely on today. Maybe it would – but we doubted it.

In terms of language, when we asked managers for their own 'headline' terms for the models, ironically they said things like 'treading water' and 'regressive' – inevitably heading towards the initial terms we had chosen.

One manager asked, 'Who would want to select, or admit they were 'stagnating' for instance?' We considered that was the whole point, to enable the organisations to take the first step to acknowledge mistakes and weaknesses, which brings the first sting of discomfort and having to confront the need to learn. The more negative the effects, the greater the urgency to choose new

---

100 See Chapter 5, The Current Mould: Four Case Studies.
101 Sumantra Ghoshal and Heike Bruch (2006) 'Beware the busy manager', *Harvard Business Review*, Winter 2006, pp. 62–70.

models to meet their future challenges though this might involve considerable change. Appropriately, the models are action-based change tools to enable appropriate actions to overcome weaknesses.

HOW TO READ THE MODELS

In reading the models, another manager said, 'Some of the headings may not be seen as a continuum but as "adversarial, either/or, too contrary, or too leading".' This may be a weakness in our guidance in that however opposed the principles appear, they should be seen more as a continuum. In the initial assessment some organisations made the point that they wanted to be, for instance, both 'better bureaucrats' and *at the same time* more 'emergent' depending on their particular challenges. Some of the highly regulated organisations dealing with patients and financial services wanted to be 'better' at both 'Today' and in building thinking capacity for 'Tomorrow'. However, this applied in the end to any organisation.

LINKING THE MODELS

The elements and structure of each model are identified separately. However, this is more a conceptual separation as in practice they leak into one another, being three parts of the same approach. The structure enables organisations to identify where change needs to occur in each separately, though once change actions are clarified, these come together, as changes in one impacts on the others.

To underline their interconnectedness, each model draws on elements of the others. For instance, the theme of 'value' runs through them all: with the business model, 'value creation' is a key aspect; with the learning model, in 'Emergent', staff produce value through their (now recognised) learning for improvement; and with the management model, in 'Tomorrow', a climate of high trust produces engagement and commitment without which 'value' will not be created at all.

At the time of writing a colleague ordered a new PC from Dell and described the experience as: 'The company is excellent, the delivery procedure is Del Boy.' We mention this because when customers make a purchase or agreement they see it as one task, not many. Thus the models and how organisations operate them in practice, should connect together.

THE MODELS FUNCTION AT A MAINLY CULTURAL LEVEL

The models are constructed round the cultural components of organisational behaviour. However, as everything is not included explicitly, they must be sufficiently comprehensive and flexible to allow virtually anything that could arise to be included. In the management model, for instance, issues to do with organisational structure can be addressed in the 'Hierarchy/Collective wisdom' continuum; and systems and processes can be addressed through the 'Bureaucracy/Emergence' one.

However, *how* these issues arise, and suggestions to improve them, have to emerge from people, and the management model will test if and how they are, or are not, enabled to do so. Such issues will test the feasibility of all the models. Similarly, the business model perhaps gives over prominence to a crucial element, the CVP,[102] while downplaying the other three elements necessary, the key resources, processes and profit formula.

The test, again, is whether different issues can be raised within the models, and our sense was that they could. The models are based on a recognition that in each, *choices* made by organisations make them effective or ineffective, sustainable or not. And how they go about improving, renewing or reinventing them is inevitably *a product of human agency* – does how they operate include how they can be changed? In this sense, the models give due importance to the people who have to work them continuously, to *their* commitment and craft.

BALANCING ADAPTIVE AND RADICAL INNOVATION

The models offer radical innovative potential for organisations. However they can also function as adaptive improvers with more than 100 separate individual improvement activities *possible*, once linked to some process. For instance, 'How can we ensure leaders emerge?' or 'Seek better market adjustment' to be more 'agile' or 'How can we tap into our collective wisdom?' Or being better at 'Today' as better 'Bureaucrats' or getting a better balance between various principles.

This is easy to claim from the writer's perspective having designed them for that purpose. However, that may be some way from an organisation's perspective which might see a cobweb of clutter, boxed incoherence, or 'management' language on stilts. Nonetheless, the models *are* meant to be demanding concept-grenades, a new way to build improvements, tackle uncertainty and more effectively provide for the future.

---

102 See p. 91, the Business Model, in this chapter.

AN ACKNOWLEDGEMENT

The idea for the three models here was based on an initial prompt – the management model in *Reinventing Management*[103] by Julian Birkinshaw which I have significantly amended to meet my specific purposes. I wondered if there was enough in his model – *in itself* – to construct the changes 'management' clearly needed. Even though there were many brilliant examples of changes in Birkinshaw's book, I felt that learning, and particularly *collective learning*, needed more explicit profiling. I have retained his grid format but made changes in the dimensions, principles, integrated their effects and spelt them out, and in the overall explanations. Though organisations may have found his assessment easier to use, this work asks them to self-assess, and the value-creating method, key to this work, invites them to explicitly improve the assessment itself, the inquiry tools. The overall result is I believe to encourage more risk.

Nonetheless, I want to pay my respects to *Reinventing Management*. Though the case for reinventing 'management' was already proven in my own experience as a manager, consultant and many years teaching MBA students, it gave me the initial idea. From it I developed an approach which would enable organisations not just to get beyond management 'failure' and reinvent it, but also to consider those areas treated separately but absolutely integral to sustainable organisational development, learning and business approaches, or models.

Some points about the models:

- they are self-improvement tools;

- they serve as heuristics;

- they are designed as an innovative way for organisations to 'get to know themselves anew' by assessing the state of their current approaches or models to decide if they need to make new choices about them;

- they are meant to give a sense of direction particularly using the 'Effects' so organisations can decide if they have an appropriate direction of travel to meet their current and future challenges;

---

103 Julian Birkinshaw (2010) *Reinventing Management* San Francisco, Jossey-Bass. This is a great storehouse of management innovations. Birkinshaw is also a co-founder, with Gary Hamel, of MLab, a forum for 'Management 2.0'. MLab meetings take the shirt and tie off 'management' and give it a rhythm to dance. It creates a unique, idea-reverb climate which any business school would give two chairs for.

- they are not meant to be absolutes, hermetically sealed from each other or sanctified theory, rather they are a mess of possibility having emerged from contemporary change-practice with all its limitations. The whole point is to get organisations to a point where they can make meaningful *new* choices about the models they now need.

The Management Model

The choices made about how organisational effort is organised (the *how* of business)

How is your management model changing?

Dimension	Principles	Continuum	Principles
Managing direction	**Hierarchy**	⟷	**Collective wisdom**
Managing means	**Bureaucracy**	⟷	**Emergence**
Managing capacity	**Today**	⟷	**Tomorrow**
Effect	**Static**	⟷	**Agile**

Today	2 years on

Explanation of Terms

Hierarchy	Collective wisdom
Goals and direction are set through authority of managers; leaders are ascribed	In certain conditions, collective expertise of large numbers can produce better decisions and forecasts than a small number of experts; once confident, oblique principles are adopted (goals pursued indirectly); leaders emerge
Saying: *The boss/manager knows best*	**Saying**: *More open sourcing will accelerate 'wisdom' – or learning*
Bureaucracy Work is structured through formal rules ensuring consistency, maintaining tradition	**Emergence** Purposive self-organising occurs with actors working more independently, taking responsibility for co-ordinating their work
Saying: *Use the signoff procedure – or else*	**Saying:** *Let's self-organise to get there faster*

Today	Tomorrow
Concern for control; little staff discretion; most energy consumed in daily operations; works predictably; 'permission culture'; 'development' is more of the same; extrinsic motivation	Concern for trust; staff autonomy; high improvement and innovation rate; freedom in how work is done; 'forgiveness culture'; stretching rather than striving; challenging climate; intrinsic motivation
Saying: *Limits are limits*	**Saying:** *The more challenging the goal (purpose) the more other goals will be reached*
Static Has a fading respect; traditional; inflexible; 'job for life'; comfortable; long staying staff	**Agile** Flexible, seeks continual successful market adjustment; potentially stressful; high trust leading to sustained high performance; long list of people who want to work there
Saying: *Tomorrow is more of today*	**Saying:** *With engagement, tomorrow begins today*

The three 'dimensions' or key activities are:

- *Managing direction*: how purpose and direction are established and maintained.

- *Managing means*: how achieving our purpose through performance is maintained.

- *Managing capacity*: how we develop our resources to meet our purpose and continually emerging challenges.

The dimensions are the essential structures of any organisation which need collective effort to operate. They include not every aspect of management but the encapsulating, generic ones relevant to this field and this approach.

Each dimension is followed by a set of 'principles' expressed along a continuum. 'Principles' are the underlying beliefs which inform work in practice, that is, how staff would experience it in action. The principles also recognise the strengths of bureaucracy and hierarchy in, for instance, maintaining tradition and that certain activities may mean organisations want to be better at *both* 'bureaucracy' (having better systems) *and* 'emergence' and want a more effective balance to meet particular challenges. At the end of the grid are 'effects' intended to capture the consequences of using particular principles in practice.

Key aspects and concepts

- A key feature is the elimination of 'debt'[104] by not accruing it in the first place but by developing goodwill and commitment instead. This is designed to reverse the model creating disengagement and unchallenging work, with the effect of 'body here, mind elsewhere'.

- In each principle, the left-hand side is broadly more concerned with control while the right is more concerned with trust. For instance, control (in practice more *enabled self*-control) is maintained through greater trust which is manifested in a 'forgiveness rather than permission' culture, with more experimentation, and a higher improvement and innovation rate.

- The 'Today/Tomorrow' principle, however dramatically expressed, is designed to get beyond any wishful thinking around 'we *always* think of the future' and enable organisations to recognise that if they are overbalanced into 'Today' they will have a limited 'Tomorrow'.

- The three models are interlinked for stronger use: for instance, 'purposive self-organising' and 'staff taking "greater responsibility for work co-ordination" in the management model, along with "forums emerge as problems emerge" in the learning one, and how "the customer value proposition" actively drives discussion' in the business model, *together* have the effect of 'making work whole' so that staff control and improve it from beginning to end.

---

104 'A legacy of traditional management … it accrues not good will or commitment but what is best understood as organisational debt … where over time, staff with least official power (and others) find unofficial ways to reclaim it … a "forced" pay back in the form of 'creative noncompliance' in The Three Models: Facing the Future – the Management Model (p. 84) in this chapter.

The Learning Model

The choices made about how organisational thinking is mobilised (the *what best next* of business)

How is your learning model changing?

Dimension	Principles	Continuum	Principles
Focus for Learning	**Individual**	⬅➡	**Collective**
Sources of Learning	**Traditional**	⬅➡	**Emergent**
Type of Learning	**Superficial**	⬅➡	**Deep**
Effect	**Asphyxiation**	⬅➡	**Resilience**

| Today | 2 years on |

Explanation of Terms

Individual	Collective
The most powerful dispense 'knowledge'; occasional; disconnected; any sharing is based on didactic and 'subject-based' methods	'Productive interference' between individual learning and organisational practices; learning is named, claimed, shared and improvement-leveraged; connected; there is a powerful organisational learning culture informed by vision and values
Saying: *It's up to staff to learn – if they want to*	**Saying**: *What can we learn from that?*
Traditional Staff are consumers of learning; restricted access; traditional training; a 'drain on budgets' yet little ROI analysis; if ROI used, no awareness of the cost of not learning; large cost in 'unlearning' needed for sustainable improvement	**Emergent** Staff are producers of learning; democratic access; open climate of high trust; forums emerge as problems emerge: for example, 'promising practice', creative problem-solving techniques; envisioned experiments, risk-projects led by staff; ideas into impact; managing innovation system; skunkworks; confident; multiple sources; many routes to 'excellence'
Saying: *Ask the experts*	**Saying**: *Here's some news we can use*
Superficial Learning-lite: facts, data, top-down; useful though limiting; satisfied with first returns; learning wrong things, for example, 'unaccountable disengagement'; fearful, compliant; marginal; fire-fighting	**Deep** Rate of learning increases as environment changes; acknowledges and tackles emerging issues; does more complex things better year-on-year; work is an engaged improvement conversation; iterative, persistent, challenging; all activities deeply mined for learning; transparent 'knowledge management'; future-fighting
Saying: *Didn't work before – do what we always do*	**Saying**: *Don't just try harder – learn harder*

Asphyxiation Diminishing returns; repeated failure; dependent staff; increasing costs; opportunities missed	**Resilience** Sustained high performance; agile; high anticipation reservoir; uncertainty-bounding; independent, politically-skilled staff; learning is organisation's oxygen; restful cerebrating
Saying: *We're always too busy to think here*	**Saying**: *The more the challenges the greater the options*

The three 'dimensions' or key activities are:

- *Focus for learning*: where is learning concentrated (people)?

- *Sources of learning*: where does learning come from?

- *Types of learning*: how deep is learning?

Each dimension is followed by a set of 'principles' expressed along a continuum. 'Principles' are the underlying beliefs which inform work in practice, that is, how staff would experience it in action. In building the learning approach we had previous experience of using a range of models including Boydell and Edmondson[105] but we wanted our model to raise more explicitly the profile and primacy of learning, how to spot its need, how to tackle barriers to collective learning, the ultimate value-creator, and to recognise its interrelationship with – and current negative dependence on – a management model.

The principles break each dimension down into separate, feasible, measurable activities. They include not every aspect of learning but the ones which this work claims are commonly neglected, and are most critical for change and development.

At the end of the grid are 'Effects' intended to capture the consequences of using particular principles in practice.

Key aspects and concepts

- A key feature is 'increasing the rate of learning as the environment changes', designed to frame a process necessary not to 'control' change but adjust to and 'ride its waves'.

---

105 Two excellent models: Boydell 4 Stages of Organisational Development: Doing things anyhow, Doing things well, Doing things better and Doing better things. Also Edmondson Organisational Learning expressed in terms of psychological safety: Anxiety, Apathy, Comfort and Learning Zones.

- In each principle, the left-hand side is broadly more concerned with common, and inherited, forms of learning while the right outlines more what are increasingly seen as necessary forms (and types) to enable effective development. For instance, staff being 'producers of learning' rather than only its 'consumers' means they are more alert and have a greater variety of sources to draw on so 'forums emerge as problems emerge', including purposive use of social media; and their repertoire and capacity continually extends so the organisation can do more complex things better year on year.

- 'Productive interference' in the 'Collective Learning' principle is designed to get beyond wishful thinking around for instance, 'our budget for development has always been X per cent' and therefore assume learning occurs, and push organisations to not just improve their development 'return on investment' but to change their learning paradigm. Having to assess their balance between 'fire-fighting' and 'future fighting' reinforces this.

- Reinforcing linkages between models: combining 'multiple sources of learning', in the learning model, along with 'freedom in task-discretion as to how work is done' in the management one and how 'how to capitalise on new opportunities' in the business model, ensures their work is 'future-infected' rather than the present simply infecting it.

- This work makes one other radical claim: *the learning model is the midwife, the lubricant, for the other two models.* That is, the first inkling that change is needed tweaks not the specialist in us but the learning central nervous system; that we frequently deny or resist it, or commonly minimise it, is a sign that we dread its messy calling.[106] The only antidote, however sweaty the journey, is bringing it into the conscious uplands, naming it and using it: individual learning and its gateway, collective learning.

---

106 This is developed further in The New Models: Interdependence and Learning as a Midwife earlier in this chapter (p. 122).

The Business Model

The choices made about how organisational value is created and delivered (the *what* and *why* of business)

How is your business model changing?

Dimension	Principles	Continuum	Principles
Current Business Model	**Implicit**	⬌	**Explicit**
Organisation focus	**Inside out**	⬌	**Outside in**
Value	**Value subtraction**	⬌	**Value creation**
Effect	**Stagnation and decline**	⬌	**Growth and renewal**

Today	2 years on

Explanation of Terms

Implicit	Explicit
Limited awareness of current BM and how it works; one only, or very mature BM; 'how can we plan in such an uncertain business environment!'	Keen awareness of how BM delivers value; how the BM elements cohere; and BM as a 'theory of business' – flexibly; how use it to capitalise on new opportunities; a potential 'white space invader' – unmapped territory outside core business
Saying: What's wrong with more of the same!	*Saying: How can we link customer value and a profit formula? (see below for BM elements)*
Inside-out Opaque windows – internal views dominate; environmental scanning discouraged; customers 'don't know what they really want'	**Outside-in** Sky-high overview of environment; mapping and tracking competition; CVP actively drives discussions; the job a customer 'needs to be done' (the outside) is actively internalised (brought inside); creative customer engagement
Saying: That kind of thinking is not my job	*Saying: How can we meet customer needs faster, better than they currently experience?*
Value subtraction Great barriers to 'value'; staff work in silo-units, disconnected ways, attritional discourse; delays and arguments are routine; 'rules are rules'; rigid planning; improvement ideas are ignored; compliance is the greatest value	**Value creation** Sources of organisational 'wealth' are (1) the thinking (learning) of engaged staff and (2) robust customer engagement; customer unmet and unsatisfied needs are actively sought and capitalised on; whole-organisational interdependence; value-creating activities identified early on; move from company push to customer pull
Saying: Why should we know what 'value' is?	*Saying: Value is sustainable organisational wealth*

Stagnation and decline	Growth and renewal
Business is at an unrecognised mature stage in the life cycle; planning is a mix of more of the same/hope for the best'; 'the bottom line is the only line that matters in judging performance...'	There are a number of BMs in operation; capability is developed and exploited; BM innovation is seen as a toolkit for conquering the unknown
Saying: *Business models – just theory really*	**Saying**: *If there are more opportunities than we can grasp – which are key?*

See 'The Three Models: Facing the Future – The Business Model' in this chapter.[107]

The three 'dimensions' or key activities are:

- *The current business model*: how well is it known and to what end?

- *Organisation focus*: is concentration internal or external and to what end?

- *Value*: what is it and how is it generated?

Each dimension is followed by a set of 'principles' expressed along a continuum. 'Principles' are the underlying beliefs which inform work in practice, that is, how staff would experience it in action.

The principles break each dimension down into separate, feasible, measurable activities. They include not every aspect of business but those the work claims are commonly neglected, and are most critical for change and development.

At the end of the grid are 'Effects' intended to capture the consequences of using particular principles in practice.

Key aspects and concepts

- A key feature is 'value creating': this starts with the customer, where unmet and unsatisfied needs are actively sought and capitalised on.

- In each principle the left-hand side outlines broadly more limited business model thinking (occurring in current approaches) while the right outlines more ambitious, developed ideas which some

---

107 Mark W. Johnson (2010) *Seizing the White Space: Business Model Innovation for Growth and Renewal*. Boston, MA, Harvard Business Press, p. 4.

organisation used to develop faster. For instance, all staff 'having an awareness of how their business model delivers value' along with 'mapping and tracking competition' ensures 'increasing capability is developed and exploited'.

- The 'Inside-out/in' principle expresses anew what is involved (and the change-leadership needed) in the journey from 'not my job' to 'customer 'needs' *are* my job'.

- Reinforcing links between the models: 'sources of organisational wealth are the thinking of engaged staff' and 'robust customer engagement' and 'interdependence' (business), along with 'connected' (learning), and the enabled 'challenging climate' (management) can be a sustained source of 'value creation' for organisations.

The Research Sequence

The purpose was to test if the organisations could get to their next stage of 'development' *faster* using these three new models.

It involved the organisations in:

- using the new models to assess where they were now and wanted to be two years on;

- identifying their current and future challenges;

- identifying their current three models, however implicit, their 'theories-in-use' and their adequacy in meeting these challenges;

- where necessary, making explicit choices about new models and testing their validity and usefulness;

- identifying the next stage of their development and integrating this into new business plans;

- applying the new models to activate this stage (identify, inform and develop).

It also involved:

- testing out a new 'value';

- using the value-creating inquiry method.[108]

GETTING INTO PRACTICE: THE SUPPORT

For participant organisations, consultancy support was offered by Critical Difference. It consisted of enabling the organisations to interpret and use the models, develop their next stages, and involved interviews and author/consultant availability. It also involved facilitating meetings with all the organisations together, and with whole staff groups of the established organisations. These were very productive collectively[109] and resulted in further development meetings led by the founders themselves. This was consistent with the value-creating method, that organisations would take charge of using the models themselves, independently.

Coaching by Winning Pathways Coaching, taken up at a one-to-one level, was also extremely valuable in accelerating learning and enabling some founders to construct new choices both individually and organisationally. It confirmed a long-standing author belief that without coaching, significant development risks take much longer, or fail entirely.

---

108 See Chapter 4, Research Method or Inquiry Approach.
109 See details in Chapter 8, What Occurred and What We Learned.

PART III
The Application

7

Applying the New Models

This chapter consists of:

- Participant organisations and starting by building on their current strengths.

- How the models were introduced to participants.

- How they completed an initial assessment and the outcome.

- A note on theories used (with an Appendix).

- A detailed analysis of each organisation in a 'Summary and key aspects' of each through the models including: the key characteristics of their current models; their key challenges; purpose; performance; and adequacy of their current models to meet these. This is followed by emerging issues; their theories-in-use[1] and the implications; their future challenges and adequacy of their current models to meet these; their next stage of development and finally key tasks to enable them to meet their next stage and their choice of models to activate it.

Please note: Though the structure is broadly the same for all five organisations, it is changed slightly for the start-up and selling-on organisations because of their particular stage of development. These both raised specific issues about the models themselves and this work, which is examined in the 'summary' of each.

---

1   The different theories-in-use are outlined in 'All together now' below (and more fully in Appendix 2). This includes an outline of the history and experiences of small businesses but also how explaining behaviour of people in organisations involves psychological and sociological theories, and economic and above all political theories, as well as management, learning and business ones. Just as managers do not encounter problems as neat 'subjects', neither do organisations. In the end, understanding organisational behaviour and particularly change, might be a case of what theories are *not* relevant.

The Organisations

The participant organisations were, by category:

ESTABLISHED

Believe

Established: 2000 (and previously for five years).
Size: Four full-time staff, many volunteers and around 250 clients (continually expanding).
Type: Registered charity (Private, limited by guarantee).
Purpose: 'Helping people reconnect with their homeland.'

Health House

Established: 2004 as part of an overall social enterprise company.
Size: Around 20 staff (full and part time), approx. 4,000 patients (stable over five years).
Type: Private limited company.
Purpose: 'Providing NHS care for patients with some private services.'

Philosophy Football.com

Established: 1994.
Size: Three full-time, two part-time staff with some highly resourceful, well-connected associates.
Type: Private limited company.
Purpose: 'Sporting outfitters of intellectual distinction – we present ideas in the form of t-shirts as low cost vehicles for our politics and sporting interests.'

START-UP

Social Stock Exchange

Established: Will commence trading in 2012.
Type: Private limited company.
Size: Four to ten full-time staff envisaged.
Purpose: 'To contribute to changing the world by funding social mission organisations.'

'SELLING-ON'

Cognac

Established: 2005.
Type: Private limited company.
Size: Four to seven staff (varies).
Purpose: 'To communicate anything in ten minutes.'

The Journey of the Models: Building on Current Strengths

It is important to be respectful to participant organisations and recognise their current achievements. They didn't 'need' this work in the sense of not surviving without it, though certainly they can benefit from it – at least initially anyway, according to the author.

As stated in each of the 'Summary and Key Aspects' below, the established organisations and the selling-on one had all been trading effectively for some time and had developed significant strengths, reputations and individual ideas of 'success' as part of their unique identities. This means that unlike some more well-known companies which are frequently bought and sold, they *know who they are and what they are there for* – which many companies might seem to have forgotten.

Together these characteristics meant they also had unrealised potential, a challenge which this work offered the opportunity to realise. In conventional business terms they had reached a point where they could 'develop', depending on how this was interpreted. Each established organisation was at least ten years old, had proven sustainability, was 'profitable' and *could be open* to new market opportunities. While the work had set out to involve them in identifying (and possibly changing) the thinking behind their thinking, it also involved them in identifying the challenges behind their challenges – including any 'development opportunities' – at an organisational level but also for the founders, at a personal level.

INTRODUCING THE MODELS

In this initial stage, we first made clear:

1. *The purpose*: to test out the claim that using the three models would enable organisations to get to their next stage of development *faster*.

2.   *The potential benefits*: that applying the models would involve
      identifying their current challenges, their next stage of
      development, the adequacy of their current models to meet these,
      and the opportunity to make explicit choices about new ones, a
      sort of *organisational rebooting* – if necessary. It would also explore
      new 'value'. We also suggested that depending on the challenges
      they faced, while small improvements might result from using the
      models, they are designed to produce more radical developments.
      The organisations were already functioning effectively at various
      stages of development so their current planning would make
      clear what their current models were and how they related to
      the models. There was another potential benefit: that the tools
      are self-assessment ones and could be used independently by the
      organisation themselves, an overall intention of the work.

3.   *The unusual nature of this journey*: using the value-creating method,
      (or inquiry approach) we were starting imperfectly in order to get
      started, while aiming to improve as we progressed. This should
      lead to reciprocal benefits: for the organisations, assessing their own
      performance and considering how to meet their next challenges,
      and for us, with their help, testing out and improving the inquiry
      tools themselves.

TAKING A RISK AND BOUNCING-IN THE ORGANISATIONS

To generate understanding of the models as assessment tools leading to new
actions, we employed the value-creating method – 'Use learning as a bias
towards action and trust it, the first risk' along with 'Embrace the management
of uncertainty – take risks beyond *knowing*'. The purpose of the initial assessment
was less to be 'scientific' but to create an entry point for the venture, a friendly
bouncer, bouncing the organisations *in*. Regardless of where they placed
themselves on the models, we wanted them to explore their own thinking,
bring evidence to justify their judgements, and relate this to their current and
future performance. It was the start of an extended thinking process about how
to construct their futures – along with their present planning.

THE FIRST EXPERIENCE IS THROUGH LANGUAGE

The organisations' first actual experience of the models was less by way of
benefits and more through their *language*. We wondered how they would see the

tools: as just 'management theory', too remote from practice, too revolutionary, or imagined; or as a cluttered cobweb, management language on stilts?

We worried about these even if they begged the precise question we sought to answer: what are their current management, learning and business theories? And even if we knew a stronger understanding would emerge as they began to apply them. We may have underestimated the degree of persistence we all needed to pursue them for the purpose intended. We reassured ourselves that the models are *meant* to be demanding and part of the job was to bridge the practice between their everyday 'operational incontinence', as one manager put it, and risking new thinking to tackle it.

AVOIDING FALSE RESEARCH

We also wanted to avoid *false research*. This is the process, however sophisticated, of simply renaming what is already being done in the language of the 'researchers'. We wanted to find out their current models, how they had been chosen, their language and use, and how this related to the models.

At this stage, depending on their current models, a potentially dangerous perception arose that our intention was to prove their models 'wrong' or limited (see Chapter 8, What Occurred and What We Learned). To counter this, we restated that the work included *their view* of the adequacy of their current models in meeting their challenges, and that the whole point of the work was to test out the claim of 'faster' development using the models.

COMPLETING THE INITIAL ASSESSMENT

To test the claim and get the journey going, we used the assessment to 'start imperfectly but meaningfully' informed by the method, to:

1.   familiarise managers and their organisations with the overall aims and methods of the inquiry and build a relationship between them and the materials, and between the author and the managers;

2.   assess where they are now and wanted to be in two years time;

3.   increasingly become more accurate with the language and evidence, and bridge any gap between where they thought they were and where they actually were;

4.   reciprocally, improve the inquiry tools;

5.   over time, identify their challenges, the adequacy of their current models, their next stage of development and the models needed to activate this.

THE OUTCOME

As the initial activity, this was meant to be rigorous. It didn't matter where managers placed their organisations – greater accuracy would come with greater familiarity with both materials and their own needs, possibly seen in a new way. In strictly assessment terms, it was weak in validity and reliability – for instance, some organisations expressed preferences rather than where they realistically were – but it was certainly meaningful. The process generated appetite, engagement, discomfort and some weakness in the guidance: some of the principles (for example, 'Hierarchy/Collective wisdom' or 'Bureaucracy/ Emergence') were seen as being in opposition, or adversarial, rather than as part of a healthy continuum where a strengthening of both might be required. For instance, some heavily regulated organisations sought 'better bureaucracy' *and* 'more emergence'. This could apply to the others, too.

Another issue was that as well as handing new concepts, all the organisations were themselves completing assessments *of their own* organisations; this resulted in some over generous findings. Nonetheless, this stage realised its purpose: to get going meaningfully then begin the process of returning with more rigour for more evidence.

GETTING BEYOND THE START

As mentioned in Chapter 2,[2] everything did not go to plan. The start was uneven and seemed to lack impact, an impatience-driven focus on my part. I soon realised that for the organisations, meaningful 'models-based work' was dependent on their own internal rhythms – when they felt they could use them, they would. As one manager said, the models acted as 'think-detonators' – as they were applied, the organisation began to realise that they 'were *not* just more of the same' – which was just the starting impact we would have hoped for!

---

2   See Chapter 2, The Purpose, the Organisations, the Journey, the Start – The Journey: Building the Transport System.

After about three months, having worked with each organisation individually, we convened a workshop for them all, the first time they all met. To capture the thinking-feeling at this point, as another manager said *'real development necessitates demanding tools...'*

All Together Now: A(nother) Note on Theory

In the following analysis of the organisations, one section is called 'Theories or Parts of Theories-in-Use Which Could Limit Development and New Ones Which Could Aid Development'. This might seem a little clumsy but as one manager said, theory gets 'where even dirt doesn't'. The different theories-in-use includes an outline of the history and experiences of small businesses[3] but also how other equally significant theories occur and influence practice.

Current practice in each organisation is informed by particular theories, however implicit, whether they are seen as 'just practice', 'no theories at all', or simply unacknowledged. For instance, managers claiming they want to 'consult' staff but then seek limits on any ensuing action, draws on theories of command and control from 'scientific management'. Similarly, managers using external courses and training for 'learning' as normal practice, are drawing on academic theories of learning with set subjects and didactic, instructional methods *for staff consumption*. And managers using separated roles and structures draw on traditional organisation and business theories.

However, theories of psychology also operate in organisations and could explain, for instance, why some managers do not challenge accepted thinking even where it does not work, or how the 'family model' is used to understand organisational structures, or sociologically, where certain groups, for example white middle class men, come to dominate senior business positions. Though it may seem obvious that explaining the behaviour of people in organisations involves psychological and sociological theories, we also need economic and above all political theories, as well as management, learning and business ones. Just as managers do not encounter problems as neat 'subjects', neither do organisations. And the artificial separation of these as into 'subjects' simply adds another barrier for managers. In the end, understanding organisational behaviour, and particularly change, might be a case of what theories are *not* relevant: after all 'organisations' are just 'society writ small'. One famous author on understanding organisations commented *reflectively* that organisational

---

3   Included in Chapter 8: What Occurred and What We Learned.

phenomena should be explained by the kind of contextual interpretation used by an *historian*.[4] In the end whatever aids understanding should be used, regardless of whatever name it's been lumbered with (see Appendix 2).

Note: the following diagrams are summaries from the assessment of the three models[5] completed by each organisation based on the 'Effects' they identified now and what they seek two years on.

Organisation: Believe

SUMMARY AND KEY ASPECTS

Stage: Established.

The 'Effects' of their current models: **Now** (black circle) and 2 Years on (grey circle).

Source: Initial assessment.

		1	2	3	4	
Management Model	Static		●		○	Agile
Learning Model	Asphyxiation			●	○	Resilience
Business Model	Stagnation/ decline			●	○	Growth and renewal

> *'We are our clients' last resort – when everybody else has given up on them.'*

---

4   Charles Handy (1985) *Understanding Organisations*. London, Penguin Books, p. 13.
5   See the complete models in Chapter 6 and Chapter 12.

Key characteristics

The management model: is based on consensus, professional self-managing, high trust and autonomy, and regular reviewing, as a collective.

The learning model: is flexible, with 'many routes to excellence' through emergent practice; individual, informal learning predominates.

The business model: explicitly expresses client value: 'Encouraging self-worth and independence.'

Purpose: 'Helping people reconnect with their homeland.'

Performance: Over ten years (incorporated 2000) it has grown significantly as an 'agency of last resort' with a 10 per cent client increase in each of the last five years, performance appropriately measured and improvements year on year. It makes fruitful contact with 'hard-to-reach' groups, by word of mouth, networks of agencies and carers, and is well respected with an established reputation for excellence from clients and referral bodies.

Adequacy: Current models are adequate to meet current challenges so far.

EMERGING ISSUES

On reflection, the initial assessment was fairly accurate and used the principles as a continuum, identifying the need for greater strength at both ends of, for instance 'Bureaucracy and Emergence' and improving 'Today' as well as 'Tomorrow'.

The Management Model: 'Humanist managing' is offset by rigorous concern for behaviours which enact their values of reaching out, reconnecting and building trust; 'consensual' decision-making can mean key decisions left to the founder(s); this can result in an offloading of leadership as opportunities emerge in an increasingly complex environment and taking risks needs to be collectively *shaped* with nimble actions and faster learning.

The Learning Model: This needs to balance functional learning, for example health and safety and safeguarding, with outward-facing collective learning on business development.

The Business Model: Immense solidity is given by a highly mobile, skilled team who persevere with complex cases which other agencies have given up.

Overall: 'The need to look outwards more and also to trust, celebrate and exploit our success.'

Theories or parts of theories-in-use which could limit development and new ones which could aid development

The Management Model seems based on a one-to-one counselling approach, itself based on humanist theories of meeting peoples' emotional needs; for the organisation to develop, collective wisdom theory could be used more for instance 'friends' become trustees, and use their business experience to maintain continuity and reputation, 'manage means'[6] more, and contribute to more agile decision-making on rapidly emerging issues.

The Learning Model is based on traditional learning theories which accepts individual learning as an effective channel and voluntary sharing as 'information-adequate'; however learning for mandatory qualifications and learning for *resilience* have different ends and the 'significant learning'[7] required for their next stage needs the latter; in a changing sector landscape new knowledge management theories to mine and extract *value* from what is learned needs a structured *system* to 'extract and pump learning through the organisation' to address problems as they arise. Facing *new* problems arguably, should be their natural state of development.

The Business Model based on creating client value, is successfully 'settled'; 'outside-in' is well embedded; the performance confidence this has built up could be 'exported' to other sector organisations to generate income, with a value-driven, more entrepreneurial approach – for example, 'Enabling organisations to bring independence home.'

---

6   From the Management Model in Chapter 6, p. 138. '*Managing means: how achieving our purpose through our performance is maintained*'.

7   This task integrates all three models and requires 'significant learning' which involves 'a certain amount of pain, connected with the learning itself, or distress connected with giving up certain previous learning … it involves a change in self-organisation – in the perception of the self is – threatening and tends to be resisted … it involves turbulence within the individual and the system' Knud Illeris (2004) *The Three Dimensions of Learning*. Gylling, Denmark, Roskilde University Press, quoting Carl Rogers (1969) *Freedom to Learn*. New York, Merrill.

EMERGING CHALLENGES

The client group and the 'social need' for the service is expanding; maintaining current performance with reduced or flat-lined funding over the next three years; generating independent revenue; becoming more entrepreneurial; balancing 'democratic flexibility' with more formal structures and more developed management skills; how to embed social media for greater organisational impact; the need (in the absence of greater funding) to further develop the volunteer side and prepare for younger immigrants.

CURRENT MODELS ARE UNLIKELY TO MEET THESE EMERGING CHALLENGES

Next stage of development

While not in a position 'to grow in terms of staffing', they will 'develop'[8] by bringing ideas 'from a latent to a visible state', and 'to maturity', in the form of '*growth through direction*'.[9] This involves a new property strategy, an income-generating approach based on its own successful development; an education campaign; and 'authoritative marketing'. They also choose new models: Agile Management, Resilient Learning and Business Renewal to activate this development.

Development tasks[10]

> '*We need to be more entrepreneurial.*'

To capitalise on its success, strong 'governance' and committed 'mobile team' through collective forums, Believe needs to:

- accept risk informed by the value-creating method: 'be experimental, practice rapid piloting' and increase their rate of learning in this;

---

8   This involves choices in meaning too: meanings of 'develop' and 'development' include: to unfold, reveal, bring, come from a latent to an active or more visible state, to bring to maturity, become more elaborate, more systematic or bigger; a gradual unfolding, stage of advancement, a more elaborate form. Source: OED.

9   Greiner 'dilemmas of growth' or 'pain of success' (1972) quoted in Charles Handy (1985) *Understanding Organisations*. London, Penguin. See: The Next Stage of Development in Chapter 8 including 'organisational growth' diagram.

10 As with footnote 2 above, this task integrates all three models and requires 'significant learning' which involves 'a certain amount of pain, connected with the learning itself, or distress connected with giving up certain previous learning … it involves a change in self-organisation – in the perception of the self is – threatening and tends to be resisted … it involves turbulence within the individual and the system' Knud Illeris (2004) *The Three Dimensions of Learning*, quoting Carl Rogers (1969) *Freedom to Learn*. New York, Merrill.

- use its sector leadership position and affiliated networks to become more entrepreneurial and 'sell smarts'[11] and generate income for instance by 'Enabling other organisations to bring independence to their vulnerable groups;'

- embed social media including client generated contributions, to further develop its Customer Value Proposition (CVP);

- embed more formal structures including management skills (not a risk) and learning and business forums;

- use the 'exalting ego-less persuasion' of the (co)founder, its client value creation and the power of its vivid stories.[12]

Organisation: Health House

SUMMARY AND KEY ASPECTS

Stage: Established.

The 'Effects' of their current models: **Now** (black circle) and 2 Years on (grey circle).

Source: Initial assessment.

		1	2	3	4	
Management Model	Static		●		⬤	Agile
Learning Model	Asphyxiation		●		⬤	Resilience
Business Model	Stagnation/ decline		●	⬤		Growth and renewal

'We want to be agile.'

---

11 As with Cognac, (below) the selling-on organisation, marketing and selling the process by which it became successful.
12 A good example of how every last breath of difference is garnered for competitive advantage: http://www.mckinseyquarterly.com/The_power_of_storytelling_What_nonprofits_can_teach_the_private_sector_about_social_media_2740. Accessed 4 February 2011.

Key characteristics

The management model: is based on consensus, with non 'management' terms used for organising effort; also professional, high trust.

The learning model: individual, clinical, specialised learning or 'training' takes precedence.

The business model: is based on, 'We offer different positive choices to patients.'

Purpose: 'Providing NHS care for patients with some private services.'

Performance: It has an established reputation with a constant, respected local presence; performance has been stable over five years with similar numbers of staff, patients and financial performance.

Adequacy: Current models are adequate to meet current challenges so far.

EMERGING ISSUES

On reflection, the initial assessment was 'over generous' (Director); some aspects such as trust and commitment were overestimated.

The Management Model: Most energy is consumed in today's operations, with little future–fighting; organisational direction seems static and leadership has a reactive, dependent feel; structurally, management roles need renewing for today's challenges.

The Learning Model: Needs to more explicitly embrace learning for improvement and innovation, to tackle perceptions of 'risk with patients' as a *source* of innovation rather than a barrier *per se*;[13] also collective learning forums need to lubricate business development.

The Business Model: Could capitalise on 'offering different positive choices' (above) with a broader CVP, which also recognises that quality begins with the immediate customers and leads back to funders.

Overall: 'The need to spend as much time on the business as in it.'

---

13 'Break-through Ideas for 2010', *Harvard Business Review*, January–February 2010. By contrast, key innovative ideas once given a favourable climate, need 'not be high cost, high risk or high tech' as these examples show.

Theories or parts of theories-in-use which could limit development and new theories which could aid development

The Management Model: Structurally, it seems based on traditional 'Administrative management' and organisational development theories of Henri Fayol and Max Weber[14] with specialisation and division of labour, and linkage of authority and responsibility; different theories, for instance, system theory to recognise the greater interrelations of its parts, or contingency theory, with more flexible leadership and design contingent on the circumstances faced,[15] could enable a more nimble structure to reflect the changing environment and the overall performance agility they seek.

The Learning Model: This employs theories of traditional, 'in-receipt-of' individual learning in specialised subjects, with knowledge as 'objective', and a predominantly behaviourist approach; however a bolder, diverse learning culture is needed to strive for 'Resilience'[16],which could be built on theories of innovation, divergence and creative problem solving to (1) facilitate emergence[17] and innovation; (2) to enhance capacity through greater *peer-produced* learning based on cognitive and social constructivist theories of learning; and (3) to fuel greater *interdependence*, initiate collective learning forums for faster *organisational development*. All these are designed to advance agreed and renewed organisational purpose.

The Business Model: This is now overly mature; a traditional value metric of 'contractor' funding volume and externally imposed quality audits is beginning to predominate; new business theories including the CVP can create new 'customer value' as part of a renewed, explicit business model to more effectively meet their future challenges.

EMERGING CHALLENGES

Maintaining high-quality care in a 'cuts' climate; generating 'independent' income; meeting new policy-led changes which link funding to patient satisfaction; getting greater patient feedback; capitalising on current

---

14 Henri Fayol (1930) *Industrial and General Administration*. Geneva, International Management Institute; and Max Weber (1947) *The Theory of Social and Economic Organisations*. New York, Free Press.
15 Fritjof Capra (2003) *The Hidden Connections*. London, Flamingo.
16 'Resilience' is the desired effect in the current learning model built on the principles of greater collective, emergent and deeper learning.
17 Fritjof Capra (2003) *The Hidden Connections*. London, Flamingo. Inside the organisation 'continual questioning and innovation is rewarded...' and diversity is valued and it 'tolerates activities in the margin: experiments and eccentricities that stretch their understanding', p. 107.

Government 'support' for social enterprises; making the most of their 'brand' with more focussed direction; managing possible threats from recent policy changes including ones restricting funding applications to larger businesses.

CURRENT MODELS ARE UNLIKELY TO MEET THESE EMERGING CHALLENGES

Next stage of development

'Development'[18] is by bringing ideas 'to maturity' *to renew organisational purpose.*[19] They also choose new models to activate this development which are: Agile Management, Resilient Learning and Business Renewal.

Development tasks[20]

> *'It's in our blood – we choose to work here because it is, 'nurse-led' and patients would choose too.'*

To capitalise on the strength of staff commitment Health House can use staff-led groups to:

- accept risk in the spirit of the value-creating method to 'encourage that which does not yet exist';

- renew purpose and make more of their unique status to seize new opportunities; embed self-managing in both organisational purpose and as a patient value;

- examine what can be learned from high performing 'Community-interest-Company' competitors;

---

18 This involves choices in meaning too: the Oxford English Dictionary meanings of 'develop' and 'development' include: to unfold, reveal, bring, come from a latent to an active or more visible state, to bring to maturity, become more elaborate, more systematic or bigger; a gradual unfolding, stage of advancement, a more elaborate form...

19 Greiner 'dilemmas of growth' or 'pain of success' (1972). This involves in Greiner's phases, 'growth through direction and delegation, prompted by 'crises in leadership and autonomy' See: The Next Stage of Development in Chapter 8 including 'organisational growth' diagram.

20 This task integrates all three models and requires 'significant learning' which involves 'a certain amount of pain, connected with the learning itself, or distress connected with giving up certain previous learning... it involves a change in self-organisation – in the perception of the self is threatening and tends to be resisted... it involves turbulence within the individual and the system', Knud Illeris (2004) *The Three Dimensions of Learning.* Gylling, Denmark, Roskilde University Press, quoting Carl Rogers (1969) *Freedom to Learn.* Accessed 4 February 2011.

- develop an innovative culture via small experiments for improvement to build greater trust and engagement;

- develop more 'productive interference'[21] in 'what matters' collective forums for, initially, business development;

- embed social media for more effective internal exchanges, publicising 'value', and greater patient contribution;

- keep seeking robust patient engagement.

Organisation: Philosophy Football.com

SUMMARY AND KEY ASPECTS

Stage: Established.

The 'Effects' of their current models: **Now** (black circle) and 2 Years on (grey circle).

Source: Initial assessment.

		1	2	3	4	
Management Model	Static			●	●	Agile
Learning Model	Asphyxiation		●		●	Resilience
Business Model	Stagnation/ decline		●		●	Growth and renewal

'We are 17 years old, and like everyone else, heading into an economic five year tunnel … we need to go back to Art school.'

Key characteristics

The management model: is necessary self-managing, with independent working and immense task discretion and individual responsibility for

---

21 See 'Focus for Learning' in the Learning Model, Chapter 6, p. 141.

work co-ordination, in order to 'always be agile' and be more 'porous'.

The learning model: is predominantly individual learning; a new source is by inviting business-experienced supporters to review performance and contribute to strategically developing the business.

The business model: is 'Selling enough ideas on enough t-shirts.'

Purpose: 'Sporting outfitters of intellectual distinction' 'Presenting ideas in the form of t-shirts as low-cost vehicles for our politics and sporting interests.'

Performance: Over 17 years, they have grown from being a 'hobby' to a source of income for three full-time and two part-time staff, with an expanding 25k plus customer database, and expanded production based on causes, anniversaries and people, to arrest and challenge mainstream history. They are used to thriving on 'sudden spurts' depending on the outcomes of various sporting fixtures. They also organise and facilitate events which creatively promote progressive causes with a reputation for intelligent, innovatively mixing politics and entertainment.

Adequacy: Current models are adequate to meet current challenges so far. ('The most difficult question to answer in the assessment.')

EMERGING ISSUES

In the initial assessment, the principles were used as a continuum, for instance, being better bureaucrats' *and* tapping more 'emergence'.

The Management Model: Both founders have different perspectives on all three models; they have separate functions (marketing and design) which grant independence and 'productive tension', but give low dynamism for development.

The Learning Model: Is based on individual learning which can assume collective learning; however, they seek 'deeper learning' from collective and external sources.

The Business Model: Is nominally, around t-shirt sales but with immense potential which bringing 'more imagination to their BM' and a stronger CVP could realise; also taking more risks, which the strength of their customer loyalty justifies. A priority is to 'develop our presence over a range of platforms', renew their website and include social media using their own and associate expertise.

Overall: 'Wearing our t-shirt is a powerful way of saying *who I am* – how can we build on that?'

Theories or parts of theories-in-use which could limit development and new ones which could aid development

The Management Model: is based on conventional theories of structure, control and co-ordination[22] responsively applied. However, as their various initiatives expand, there is more trust to draw on internally, for greater improvements and externally, from associates' ideas. Experienced in making current risks 'safe' they could launch further risks and seek *the multiplier effect* which historically, online purchasing gave, resulting in dramatically increased sales.

The Learning Model: Current thinking is informed by previous experiential learning which, in an uncertain climate, can overly lean towards the tried and tested. Innovation theory is used to recognise that 'not all the smart people work for us' so we can import ideas from associates.[23] They could use greater collective learning to fuel business development.

The Business Model: A strong 'producer push' informs their business thinking; also some implications of traditional small business theory apply, where the threat of 'low barriers to entry' and lack of ambition can trump development; they could explore greater business diversity by building on their uniqueness, internal capital, and customer loyalty.

EMERGING CHALLENGES

Sustainability; global price of cotton; getting more customer feedback; 'easier' barriers to entry for competitors; balancing core values with new development; recreating itself – getting younger customers; seizing the immense opportunities the political landscape offers – a right-wing government in power for an extended period; and in as one co-founder said, 'We might be mature (as in

---

22 Ultimately a functioning mix of enlightened F.W. Taylor and Elton Mayo's 'Human Relations' theories .

23 Henry Chesbrough (2003) 'The Era of Open Innovation' from David Mayle (Ed.) *Managing Innovation and Change*. London, Sage Publications and The Open University.

Greiner's model – see below) but without developing...' and using the models to tackle the implications of this.

CURRENT MODELS ARE UNLIKELY TO MEET THESE EMERGING CHALLENGES

Next stage of development

This was expressed initially in a traditional way, 'We are unlikely to expand staffing'; also the two co-founders had different perceptions: 'Steady growth (the same level) is not sufficiently demanding' as against 'Can we grow beyond our natural parish and broaden our customer base, rather than our inventory.' 'Development'[24] is by bringing ideas 'to maturity' in the form of: 'growth through direction'[25] and 'delegation and collaboration' which involves broadening the management structure and culture.

They also choose new models: Agile Management, in particular to develop greater trust and self-managing; Resilient Learning and Business Renewal, to activate this development.

Development tasks[26]

To capitalise on its success, strong customer loyalty and new opportunities in the political landscape, Philosophy Football, through collective forums, needs to:

- accept risk in the spirit of the value-creating method to 'Use learning as a bias towards action and trust it, the first kind of risk.' Embed trust and risk as key components of collective self-managing to (1) refine its structure, systems and roles; and to (2) strengthen its position and continually mobilise its thinking for greater agility.

---

24 This involves choices in meaning too: the Oxford English Dictionary meanings of 'develop' and 'development' include: to unfold, reveal, bring, come from a latent to an active or more visible state, to bring to maturity, become more elaborate, more systematic or bigger; a gradual unfolding, stage of advancement, a more elaborate form...

25 Greiner 'dilemmas of growth' or 'pain of success' (1972). For the next stage they have used Greiner heuristically rather than as a mechanistic template, to seek growth through direction, delegation and collaboration (seemingly separate phases) prompted, less by 'crisis' than the need to broaden leadership, autonomy and control. See: The Next Stage of Development in Chapter 8.

26 This task integrates all three models and requires 'significant learning' which involves 'a certain amount of pain, connected with the learning itself, or distress connected with giving up certain previous learning... it involves a change in self-organisation – in the perception of the self is threatening and tends to be resisted... it involves turbulence within the individual and the system' Knud Illeris (2004) *The Three Dimensions of Learning* Gylling, Denmark, Roskilde University Press, quoting Carl Rogers *Freedom to Learn* (1969). New York, Merrill.

- the founders can seize emerging opportunities and capitalise on being: 'Sporting outfitters of intellectual distinction' *and* the reverse!

- use their strong identity and brand loyalty to develop a more explicit and imaginative business model; seek more robust customer engagement and explore more diverse CVPs including potential niche markets, for example, customer-generated products;

- use committed associates with business experience to make them 'business outfitters of distinction';

- as intended, embed social media – establish, experiment and extend it – lead 'next-practice platforms' in their field;

- entrepreneurially mine their experience and confidence of managing highly successful ventures and cause-based events, to create greater value for themselves and other organisations.

Organisation: Social Stock Exchange

SUMMARY AND KEY ASPECTS

Stage: Start-Up.

The 'Effects' of their current models: **Now** (black circle) and 2 Years on (grey circle).

Source: Initial assessment.

		1	2	3	4	
Management Model	Static			●	●	Agile
Learning Model	Asphyxiation			●	●	Resilience
Business Model	Stagnation/ decline			●	●	Growth and renewal

'We are principled intermediaries.'

Key characteristics

The management model: is (or will be) explicitly chosen and will be outcome-oriented (not process), create autonomy, be egalitarian and will involve collective decisions; 'culturally, our early employees will write the organisation's handbook'.

The learning model: is also explicitly chosen, involving learning by doing; it encourages reflective practice, intelligent observation and persistence; it seeks to meet emerging learning 'needs' through diverse collective learning; in uncertainty, it will keep minds open and use feedback loops, to gauge different kinds of success.

The business model: is explicit: 'access to capital for social purpose organisations to make a social impact and alleviate a social problem'; it involves 'an innovative business proposition which creates value and success', depending on creating social and environmental value; and embraces social media and ethical values as essential in creating value for society as a whole.

Purpose: 'Our aim us to contribute to changing the world by funding social mission organisations.'

Performance: Their current stage is post 'proof of concept' with launch planned for mid-2012.

Adequacy: Current models (prior to testing) seem adequate, are chosen, with the business model so far being particularly effective.

Theories or parts of theories-in-use which could limit development and new ones which could aid development

The Management Model: is based on empowering and entrusting theories of management 'to be like Semco';[27] it uses Drucker's 'responsibilities' for managers.[28] There is also an awareness of best use of the founder's own cognitive style: 'Consultation and involvement is my natural style – we can change things with evidence and insight … We must be agile – with so few of us (five to ten) we will be virtually job-sharing.'

27 Ricardo Semler (1994) *Maverick! The Success Behind the World's Most Unusual Workplace*. London, Arrow Edition.
28 Peter Drucker (1991) *Management: Tasks, Responsibilities, Practices*. Oxford, Butterworth-Heinemann.

The Learning Model: is based on theories of experiential learning and also how organisations like Google and Amazon use free-flowing collective learning. Uncertainty is managed 'by not closing our thinking too early'. Leadership theories are also considered to enable distributed decision-making and autonomy. There is also an awareness of other learning theories, for example, Peter Senge[29] which can be applied as needed.

The Business Model: is based on in neo-classical economics theory and extensive theories and practice around social value.

EMERGING CHALLENGES

Pre-launch phase: raising (final) capital; offering two options: being different, while making clear to all we are not 'alternative'.

'Leading and building the business knowing what I want it to look and feel like, creating an outcomes-based company culture, and delivering on our promises.' Given the long run-in to launch, however high the barriers to entry, might competitors emerge?

Please note: Because of the particular stage of development of this organisation (starting-up) the narrative structure is changed to accommodate issues raised by the founder and the implications for the overall approach and models. There are three mini-sections: Meeting the founder's challenges to the models; how these issues relate to the claims of the work and the models; and some learning points about the models.

Meeting the founder's challenges to the models

SSE is an exciting, urgently needed venture and will use the founder's previous learning in financial investment and business-building to create significant value in this sector. Below are discussions based on the founder's claims that (1) 'Businesses do not frame themselves in terms of the models;' (2) 'Learning is not the first point of change;' and (3) how to anticipate and address possible barriers arising from 'Founder's syndrome'. The discussions are designed to convince him of the benefits of using the models.

---

29 Peter Senge (1999) *The Dance of Change: The Challenge of Sustaining Momentum in Learning Organisations*. London, Nicholas Brealey.

(1) 'Businesses do not frame themselves in terms of the models'

A (author): You have the seen the benefits of making explicit your BM – why not also for both management and learning models?

F (founder): The management one will emerge… in the beginning, with staff who have left behind the 'corporate culture'.

A: What about the power and grip of the default models – won't these inevitably emerge unless specific alternatives are built? How will the new organisation be 'Agile' from the start, with maximum learning capacity?

F: I have 'grown up on' progressive management and business theories and practices. These default models of command and control or business 'inside-out' have never been on my radar. We will also have staff committed to our purpose… and agility will be part of their DNA. 'Purpose' will be a key driver which your models might recognise more explicitly…

A: The new models are designed to encourage challenges from the inside as needed. This builds capacity so there is no need to bring it in from outside when big challenges occur, for instance, the challenging, stretching practice of 'Tomorrow' in the management model. What if a different DNA emerges – can you 'transform' it? What is the role of learning in becoming 'who we are'?

F: Staff become aware of our management model at interview. The recruitment process might be a 'safety first process' where we could use short contracts, a try-before-you-buy, and a chance to see evidence of nimbleness.

A: How can you build on this beyond the starting point, to sustain them? What of collective learning?

F: Collective learning can be taught – or learned – via management meetings where we explicitly learn from each other.

(2) 'Learning is not the first point of change'

We took two examples of the founder's journey so far:

- He assumed business would come from social purpose companies making Initial Public Offer (IPO) applications. However, it became clear that this was unlikely, so he re-focussed on those already funded from other sources but who were dissatisfied. That is, he offered them a new CVP.

- Raising capital: potential investors wanted to invest not in infrastructure but thematically, for example, healthcare, education, so he needed *'to tell our story differently'*. These are developed in Chapter 6, The New Approach: The New Models – Interdependence and Learning as a Midwife.

Both these involved *increasing his rate of learning* dictated by changes 'in the environment'; that is, changes at a strategic level, or not getting the anticipated response to key arguments or positioning, *which affect progress*. In other words, if he had not responded first, through learning, a key opportunity would have been lost. In practice wouldn't he want this from all his staff? Further analysis of this issue is below.

(3) Who 'owns' the new company? Tackling the dependence which 'Founder's syndrome' can create

Could 'Founder's syndrome' emerge in practice, that is, even if found wanting, the founder's thinking is, a priori, granted more power? The new learning model is designed to counter this (and other possible barriers) by explicitly containing a range of practices to 'democratise' learning. For instance, individual learning is balanced against collective learning so no individual's learning has greater status, and 'productive interference' should occur between individual learning and organisational practices. In this way staff actively deploy their learning as a key means of creating value and developing a 'Resilient' learning model for competitive advantage. Further, the models are also interlinked so as problems emerge, 'what best next' prompts the learning model, the management one encourages autonomy and business model encourages value creation. Further analysis of this issue is also below.

How These Issues Relate to the Claims of the Work and the Models

The founder has 'grown up on' the more progressive management and business theories and practices while the 'old/default' models of management command and control, or business 'inside-out' have 'never been on his radar'. For his organisation, default models would have no power or grip – 'the species has already evolved'. As for making his approach explicit, the founder has an 'explicitly implicit' awareness of his preferred theories for use; by this he means that it is important that different models already 'exist' within the organisation, in the thinking and experience of staff, including himself, as a resource to be used as need emerges and the organisation develops. Thus, they do not need to be 'written down' as such.

This awareness of particular approaches and theories to draw on as needed also applies in the following ways:

- *If learning is not the means of changing the other models, then what is?* Traditionally in change, learning lags, which is why most change fails, whereas in the model here, learning leads as a key element which along with other principles, enables 'resilience'. Thus change is anticipated, normal and rhythmic, rather than needed yesterday, a distraction, and resisted. The founder is confident, so far, that learning is present but implicit, available to be drawn on as needed.

- *What about the dangers of 'Founder's syndrome'?* He is acutely conscious of this and will (co)lead the organisation for a specific period and at an appropriate time, will want to move into a different role. What is important is to 'recognise' where such change is needed and access to appropriate responses. This means having an internally challenging environment *for all staff* which uses their 'implicit resources' which include the listening skills of the founder, their corporate purpose and identity, their connections in providing progressive capitalism, and customer feedback. Together, these can address 'problems' and create greater value.

- *How are the new models interdependent?* SSE's selection of their business model is a good example of how 'hidden' thinking using aspects of all three new models here, ensured it effectiveness. It is (1) explicit in its CVP and customer engagement; it (2) uses all the principles in the new business model here; and (3) it is built using principles from the other two models, 'deep' in learning, 'emergent' in management; in effect all three, interdependently.

Some Emerging Issues About the Models

These are created in the sense of the writing journey overall: I interpreted what founders said in the conceptual terms of the work.[30]

THE MODELS AS 'FLEXIBLE HEURISTICS'

For the founder, the models are best seen as *heuristics*, offering persistent questioning, where organisations can have 'their own thinking exposed'. 'Inflexible use' of the models, in seeking to make everything explicit, to map organisations or everything they do to models, can be dangerous. On the other hand 'they offer the priceless benefit of enabling organisations to re-engage with their purpose'.

IMPLICIT/EXPLICIT/IMPLICIT?

Are we being inflexible in seeking explicit models? Over-concerned with countering the danger of organisations adopting implicit models which cause current problems in the first place, and cannot enable development? What we learned here is that *the next stage of organisational development* must be explicit. The framework of the models enables this and then consciously chosen, explicit models are needed to activate the next stage. Other questions also emerged here: doesn't practice which is explicitly sought and refined, eventually become *unconsciously competent* – highly embedded and implicit, to be drawn on when needed? At this stage, has the founder, with the experience of having led various businesses, now internalised better theories which are consistent with the models here?

WHAT CHOICES IS SSE PRACTICE BASED ON CURRENTLY?

We claim a new learning model is needed to 'upgrade' learning and bring greater conviction to collective learning, which might otherwise, be left to chance. Nonetheless, the choices SSE makes now about its models, the management model – high trust, the business model – value creation, and to some degree its learning model – self-learning, are entirely consistent with the new models here. The business model is absolutely explicit. However his theories-in-use operating in the learning approach,[31] that is, his default position and automatic recourse when challenged, are to 'produce self-learning', to 'increase his rate

---

30   Henry Mintzberg (2009) *Managing*. Harlow, FT/PrenticeHall, p. 5.
31   See: Individual Learning in Chapter 6, p. 99.

of learning', to be 'iterative, persistent and challenging' in manifesting 'deep learning' all embrace the progressive practices the models contain. His learning approach may be implicit – and drawn on (as above) when necessary. But at some stage what is involved must have been explicit, must have been learned. Perhaps the issue is when. It seems clear that their acquisition and use was as a result of the learning orientation of the founder.

'SEMI-DETACHED MODELS' BUT KNOCKING ON THE DOOR OF THE MAIN BUILDING?

It seems that the learning model has prompted new questions about the role of learning and how it emerges in new, challenging circumstances. And how exactly its users name their changing thinking, which we call learning.

Given the founder accepts the inherent value of the models, perhaps he sees learning as 'the building beside the main business building', somehow semi-detached, but nonetheless populated and available. If it is not populated with the theories and approach in the models here, we still claim that the main house will eventually fall down. We still consider learning should have its own room in the main building.

This issue is given a fuller discussion here to show the uneven pathway theories and practices take, the difficulties of locating the 'parents' of habits, default positions, actions and approaches, and how without 'learning' (however characterised) they will not be found. And without finding them we cannot develop.

Note: in writing throughout, and particularly in this section and in summarising, there is a need for the writer to be aware of the *comforts of conclusiveness*: that is, the desire to wrap everything up neatly in boxes even if they bulge, but then finding on a later visit, that the box has fractured.

Next Stage of Development

Having launched, translating its 'explicitly implicit' management and learning models into practice.

To trust their choices in future models of Agile management, Resilient learning and Growth in business.

To accept a challenge from this work: to theorise learning more, build collective forums, and 'use learning as a bias towards action –the first kind of risk'.

Organisation: Cognac

SUMMARY AND KEY ASPECTS

Stage: Selling-on.

The 'Effects' of their current models: **Now** (black circle) and 2 Years on (grey circle).

Source: Initial assessment.

		1	2	3	4	
Management Model	**Static**			●	●	Agile
Learning Model	**Asphyxiation**			●	●	Resilience
Business Model	**Stagnation/ decline**			●	●	Growth and renewal

'Working hard is the simplest form of laziness.'

Key characteristics

The management model: their culture is driven by values; the staff handbook guides behaviour; there is collective planning for priorities and what next (and what not) every three months which includes direction; it is completion-focussed and each employee has 'manager' in their title; there is high discipline and high trust; their model, with a small staff of six, produces '100 per cent engagement'. In terms of performance, all staff have targets which are company not personal and a collaborative bonus system.

The learning model: includes individual learning; there is also collective learning through project debriefs and open conversations on how to work smarter; also a £1k learning budget for all staff with £200 for books; 'we know what we don't know'.

The business model: is fixed-fee consulting engagements 'Communicate anything in 10 minutes proposition'.

Purpose: 'To profitably solve someone's business problem' – making difficult things simple.

Performance: Being sought and sold as a result of successful performance.

Adequacy: Current models are adequate to meet challenges so far.

EMERGING ISSUES

In the initial assessment, the principles were used as a continuum, for example, being better at traditional *and* emergent learning,

The management model: There is ample evidence of a general move from control to trust in the form of greater:

- Collective wisdom: their quality strategy includes one day offsite planning identifying five priorities plus deciding what not to do for next three months. Also, 'we like emergence': we might decide that the Big Party is key – this involves inviting round 500 companies and individuals to an outdoor summer party in central London, bigger and more fashionable each year and renowned for its networking and contact-making.

- Deep judgement reservoir: staff aim to make decisions with *their* (customer's) key decision makers.

- Seeking to be agile: 'Like Dell, don't be successful *then* do smart things, first do smart things then be successful.'

- Structuring routine work to ensure quality: (1) 'All hygiene factors should be a process': scalable services should be product-based. 'The process sets you free' (2) The staff have clear, dynamic roles so can collectively build the smartest way of working – 'otherwise we all can end up chasing the ball like kids playing football'.

The learning model: There is ample evidence of a peer-produced learning and 'learning-conscious learning':

- All activities are mined for learning: Projects have brief, frequent catch-ups and project debrief time. 'We spend time on how we should do things here and our handbook has guidance on how to work smarter which we refresh with sustained open conversations.' Collective learning: we are always concerned for how we work together better: staff 'become redundant' by not hoarding ideas, for instance they find what's not working and improve it. 'As a result we need to do little fire-fighting and maintenance.'

- 'Pleasure learning' (business non-relevant) is also strongly encouraged, funding, for example, tango lessons, flyfishing – 'whatever lights you up'.

The business model: There is ample evidence of the BM being explicit, outside-in and based on value creation:

- Success is based not on our features but how we meet customer pain, produce customer benefits.

- Value: 'We seek to create value – we can optimise profit as part of a balanced scorecard; in the longer term the business is more than this.

- In producing your first product you need also to think of what a 'profitable second product needs to be'.

- Quoting Jezz Bezos of Amazon, when a colleague said they wanted to be the best customer service in the world, he said they wanted 'no customer service' but to give customers what they want, for example, I don't want to spend time buying car insurance I want to *have* it.

- They are strong at value creation and are also aware of value subtraction: we are always trying to find new ways of 'costing effort' (tasks for customers) and adjust pricing as our market effectiveness grew.

- They use *social media and networking* extensively: Their networking usage is very effective and admired by many companies and competitors which accounts for its high media profile and success. They initiate networks, are generous with their invitations, and host current, topical events such as Vizthink, as idea generators for media working.

Overall: The learning orientation of the founder is a key influence, and his strong awareness of the implications of his decisions and thinking, for instance: 'I hire completer finishers and seek 50/50 decisions through the appropriate groups but can adjust these as needs arise.' Actions are informed by 'decisions made on facts, making everyone's fact equal'.[32] This element of his cognitive style is crucial.[33]

Cognac have made explicit choices about their models as a result of experience and sustained thinking. 'We spent some time considering and choosing models, delaying our start by three months till we found an appropriate business model which was a selling-defined project, a fixed fee, project-based consultancy.'

'Our management model is to be agile, listening wisely and making clear decisions. Our learning model is to be Resilient: we also use unlearning, questioning the adequacy of what you think you already know by asking again if it is enough, six months on – for instance "if we were to try a start-up business now, would we start *this*?" We also ensure bespoke learning by funding priorities driven by pain.'

Our business model is for growth and renewal: 'We remember that over a long timescale all things will die.' Both 'Outside-in' and 'Inside-out' are needed. 'Even with a good BM we ask who are our *right* competitors – not every one – and act on what you find. We know who ours are.'

Among the key learning points that established and made them effective were:

- Their CVP 'communicate anything in ten minutes' became a brand promise like Fedex 'small packets delivered overnight' or 'a Hot

---

32 Simon Caulkin 'The Job in Hand: Leadership', *Public* (Public Sector Management Magazine), September 2006.
33 Philip Crosby (1996) *Reflections on Quality*. New York, McGraw-Hill. 'It is not possible to know what you need to learn', Epigram 14.

Pizza in 20 minutes' as we promise you can 'communicate anything in ten minutes'.

- We know that even a poor business model can generate income but even good ones will not solve problems forever.

- It can be as hard to make new business with an old customer as getting the initial business in the first place.

- A 'natural' business model has recurring revenue. The wrong one aims for solo transactions, which Cognac at one stage, sought to move from in order to develop[34] more sustainable relationships.

- We are disciplined: we don't tolerate 'uniform carriers' – being all dressed up in uniform yet doing nothing.

- We spend as much focus *on* the business as *in* the business.

- We tried to choose, focus, prioritise – you can't do everything.

Please note: Because of the particular stage of development of this organisation, selling-on, the narrative structure is changed to accommodate issues raised by its performance and the implications for the overall approach and models.

The Relationship of Cognac's 'Success' to the Approach and Models

1. They have made explicit choice about their models which contain many of the principles of the new models here and which work interdependently to enable sustained high performance. All their systems reflected their purpose.

2. Learning was the lubricant for the other models. The founder's statement (typical too) that 'working hard is the simplest form of laziness' is virtually a definition of the new learning model, and cannot even be conceptualised without reflective learning in practice. Each new idea was interrogated for scalability. Learning was 'close

---

34 Rita Gunther McGrath 'When your business model is in trouble', *Harvard Business Review*, January–February 2011.

to strategy', to find improvements from day one, a strategy with collaborative rhythm. It also was designed so staff 'are net productive in a week'. They sought to build a culture where staff said, 'I promise to learn... a sort of contractive learning.' Used in this way learning meant that, 'Together we know what we don't know – and what we do.'

3.   They have business appetite: even with apparently successful ventures they ask, 'Six months on, would we start this business *now*: what has changed and is it still viable?'

4.   Risk was welcomed, scoped and tamed through learning. This is in harmony with the value-creating method to 'take risks beyond *knowing*'.

5.   The founder had a clear idea of his own development journey – 'I want to become a client of Cognac' where personal and business success coalesced. To sell the company, he developed not so much the business 'truth' as the authority to say it. Building a successful business *and selling it* is an inevitable part of this continuing journey – a good example of 'grow and go'.

6.   Its strengths made it confident and attractive – not just to customers but to buyers in the market too. An example of its confidence is the unique and forthright way it expresses and enacts its values.[35]

THEORIES OR PARTS OF THEORIES-IN-USE WHICH COULD LIMIT DEVELOPMENT AND NEW ONES WHICH COULD AID DEVELOPMENT

The Management Model This is based on management and motivation theories to produce high trust and an *internalised commitment* psychological contract. Leadership theories live like well-treated plants in its practice and include: 'distributed leadership, 'leaders as readers', 'leadership grounded

---

35 In attenuated form: 'How do you summarise a culture, a view of life, in a few words? Great companies have a great culture – starting early and carried through ... impossible to capture that essence – but essential to try. Here goes: *Measure by results* Can you think harder or only smarter? We want to get out of the "hours" culture and into the "results" culture ... metrics that tell us when to celebrate and where to push harder. *No Muppets* Good people ... easy to say, incredibly hard to find ... *No Ego* It takes a lot to know nothing. *Slightly irreverent* We try hard not to try too hard. *Do the right thing* we have some ideas – but exactly how is a conversation we would love to have. That's us. How about you?' (Ends with a contact address).

in the work itself defines what is needed'.[36] Organisational capacity is continually built by everybody thinking *more*. Also *the organisation itself* seems the organising mechanism, and less 'management'.[37]

The Learning Model: This is deep learning;[38] avid reading and reflection is encouraged for theories and idea-swiping, for example,[39] 'having a hedgehog concept'.

The Business Model: This centres on value creation; they use a 'balanced scorecard' to be comprehensively aware of the 'hard' elements, for example, how they are doing financially at any time – 'we tracked revenue per head and its relationship to gross profit', and 'soft' elements including an awareness of the relationship between how staff perceive they are 'managed' and how they perform.

There is also emergent evidence of an innovative theory-in-use: *the organisation itself*, the purpose for which people come together for collective benefit, where staff and organisation become more than the sum of their parts, is the organising mechanism, *not* 'management'.[40]

Next Stage of Development

Selling the 'smarts' of the company; building another business; constructing the high enabling, entrusting models in a new company and/or in larger and more established ones.

---

36 Simon Caulkin 'The Job in Hand: Leadership', *Public* (Public Sector Management Magazine), September 2006.

37 Martin Parker 'If only business schools wouldn't teach business', *The Observer*, 30 November 2008.

38 In the current learning model 'Deep learning' is one of the principles required for 'Resilient' learning.

39 Jim Collins (2001) *Good to Great*. London, Random House. Also Verne Harnish, the 'Growth-guy', Mastering the Rockefeller Habits. http://verneharnish.typepad.com/

40 Martin Parker 'If only business schools wouldn't teach business', *The Observer*, 30 November 2008.

8

What Occurred and What We Learned

This section brings together the responses to key questions posed by the work and key learning points which emerged, and consists of:

- What occurred and what we learned as a summary, of how organisations' current models were selected; what these were; their adequacy in meeting current and future challenges; how useful they found the models; and the 'outcomes' of this work against its claims, *so far*;

- Some implications of small business theory for participant organisations;

- 'Crafting the next stage of development' the challenging *process* of getting to their next stage, the key factors involved, and the outcomes;

- 'More value': some ideas for other organisations in using this approach.

How Were Current Models Selected?

The established organisations: their models were all 'implicit', default choices.

The start-up explicitly chose its business model and refined this in practice, while the thinking needed for progressive management and learning models is 'explicitly implicit', available as a resource once they begin doing business.

The sold-on organisation models were all explicitly chosen, the actual start of the business being delayed until they were optimised.

What Were the Current Models?

For the established organisations, the current models were contradictory and benefitted from as one manager said 'being found out'. In managing their businesses none of the organisations were starting from scratch; however implicit their current models, they had an awareness of the limitations of conventional management model. Of the established organisations, Health House choose explicitly not to use the term 'management'; Philosophy Football saw it as something to avoid, and Believe sought alternatives to it. All their models had some strengths.

> *The management models*: the start-up explicitly chose and refined its business model, at this stage, its 'practical front', but also had 'grown up with' more progressive management models so knew what it wanted. With the selling-on organisation, their models were explicitly selected *and* interconnected, unlike the other organisations, and this provided a significant strength.

> For the established organisations, their implicit models were compounded by the fact that their next stage of development was also implicit. In a sense the weakness of their management models was linked to the founder's vision, in that it assumed that 'more of the same' having carried them so far, was sufficient for the next stage. However, this work aimed to enable them to explicitly identify their next stage and the models needed to activate it.

> *The business models*: with the start-up and the selling-on organisations these are explicit. The established organisations' business models could be stronger; all have immense potential which bringing 'more imagination to their business model' (as one said, which could apply to all three) and a stronger Customer Value Proposition (CVP), could realise.

> *The learning models*: with the exception of the selling-on organisation, the learning models were the weakest of current models; these broadly, privileged traditional and individual learning. Apart from some informal gatherings there were no collective learning forums, though these did

emerge during this work, nor any explicit means to challenge prevailing thinking in changing circumstances. However, with the start-up there was an explicit awareness of founder's syndrome and the need to have in-house thinking 'existing' to tackle it as it emerged.

How Adequate Were They to Meet (1) Previous Challenges and (2) Emergent Challenges in a More Uncertain Environment?

The established organisations: while their current models are adequate to meet their current challenges, they are not adequate to meet emergent ones which bring possible changes in funding, markets and policy, nor to exploit new emerging business and political opportunities.

The start-up organisation: current thinking is effective having reached its next stage (launching) fronted through its explicit business model. However the management and in particular learning approaches are 'explicitly implicit': this means an awareness of preferred theories-for-use 'exists' within the thinking and experience of staff, including the founder, as a resource, to be used as need emerges and the organisation develops. Thus, they do not need to be 'written down' as such. To be fair to the organisation this trusts risk and emergence, which the models endorse. The challenge to the organisation is how to ensure this occurs (see Chapter 7, Applying the New Models – Summaries and Key Aspects).

The selling-on organisation: is being purchased in large measure *because* its models have enabled high performance (along with other market considerations).

How Useful Are the New Models?

All the organisations thought the models were useful though with different responses depending to some degree on their theorising about stages of business development.

For the established organisations: they are extremely useful in enabling explicit choices to be made about their models and to recognise the need to explicitly identify their next stage and to 'choose and use' new models to get them there.

For the selling-on organisation: though they exemplified many strengths of their organisation, they would be 'more useful in a different form' for instance, redesigned, making clear three priorities in each principle. Some redesigns as a result of these comments are in Chapter 12.

For the start-up organisation different challenges emerged: though the models may be more useful as 'heuristics', nonetheless, the thinking their approach involves is still needed for sustainable development, the issue is how explicit it should be and how it will emerge.

What Were the 'Outcomes'?

Did we meet the claims this work made: to enable faster development, create new choices about models, develop 'new value' and behind these, the interdependence of the three models and learning as the midwife? Yes, *so far*[1] bearing in mind that this journey is by definition unfinished. The (continuing) outcomes were:

- *Faster development*: the established organisations identified their next stages[2] as 'Growth through direction', 'Renewing organisational purpose' and a more complex version of 'Growth through direction'.[3] However, getting to this stage was a considerable challenge and was a key learning point in this work and is developed further below.[4]

- *Creating new choices*: they choose new models to activate their next stage, seeking to develop towards Agile management, Resilient learning, and Growth in business, and integrated these into new business planning.

1   See Chapter 9. This journey is by definition unfinished, as the ideas progress through the organisations over a timescale longer than this book. Here we will present what we have realised *so far*. We will continue to track the progress of the ideas, as a continuing journey, and further findings will be available later via web links on the Gower website.
2   See Chapter 7, Applying the New Models – Summaries and Key Aspects plus The Next Stage of Development, for definitions of development and the challenging journey to this point.
3   Two of these are terms from Larry Greiner 'Evolution and Revolution as Organisations Grow' (1972) in Charles Handy (1985) *Understanding Organisations*. London, Penguin. One organisation used this heuristically rather than as a mechanistic template to seek growth through direction, delegation and collaboration (seemingly separate phases) prompted, as they said, less by 'crisis' than the need to broaden leadership, autonomy and control. Details in each 'Summary' in Chapter 7.
4   See p. 191, Crafting the Next Stage of Development.

- *'New value'*: was developed by exploring new CVPs and customer 'need' as 'advantageously slippery' and of infinite variety'[5] resulting in: greater client contribution in complex social processes to address organisational issues; embedding and enacting self-managing for customers and the organisation; and exploring new customer-generated product demands.

- *Interdependence and learning as midwife*: each case of 'new value' began with the organisations having doubts about current adequacy to meet their challenges of creating more diverse business, which in turn, unearthed the need for a different management approach. This however, turned out *not* to be the primary 'problem' which was around learning – and what type.[6] It meant recognising the need for learning and indeed 'significant learning'[7] *first*. This was also needed for getting to the next stage. Thus, in practice, the models were interdependent with learning as midwife, and in turn, not *letting learning in* was identified as a defensive routine, as 'what we've done before'.

A key process in the work was how the organisations identified and shaped their next stage of development. This was highly significant and it is outlined in detail below. This is followed by 'More 'Value': Some Ideas for Other Organisations in Using This Approach'. More detailed conclusions about the work *overall*, are in Chapter 9.

A NOTE ON THE HISTORY AND EXPERIENCES OF SMALL BUSINESSES

Small isn't large in miniature

As all the participant organisations are small, with less than 20 staff (full and part time), it is useful to look at the history and theories of small organisations.

How are companies 'organisations'? Are they just 'society writ small' containing the values and contradictions of the society they spring from, or are effective ones somehow more than this? How does their form and purpose distinguish them?

---

5   See Chapter 6, The Three Models: Facing the Future – the Business Model.

6   See Chapter 6, Building the New Models – the Learning Model. 'Deep learning' is needed to build 'Resilience'.

7   As stated in each organisational 'Summary' in Chapter 7, 'significant learning' involves 'a certain amount of pain, connected with the learning itself, or distress connected with giving up certain previous learning … it involves a change in self-organisation – in the perception of the self is threatening and tends to be resisted … it involves turbulence within the individual and the system' Knud Illeris (2004) *The Three Dimensions of Learning*. Gylling, Denmark, Roskilde University Press, quoting Carl Rogers (1969) *Freedom to Learn*. New York, Merrill.

Each participant organisation is still led by their original founders and they are at different stages of development. We need to remember that life for small organisations can seem uncertain yet predictable, at the same time. Around 90 per cent fail or merge within their first few years, or with time and survival, many founders do not want to grow beyond their present state. Many barely make ends meet.

Also the lifespan of both leaders and organisations is shortening. Some organisations here are well established (trading for 17, 15 and seven years) which means that as their markets are mature and they should be seeking ways to be – or stay – agile, resilient and inventive. All in some way share the history and experience of small organisations and how they develop – or don't. The evidence is quite sobering. Small businesses, and this include many bigger than the ones here, have always comprised more than 50 per cent of the developed economy.

But only a small minority, say 5 per cent, make a contribution to growth or jobs, or indeed make much money for their owners. Also small firms are not large one in miniature. There is no natural path that takes them from 'small' to 'large' or from 'struggling' to 'successful'. The bigger fledgling firms grow the more irrelevant – or even counterproductive – become the qualities that first won them their success. Only exceptional entrepreneurs (a term we apply below to the organisations here) have the will and the capacity to adjust. Of successful entrepreneurs, almost all attributed success to exceptional execution of ordinary ideas, or by nothing more than arbitrage: buying cheap and selling dear to customers lacking the complete information they would have in more stable market conditions. These needed to have iron self-control – be able to live with rejection and be highly perceptive. Contrary to accepted wisdom, the qualities usually thought of as entrepreneurial, risk-taking, break-through creativity, foresight, grand ambition, power and administrative abilities – are all secondary. Fully 40 per cent of the successful entrepreneurs had the benefit of neither unstable markets nor a unique product. All they had in effect was 'hustle' – drive, energy and ingenuity in meeting customer demand. Even the so-called capital shortage for small companies may be a fallacy – as Bhide points out, the whole point of entrepreneurship is substituting brains and hustle for capital'.[a]

---

a   Simon Caulkin 'Small's no great thing', *The Observer*, 9 December 1999.

The Next Stage of Development

SOME IMPLICATIONS OF SMALL BUSINESS THEORY FOR PARTICIPANT ORGANISATIONS

The next stage of development was clear and explicit for the start-up and selling-on organisations. However, this was not the case for the established organisations and emerged as challenging, complex and contradictory. Though they shared some of the history and experiences of small businesses (above) each was 'established' in quite individual ways. Their business ages were roughly 17, 15, and ten years – the last including prior to being established in its current form. Though their next stage of development was as one manager said 'taken for granted', coming anew to it via the models, prompted some critical considerations, and some agonising, and meant it had to be more than simply repeating previous plans. This provided ideal grounds to test the models and their claims, as outlined below.

CRAFTING THE NEXT STAGE OF DEVELOPMENT

This involved considerable time and thinking in all the organisations. We had now worked with them for some time, increasing their familiarity with the models. As one said, even if some seemed at the 'left-hand side' of the grids in their initial assessment, this is already a 'value-subtracting' way to perceive the tools. Alternately, viewing them as a continuum enables either/and rather than either/or and immediately sets them on a value-creating path. As well, any current 'illness' they are experiencing, again as another manager put it, is not life-threatening and the models could show the way to needed improvements.

However, *the process* of getting to the next stage for the established organisations, to identify, grasp meaningfully, agree collectively and integrate into their new business planning, *was the most difficult* and is given here a detailed explanation.

FACTORS INVOLVED (WITH THE ESTABLISHED ORGANISATIONS

i.   The implications of their next stage being implicit (as with their current models);

ii.   Interpreting 'development' and constructing choices about it;

iii.   Using what they have 'established' including identity, purpose and risk – to founders and customers;

iv.   Recalibrating 'success' and as one said, 'entrepreneurship-cleansing'.

These factors are now examined in detail.

(1) Having an implicit next stage: barrier or bridge?

How can *implicit development planning* be a barrier to development? It was initially expressed conventionally as 'we are unlikely to grow in terms of staffing' and 'we are unlikely to expand staffing'. This might explain why, though effective, they had some of the limiting experiences of many small firms, (above) having modest levels of development and being 'hidden' in their own sectors. Nonetheless they all had immense potential. Meeting other participant organisations including the selling-on one, enabled them to see that 'taken for granted' or implicit thinking which inevitably led to 'more of the same', could not be disguised as 'development' any more. However, this realisation also brought into play other ideas including risk, entrepreneurship, direction and leadership. Their next stage was in fact significant 'organisational development' and this would involve considerable argument and discussion or 'contestation' (below).

(2) Interpreting 'development': crooked journeying

'Develop' or 'grow' can seem conventionally simple: employ more staff, expand and become more profitable. However, we asked if this was actual 'development' or is more promising, ambitious 'growth' (needs explaining too!) possible? It involved making choices in its meaning,[8] the key ones being: 'to come from a latent to an active or visible state', 'to become more systematic' and 'to bring to maturity' through a gradual unfolding.

Also, as one manager said 'growth as development' might result in its opposite, a lack of development; for instance, as an organisation 'grows' someone can offload work 'they don't like, aren't good at, or judge less important, so they never get better at it'.

There are also some necessary stages larger companies undergo in dealing with change productively, which includes among other things, 'reinventing their distinctive business models' to fit prevailing condition and '*contestation* – respectful difference that grows out of conflict' growing from the creative tension of civilised disagreement.[9] Was this 'stage' necessary for the established organisations and how could they handle it?

---

8   Oxford English Dictionary meanings of 'develop' and 'development': unfold, reveal, bring or come from a latent to an active or more visible state, to bring to maturity, become more elaborate or fuller, more systematic or bigger; a gradual unfolding, stage of advancement, a more elaborate form.

9   Stefan Stern 'Master the mix of continuity and change', *The Financial Times*, 20 January 2010.

(3) Identity

Conventional corporate behaviours do not attract the established organisations. They are animated as much by what they stand for as what they are against, their identities having been forged 'against the grain'. 'Development' is based on their perception of value, their ambition, politics and worldview. 'Success' is more complex than traditional ideas of business 'expansion'. It is subservient to the value the founders get from their work, including as one manager said, 'the flexibility and freedom in how they work', control over its purpose, and above all, engaging and managing their contribution, to 'make a difference'. However, they do have 'high achievement motivation'.[10]

(4) Age, growth, pain, success...

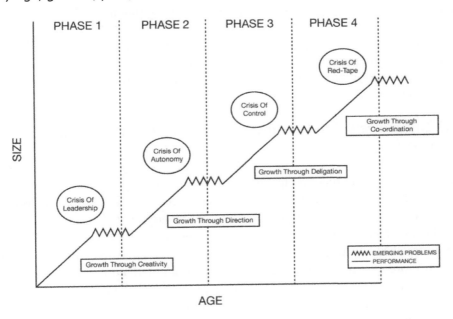

Figure 8.1   Organisational Growth: 'Professional noticing: naming pain and responding'

To help examine the next stage of development, we used 'Professional noticing', a prompt based on Greiner's organisational growth model[11] (see Figure 8.1)

---

10 Robert Kelsey 'Slow and steady', *RSA Journal*, Spring 2011, p. 31.
11 Based on Larry Greiner 'Evolution and Revolution as Organisations Grow' (1972) quoted in Charles Handy (1985) *Understanding Organisations*. London, Penguin Books. It was the phrase 'The pains of success' which attracted the organisations in this exercise. It seems to have been removed in later versions.

phases of growth punctuated by types of 'crisis'. We considered the phases could broadly apply to smaller organisations so we broadened 'growth' to 'development' (2, above) and focussed on jagged, 'painful' periods, where problems emerge and performance at best, stalls. As the organisations said, because these emergent problems are difficult, and come in different headings than Greiner, they are frequently *'professionally unnoticed'*. They occur, ranging in many forms, including 'crisis' irrationally expressed; crises not neatly separable, for example, crises of leadership, autonomy and control experienced simultaneously; being unskippable; and maybe not as 'crises', to stimulate the next stage. Further, different growth responses are possible – including a simultaneous mix of those in Figure 8.1. However, the kind of response made is crucial and the 'pains of success' can only be experienced with the appropriate developmental response. This naming and responding was excellent in further making explicit the established organisations' development thinking.

Linked to this, though 'success' was not a claim they would make, there was also an emergent feeling as the work progressed, that they could be 'more successful in conventional terms'. So what was 'success' now for them and what could it be?

(v) 'Entrepreneurs' and seeking 'success': humility or a concept devalued?

Success and entrepreneurship are linked in the history of small businesses. Did the founders here feel they were entrepreneurs? Yes but mildly so, as one said, because of common myths about entrepreneurs that they are 'confident, optimistic, charismatic, inspire people … they know they are good'. This is 'how celebrity entrepreneurs describe *themselves* … conveying an image of entrepreneurship that is aggressive, short-sighted and unfair, not least because it alienates and excludes so many potential entrepreneurs … stopping many because they fear that they do not fit the stereotype of the "maverick" entrepreneur'.[12] As mentioned above, if the founders in this work are entrepreneurs it is because of the freedom and flexibility their work provides.

When writing this section I came across the following: 'Most stories taking place in the world today have nothing to do with the vocabulary we are continually bombarded with, that of "success" and "progress". They are

---

12 Robert Kelsey 'Slow and Steady' *RSA Journal*, Spring 2011, p. 33. Also quoting Mike Southon and Chris West, *The Beermat Entrepreneur: Turn a Good Idea into a Great Business*. Prentice Hall, 2002.

about the recognition of endurance and courage.'[13] This sense of endurance and courage did include the established organisations in a way somehow 'success' didn't and they did articulate 'success' in a profoundly different way:

Organisation 1: 'After 30 years of dependence you may have given up on yourself – we haven't.'

Organisation 2: 'You don't need doctors to run primary health care – we do it better'

Organisation 3: 'Who said the Left can't run a successful business?'

The term 'success' also had a lukewarm reception from *other* founders of small organisations I interviewed. As one said, it was in danger of being a 'smug-balm', and another 'hydra-headed'. This organisation had a particular 'development' approach: it set out to get business through referrals. It grew rapidly by regarding marketing campaigns as 'failure with current customers, as the service you provide is not good enough to turn them into advocates'. This meant growth in a way which minimised *risk*. 'Success' was a 'by-product of doing well for others, building relationships and communities', a classically oblique – and successful – approach.

This might help the established organisations to renew their initial risk and give their understated idea of success more direction and purpose in a more explicit 'next stage'.

As 'practical visionaries'[14] the reasons they started their companies are still present.

Nonetheless as this work progressed, the seeking of 'conventional success' did emerge. And why not? The organisations had, again implicitly, framed 'success' as part of their mission and individuality. However 'development' for any organisation is having the confidence – *and performance* – to individually frame it but also articulate what their *more* successful business would involve.

---

13 Nicholas Wroe interviewing John Berger, *The Guardian*, Review, 23 April 2011.
14 Some of these successes deserve more than a footnote: for instance the brilliant inventiveness of Philosophy Football creating 'Makana FC' t-shirts, the team formed by the ANC on Robben Island, and giving them to the remaining ex-prisoners during the 2010 World Cup and also producing t-shirts to mark the 70th anniversary of the opening of the 1941 second front against Nazism, in Russia, with its 'To Victory' slogans and support for those 'in the city of Lenin' (under siege for two and a half years) messages in Russian.

This also means re-interpreting 'entrepreneurialism'.[15] This in turn, would mean posing conventional, yet difficult questions, such as why would someone invest in your organisation? What would a 'friendly' venture capitalist seek? What would they see as 'potential' and what growth avenues does this kind of traditional questioning release?

Mainly because of their backgrounds, each had to go through a 'contestation' process themselves internally, to reconcile the 'hydra' nature of success, renewing fought-for identity *and* 'being more profitable' in their own terms. However, this also meant recognising that the reason the next stage of development was initially resisted was because it requires 'significant learning'[16] and *acknowledging* that learning is needed. This is a crucial aspect of this work and strongly informs the 'developmental tasks' each organisation must tackle to activate their next stage.[17] This underlines an initial claim of the models, that the learning model is 'the new politics', is where the first change-engagement occurs (even if initially denied) and is key to change.[18]

Also this raised the issue of what would 'success' for this work be? One indicator is that organisations can use the models to self-assess, as a pathway for radical 'development', and continuous renewal beyond adaptively improving their service.

(vi) Accepting the challenge

The established organisations accepted the challenges and identified their next stage of development, how to activate this through changed models, and integrate this into new business planning. These included 'adaptive changes' which initially we frowned on, thinking they could emerge from any intelligent questioning, rather than the radical changes we assumed possible from the models. These adaptive changes included (1) changes in structure and in founder roles (and other staff) to enable founders in particular to seize and lead new opportunities; and (2) in more robust and efficient systems, traditional

---

15 See Chapter 8, p. 194 – '*Entrepreneurs' and seeking 'success': humility or a concept devalued?*

16 'Significant learning' involves 'a certain amount of pain, connected with the learning itself, or distress connected with giving up certain previous learning … it involves a change in self-organisation – in the perception of the self … is threatening and tends to be resisted … it involves turbulence within the individual and the system' Knud Illeris (2004) *The Three Dimensions of Learning*. Gylling, Denmark, Roskilde University Press, quoting Carl Rogers (1969) *Freedom to Learn*. New York, Merrill.

17 See individual detail in Chapter 7, Applying the New Models – Summaries and Key Aspects.

18 See Chapter 6, The New Models – Interdependence and Learning as a Midwife.

responses to growth *or age*. We call them adaptive because even when adopted, the need for more innovation is not diminished nor met by them. A range of issues along the journey helped leverage acceptance by the organisations of the challenge of this including:

- *The soft issues*: perhaps experiencing the sapping challenges of 'keeping going', or diminishing returns, where greater energy is needed each day, or in the words of Studs Terkel earlier, they felt 'more torpor and less astonishment'.

- *Collective learning forums*: the open learning forums and workshops with all the organisations together and experience of the sold-on one, with its explicit models and explicit entrepreneurial approach.

- *Emergent opportunities*: their current models not enabling them to meet their challenges (see Chapter 7, Summaries and Key Aspects) and emergent opportunities including: using their 'core business' for a more entrepreneurial focus; exploiting and combating a more right-wing political agenda; using the 'ascendancy' of social enterprises; more innovatively meeting the needs of the expanding immigrantvulnerable; and more explicit business-focussed use of social media.

Restating, or rebooting their businesses, would capitalise on their undoubted strengths and as one said 'the next stage of development means not backing into the limelight any more'.

(vi) Reaching 'the next stage of development'

The detailed 'outcomes' are above. As part of these, with their definition of 'to develop' stated first, each established organisation identified their next stage as:

1. to bring ideas 'from a latent to a visible state' for 'growth through direction' including a key imperative 'we need to be more entrepreneurial';

2. to bring 'ideas to maturity' to 'renew organisational purpose';

3.   to bring 'ideas to maturity' in the form of 'growth through direction'.[19]

They also choose new models to activate it, to seek to develop towards: Agile management, resilient learning, and growth in business and integrated these into new business planning.

For some founders, the 'significant learning'[20] driving 'development' also meant constructing new personal options, including changing role and broadening self-managing explicitly.

More 'Value': Some Ideas for Other Organisations in Using This Approach

A key aspect of this work was its claim to develop *new value*. The original working definition of creating value (from Chapter 4, Research Method or Inquiry Approach) still applies here. 'Any process which adds something more … so that as a result, it is stronger, better, fitter or more open and is the source of, or contributes to more "developmental" choices. It means for whatever issue, as a result of it, *you have more at the end than what you started with.*' Developing value began with the CVP but many different value-creating 'activities' emerged. Twenty of these are outlined below.

Further, in the spirit of one principle of the value-creating method, 'to manage uncertainty and take risks beyond knowing' this section is presented in an innovative way, with 20 headings, synoptic comments, and brief, buzzy guidance for new possible users in the form of traffic lights.

'More value' is really a journey in gradual sense-making, doubts and all. It includes the responses of the organisations and my own, intertwined, at various

---

19 Larry Greiner 'Evolution and Revolution as Organisations Grow' (1972) in Charles Handy (1985) *Understanding Organisations.* London, Penguin Books. This organisation used Greiner heuristically rather than as a mechanistic template to seek growth through direction, delegation and collaboration (seemingly separate phases) prompted, as they said, less by 'crisis' than the need to broaden leadership, autonomy and control. Detail for each is in Chapter 7, Applying the New Models – Summaries and Key Aspects.

20 Integrating all three models 'significant learning' involves 'a certain amount of pain, connected with the learning itself, or distress connected with giving up certain previous learning … it involves a change in self-organisation – the perception of the self is threatening and tends to be resisted … it involves turbulence within the individual and the system' Knud Illeris (2004) *The Three Dimensions of Learning.* Gylling, Denmark, Roskilde University Press, quoting Carl Rogers (1969) *Freedom to Learn.* New York, Merrill.

implicit 'stages'. It should be read in parallel with Chapter 11, 'The Journey' which tracks the internal journey of the writing/writer, the difficulties, real and imagined, internally and externally, the doubts from banal to Olympic-scale, and how to use what can be learned from conducting such an experiment. The section also needs to be read in conjunction with Chapter 9, 'Conclusions and Benefits' which further develops what has been learned in the work overall.

1   LANGUAGING ABOUT

The organisations' first experience of the models was through their *language*. Soon their own terms and the models mingled and eventually the language of the models became common currency. We underestimated the persistence all partners needed to pursue them purposefully.

Key learning point

A key part of learning is acquiring a 'new' language. All managers should be 'bilingual': using management language and making sense of it.

2   'NORMAL' ALWAYS NEEDS STRETCHING

Working with the three models gave an initial energy boost to the established organisations in identifying their challenges, next stage and how the models could tackle anew, their barriers. As one manager said, the continued dialogue about his organisation's current and new models was exactly the 'psychotherapy they needed'.

Key learning point

After a while, as what was 'challenging' becomes just 'more of the same' – a great energiser is 'how do you want to develop?'

3   THE MOON NOT SIXPENCE

Initially some organisations tried a sort of 'fit-up' by throwing their problems, for instance, marketing or staff morale at the models and requesting they solve them. We said they could, but more radically, the models would enable them to also tackle the conditions which had created these problems. This adaptive tendency emerged in legitimate developments such as improving a website, or having 'training in leadership' which we considered necessary though not sufficient to get to the next stage of development. However, the 'adaptive changes' we initially tolerated, thinking they would not diminish the need for more innovative, radical change promised by the models included changes in structure, founder roles and in more robust and efficient systems. What we learned is that whatever the improvement prompt, if the desire to change is ignited, don't 'diss' it. So the title of this section should be the moon *and* sixpence.

Key learning point

Rekindle the large ambition the organisations had when beginning.

See adaptive effort as untackled defensive routines.

4 SINS OF OMISSION

Early on I realised that the exercise seemed 'remote' for some organisations. What difference did it make where they placed themselves on a grid, or in two years' time, as the assessment asked? I then realised that I had left out a crucial process: that to get to their next stage we had to prove that the thinking that got them to their current stage would not be enough to get them further. This was a challenge of not so much 'proving' their current theories 'wrong' as *limiting development* even though they seemed to be working effectively now – quite a risk. Identifying their theories meant going back to hussle more time with them. Greater engagement occurred by not just pitting their current thinking against their identified challenges, threats, trends and other variables, but also against more appetising emergent opportunities. Overall these made their current position seem, as one said, 'static'. This was a stage of serious grappling.

Key learning point

Identifying what is ineffective is not enough.

What is the greatest sin by omission an organisation can commit? And how can they be forgiven?

5 STARTING THE RIGHT FIGHT

The key 'argument' was round what is your next stage of development? Within the established organisations it became an argument with the *claim* that whatever their next stage, they already do it. Further, that next stage, as their current models, was implicit, as if assuming it would occur *automagically* through what they normally did. One suggested their improvement strategy – also implicit – *was* their next stage. In these circumstances, participants need to internally *contest* their development collectively, without which 'progress' is highly unlikely. Also 'future-fit' models cannot occur by default – they need conscious choice, fuelled by the explicit stating of the next stage.

Key learning point

Encourage strategic differencing – fighting with ideas-pillows and future-ambition – *from a standpoint of commitment*.

    'Arguing.'

6 THE FIRST DUTY: THINK

The questions 'how adequate are your present models?' and 'what are your theories-in-use?' were very difficult to answer. Though all the organisations had different means of measurement, none (apart from the selling-on one) had measured the influence of their three models *on their performance*. Thinking anew was initially difficult.

Key learning point

Aim new thinking at old, even 'unimagined' problems but make it more than 'new ideas in the old bottles of perception'.

7 THEORIES-IN-USE OR 'BLAMING THE PARENTS'

All organisations accumulate habits, actions and practice whose 'parentage' – the theories they spring from – have long been lost or forgotten. These actions and practice, the 'orphans', need handing back to their parents so their real homes can be located. Effective organisations should not be orphanages but 'adultages' of practice where the theories which inform *current practice* are explicit to address the issue, 'Are they what we need now?' For instance, if limiting decision-making from authoritarian managing occurs, naming this as belonging to command and control theories, can begin to go some way towards changing it. Broadly, whatever current theories, they lead back to the need for greater agility, resilience and renewal, as in the models here.

Key learning point

Organisational business should be 'living *on purpose'*.

 Implicit planning = AMBER.

Don't assume the next light colour: it could be RED.

8   RUST, TRUST AND GOLD DUST: ENGAGEMENT, TRUST AND COLLECTIVE LEARNING

Ironically, having set out to locate evidence that greater trust, engagement and collective learning enables high performance, we found facilitating workshops between and among the organisations considerably strengthened engagement, trust and collective learning. Some issues which then emerged surprised the organisations themselves: for instance, that they could despatch considerably more than previously thought *if their processes connected*; how their business model was 'sticky' and developed loyalty but had very low barriers to entry; and the widening gap between staff and founders' awareness of organisational values.

Building collective learning in the workshops – and after – was highly effective with founders/leaders and their staff, to engage organisational development. This occurred faster than through individual learning and the collective forums can also challenge possible dependence on the founder's learning. As well, staff can increasingly use the models themselves to continually assess development and build independence. Trust is also generated through actions emerging from the workshops which generates a 'start imperfectly' (a principle of the method) and learn faster approach.

Key learning point

The three key enablers to engage *collectives* are building greater trust, engagement and collective learning, without which new 'development' is unsustainable.

9 TACKLING FOUNDER'S SYNDROME

The practice of the founder usually emerges first under the heading of the management model. A key challenge is where a founder's vision may have reached its limits or where risks previously undertaken now need significant upgrading, or as one manager said 'a significant inducing of breathlessness'.

Key learning point

There is a reason 'I did it my way' is sung at funerals.

10 RISK AND TRUST ARE TWINS

If the inquiry journey is made meaningful, anything missing in the planning will be easily embraced. We worried about the risk of not including 'everything', for instance, should the organisations complete a threats and trends analysis, or the founders a personality inventory, or should we observe their *practice* (the need for which we intuitively understood from earlier experience of seeing adult teachers – and managers – in situ rather than merely talking about their practice)?

However, when such issues did emerge they were easily 'housed' and discussed under the most appropriate principles of a model including leadership, product design and evolution, processes, identity, marketing and branding. 'Risk' also emerged and is included as a crucial element in the development tasks for each organisation (see Chapter 7, Summaries and Key Aspects).

In all this, we used the value-creating method, for example, 'use learning as a bias towards action, and trust it, the first risk' and recognise that the organisations and ourselves are 'more than their brain: the lived life has contradictions'.

Key learning point

Trust the thinking you have already done in this, the method. If thought through it will enable value creation. And because you can't do everything doesn't stop you starting something –meaningfully.

Closed method: all the thinking is done prior to use.

Open method: improve as you progress.

11   WHAT'S AN 'ENTREPRENEUR' – AND DOES IT MATTER?

Differences between the founders and their organisations emerged, for instance, some of the established organisations had been going for 17, 15 and seven years and their journey could seem to other colleagues as somehow 'finished'. By this we mean their initial success indicators were already realised along with their continuing distinctive contribution. How *their service* was seen was more important than how *they* (the founders) were seen. Terms like 'entrepreneur' needed detaching from its myths.[21] One manager characterised it as 'hogging, *yet dimming* the limelight'. However the journey of the sold-on organisation is explicitly and responsibly entrepreneurial, with more learning and more risk. Its current stage is selling its 'smarts': the products, processes and thinking which made it successful. The founder's next stage is to build another business, a key difference compared with the established founders in strictly entrepreneurial terms.[22]

Key learning point

It is only the 99 per cent of entrepreneurs that give the others a bad name! If confidence, talent, charisma and being inspiring are myths, then optimism, self-knowledge, self-determination and freedom to make a difference in contribution are not.

If the Entrepreneur = high maintenance.

---

21   Robert Kelsey 'Slow and steady', *RSA Journal*, Spring 2011, p. 33. Also quoting Mike Southon and Chris West (2002) *The Beermat Entrepreneur: Turn a Good Idea into a Great Business*. London, Prentice Hall.
22   See Chapter 8, p. 194 – '*Entrepreneurs' and seeking 'success': humility or a concept devalued?*

If the Business = high maintenance.

12   THE 'QUICKEST' ROUTE IS HAVING A TICKET TO WHATEVER ROUTE EMERGES

This work claims that using the models will enable organisations to get to their next stage of development faster. However, as we discovered, this turned out to be the reverse: identifying and committing *to the next stage* is more likely to be faster. Obvious? Not without starting with a mangled assumption in the first place! And the payoff for this work: whatever the next stage it still needs new models to activate it.

Key learning point

Don't avoid detours, they may be the destination.

13   IF THE BUS IS 'DEVELOPMENT', LEARNING IS THE DRIVER

How can organisations best *learn how to learn*? With participants, most assumptions were made about how an implicit learning model would suffice – and with others we interviewed. There was a feeling that somehow learning is successful because it is not 'resisted', that it occurs automatically, that people learn on the job even if there are no explicit forums or pathways, that management and business models will somehow engender it, or that once the need is recognised, traditional methods will do.

The claim made in this work is that having an explicit learning model will generate greater thinking capacity. To invest in learning is to create continuous organisational 'wealth' and 'learning-conscious' learners.

If the business model is the playmaker the learning model is the ball. Think how the Barcelona football team became 'insulted' when they give the ball away and how they get 'armed' to redouble their efforts to get it back. The equivalent with learning is being able to increase your rate of learning when things around you change. And not being satisfied with thin answers to your question, 'What can we learn from this?'

Key learning point

Learning will always enable you to break the speed limit – your competitors' pace.

14   EARNED BENEFITS

All the organisations had different 'frontline headaches', as one manager put it, and also had similar ones, from everyday operational to more fundamental ones. One had initially 'refused' to grant themselves the reflective space to address them but once an opportunity arose, though externally prompted, it generated will and energy, their presenting issues soon emerging as symptoms of something more fundamental – which eventually led back to the need for new models.

Key learning point

The journey provides reflective, challenging space to enable the organisations to think their way to 'developmental independence' rather than having to depend on external forces. As one manager said, strengthening their thinking capacity to 'solve their own problems, particularly what next...' and in doing so becoming more agile and resilient 'is the greatest value'.

 : I'll do it for you.

 : I think I'll think about it...

15   EMBRACE SOCIAL MEDIA

'We participate therefore we are.'

Social media is used currently or will be more fully in the next stage of development of the established organisations. Social media is attractive because it promotes a more 'democratic' horizontal, information flow, challenges the vertical flows of previous models and gives greater 'freedom' for contributors (see Chapter 3, Context: Collapsonomics, Change Gridlock or More of the Same? Or Just a Bonfire of the Certainties?). Significant learning conversations around 'what matters' can be initiated, developed and sustained over long periods, creating greater value for participants but will need an appropriate learning culture to be negotiated in advance, offline.

At a more general level, social media helps 'free up organisational problems' to sympathetic groups internally and externally: for instance, Lilly Pharmaceuticals needed to hire many pharmacists to recapture markets lost by declining Prozac patent revenues. Unable to answer the problem internally, they set up an internet-based, problem-solving forum open to any scientists, offering to pay for solutions, and creating a global virtual research and development capacity, eventually launched independently as InnoCentive[23] becoming highly successful with other companies following suit.

In this work social media was used to get responses from our networks, to my question, 'What is the best value this work can provide?' These included 'rebooting their organisations' (a well-known radical business journalist); 'be an original thinker' (professor and author on management innovation); and 'get a better title than "Trust, Engagement and Collective Learning" – try "Because Things Change – You Need Help" or "Be Your Own Model"' (Management Babylon Group).[24]

Key learning point

It is worth repeating: *none of us is as smart as all of us* (Warren Bennis).

16   PAYBACK

A key principle of the value-creating research method is 'Be reflexive' where the organisations were asked to use and improve the models. Feedback ranged from complementary to quizzical and included:

- *'How did you know*?': one co-founder said the 'sayings', as part of the overall 'explanations' at the end of each principle were 'greatly illuminating'; another said they were 'frighteningly accurate' about their company, mirroring exactly where they were under many of the headings.

23 Alexander Osterwalder and Yves Pigneur (2010) *Business Model Generation*. New Jersey, John Wiley, pp. 114–115.
24 *Management Babylon*: a group of ex-Open University Business School MBA graduates, experienced, creative managers, seeking new ways to 'manage'. Convened by Critical Difference.

- *Becoming ambidextrous*: 'improving both sides' to include improvements at the left-hand side of the models for instance in the management one: becoming 'better bureaucrats' or a 'freer hierarchy', or in the learning one: stronger 'individual learning but aimed at interpenetrating 'collective learning'; or in the business model: converting customers 'inside-out' views.

- *Language as lubricant*: in initial mapping of the models against their practice there wasn't an 'exact fit' so we encouraged the organisations to use their own language and experience – and make it stretch till it does fit.

- *Improvements*: the selling-on organisation suggested we 'simplify' the models and redesign them stressing the priorities of each; another suggested they were 'hard to grasp' and sought help from one of their own management review colleagues, while another suggested they were best used as heuristics. These 'redesigns' gave us new resources and are included in Chapter 12.

Key learning point

If everyone 'seeks to understand' *first*, far greater value will ensue.

17   BREAKTHROUGH: LEARNING FROM ACTION

The greater the application of the models, the greater the dividends: one founder said, surprising herself, 'I now realise we are using the old model of learning, with "expert" inputs from subject specialists, when we need a collective forum where we share what we ourselves have learned, to develop the business – where we *produce* learning.'

In another organisation, having assumed limited interest, we were again surprised at an early asking of, 'How do we apply these?' Once applied, the organisations then had to turn 'ideas' they favoured under each principle into a processes.[25] This was helped by redesigning the models as priorities[26] (see Chapter 12).

---

25 Donal Carroll (2008) *Know Learning, Know Change.* London, Critical Difference, where behaviours based on agreed values are turned into a process to 'activate' them fully. Available from the author.
26 See 'Improvements' in number 16: Payback above.

Key learning point

For learning, 'practice is not its medium it is its measure' (John Seely Brown).[27]

Go away and reflect on your practice.

Reflect on your practice *then* act on your reflections.

18   SUCCESS

'Success' is eagerly sought, frequently claimed but can also be a form of premature exhilaration. As a cold-headed business term, *none* of the organisations used it, giving the impression it was strongly disliked and seen somehow as 'self-praise is no praise'. As one manager said, it is not 'cuddly' and another, 'It's like an actor using the word "Macbeth" while being in it.' Nonetheless, as the work progressed, the seeking of 'conventional success' did emerge. And why not? These organisations had framed 'success' as part of their mission and individuality. Part of 'development' for any organisation is how to express, create, recognise and celebrate success while having the confidence to individually frame it; this means becoming *more successful* by reconciling the apparent contradictions of established identity and becoming more profitable in their own terms.

On the other hand paradoxically, its absence does not mean a lack of success.

One overall success indicator for this work is that organisations can in future use the models to self-assess and as a pathway for radical 'development' and continuous renewal including and beyond improving the service or sharpening commitment.

Key learning point

Success is self-shackling unless obliquely sought.

The 'dumbing down' of success begins with being applauded for saying your own name or thinking success occurs through completing a business plan.

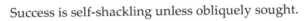

27   See Chapter 6, The New Models – Interdependence and Learning as a Midwife.

19   FINDING PATHWAYS FOR ENGAGED IDEAS AND VALUE-CREATING

From this work we can see that value is produced by *engaged minds at work* through their discretionary effort, but that is simply the first ingredient. To be effective, other ingredients are needed, for instance a climate where new ideas eliminate rank, and a pipeline of possibility for them, a pathway into life initially through experiment. This 'pathway' however, must be protected collectively – as an organisation. Only one organisation had all these aspects, the selling-on one, part of its success.

Key learning point

Value-creating needs to eliminate highly trained pessimists ('managers', as one participant called them) and the weed-killer and 'idea-minefields' they have planted, by supplanting these with trust and hope.

20   'MANAGERS ARE MORE INTERESTED IN PATTERN RECOGNITION'[28]

Some patterns which emerged through the work are:

- In organisations where there is a weak or implicit learning model the management model determines it.

- The old management models require more managers. Fewer managers are needed if there are more 'purpose carriers' than 'uniform carriers' (those apparently organised who do nothing, the term used by one founder). In contrast, in his, the selling-on organisation, all staff had 'manager' in their title to emphasise shared purpose and a movement in models from 'management' to 'self-managing'.

- Better models = fewer managers: the biggest organisation in this work was the medical one with 20 staff (full and part time). However, without explicitly seeking an agile management model as expressed here, the need for more managers and more 'managing' will always

---

28 George Yip 'How to make research relevant for managers', *The Financial Times*, 14 February 2011.

emerge, regardless of size. This seems to be what is occurring with the largest one.

MORE 'VALUE'!

As well as the different value-creating examples above, we also said at the beginning of this section that 'developing value began with the CVP' as a crucial part of a renewed business model. In the collective workshops each organisation explored their CVP for 'new value'. This also involved our claim[29] that customer need and value can be 'advantageously slippery': if 'need' is the new commodity then it is of 'infinite variety and infinitely negotiable'. The established organisations began customer value-creating in the following ways:

- For Believe, negotiating greater client contribution particularly on re-establishing community links, while affirming that this 'normalising' does not disrespect client experiences or the self-determining distances they have travelled.

- For Health House, *embedding and enacting* self-managing: for patients, as a value, and for staff as a new management dimension of 'agility'.

- For Philosophy Football, exploring and negotiating new customer-generated product demands to develop new markets including niche ones.

UNFINALLY, AN END AND A NEW BEGINNING: IT'S ALL OVER BAR THE DOUBTING

For experiments such as this a crucial element is the ability to increase your own rate of learning. This means always returning to key questions, always conceptualising, if 'stuck' having conversations in any form that ignites the imagination, and seeing 'doubt' as an organic tool for development. Don't cry harder, think harder: for every unsympathetic audience network up a new one. And... work back from the horizon.

Key learning point

It's never over. The 'ending' must be an invitation to others to improve it.

---

29   Chapter 5, The Three Models: Facing the Future – the Business Model plus Exploring Customer Need and Value.

9

Conclusions and Benefits

These are the conclusions of this year-long experiment in applied business research. The work overall should be seen in the light of *creating value*, its signature, and one it should be judged on.[1] The section consists of conclusions, benefits and 'free transfer', key ideas from the work for others to use and which is located in the next section.

Structuring the Conclusions

These are[2] structured round the following questions:

- Did the work with the three models enable the organisations to get to their next stage of development *faster*, its initial claim?[3]

- Did the approach enable other benefits and achievements for participants, or others?

- In the case of the established organisations, could other forms of intelligent interrogation have led to identifying improvements or the next stage of development?

- How can we separate the effect of the models from other variables operating in the organisations at the time?

- Is there any opposite evidence, for instance, a counterfactual case, where organisations reached their next stage faster *without* using the models?

1   This began with the Inquiry Approach continued through Chapter 8 and concludes in Chapter 10 with 'Ending with a Start – Value-creating: *A Little Yes – Because You Can*.
2   Based on more the comprehensive analysis in Chapter 8, More 'Value'.
3   These 'developments' are identified in each organisation's Summaries and Key Aspects in Chapter 7.

We want to address rigorously, while recognising that such experiments take time to get the ideas being tested dirty with practice. We also need to reflect the open-ended nature of the inquiry, a journey which is by definition unfinished, as the ideas progress through the organisations over a timescale longer than this book. Here we present what we have realised *so far*. We will continue to track the progress of the ideas, as a continuing journey, and further findings will be available later via web links on the Gower website.

The counterfactual case – we didn't conduct any different experiments – is covered to some extent, in the claim at the end, that the overall benefits and achievements of the method and approach could not have been developed by other approaches.

Conclusions

1.   Applied business research is possible in a restricted timescale if seen as 'experiments in learning' and conducive relationships established so benefits for all partners accrue.

2.   All the organisations are effective at their particular stages of development (starting-up, established and selling-on), *so far*, though the established three organisations have significant undeveloped potential.

3.   With the established organisations their current models of management, learning and business are 'implicit' having been default rather than conscious choices. Nonetheless they are sufficient to meet their current challenges.

4.   The vision of the founders of the organisations is crucial in how they see themselves as businesses: the established ones have built deep-seated identities around knowing who they are and what they stand for, which informs their perceptions of 'success', of 'entrepreneurialism' *and* their next stage of development.

5.   For the established organisations their current models are not adequate to meet emerging challenges in a more uncertain environment or to seize the opportunities from the changing landscape with, for instance, greater social needs of the vulnerable,

a more right-wing political agenda, and the 'ascendancy' of social enterprises.

6.   Their next stage of development[4] (before they experienced the initiative outlined here) is also implicit, or as one manager said 'taken for granted', and broadly, more of the same. Thus building a new next stage 'developmental platform' becomes a *key business battleground*. It brings together their history, leadership and ambition, requires significant collective argument and discussion,[5] and an examining of the relationship between being 'established' and new developments 'becoming visible'.

7.   The use of the inquiry tools and overall approach enabled the established organisations to get to their next stage of development faster, and to make new choices for their three models to activate it. It is probably more accurate to say that the choice involves them *in seeking to develop* the agility, resilience, and growth which the new models enable. They also recognise this requires 'significant learning', the interdependence of the models, that changing one is not enough, and the learning model as 'a midwife' for the others.[6]

8.   'New value' emerged for the established organisations by exploring their Customer Value Proposition (CVP) and perceiving customer 'need' as 'advantageously slippery' and of 'infinite variety'.[7] This resulted in different value creation for each, namely: greater client contribution in complex processes to address organisational issues; embedding and enacting self-managing for customers and the organisation; and exploring new customer-generated product demands.

9.   Effectively identifying their next stage of development proved a confirming catalyst in then choosing models and practice, not the other way around as we had started!

---

4   See choices involved in 'The meaning of development' in Chapter 8, What Ocurred and What We Learned.

5   Or 'contestation': a form of respectful strategic *differencing* that grows out of conflict – in this way dynamic businesses grow from the creative tension of civilised disagreement. Stefan Stern 'Master the mix of continuity and change', *The Financial Times*, 20 January 2010.

6   See 'Significant learning' in Chapter 6, The Three Models: Facing the Future – the Learning Model.

7   See Chapter 6, The New Approach.

10. Though social media was used, it was marginal. However, the next stage for all involves risk, to take greater advantage of social media, and as one manager said, 'Exposing ourselves more publicly while being more cool…'

11. The selling-on organisation had explicit models, highly consistent with the ones here, which produced higher performance and were instrumental in its being pursued and bought by a larger company. The founder had an explicitly entrepreneurial mindset of 'success'[8] and of 'growing and going', that is, building a company, selling it *and how it became successful,* and then going on to build another company.

12. The starting-up organisation had an explicit business model which was instrumental in its success so far. Using the founder's awareness of more progressive management and learning approaches, these could be *'explicitly implicit'* that is already 'existing' in the organisation and available as a resource for emergent needs. This, in his view, was evidence of an 'Emergent' learning approach, with autonomous staff as producers of learning (see Chapter 6,'Building the Models' for detailed principles).

13. Finally: the overall approach provided another key benefit – as one manager said about the next stage of development – 'It is not a blank page in the sense of thinking as before. Using the models can provide a competitive edge enabling them to plan their business futures, handle challenges and threats, analyse the "right" competitors, and be clear what the future would ask of them *which other approaches would not have developed…'*

Benefits

A range of benefits from the overall approach also emerged. They included:

- *Starting:* launching a meaningful experiment to get new ideas into a 'research field' and beyond.

---

8 A member of the BBC TV programme 'Dragons Den', Peter Jones, that effective 'enterprise is not the mechanics of setting up a business but a state of mind, a confidence that you have the knowledge *and the right mindset to be successful.* Quoted in *Times Educational Supplement,* FE Focus, 27 August 2010.

- *Building tools*: for all the organisations, and particularly the established ones, having the tools to self-determine an improvement or development journey at their own pace, *independently*.

- *Exploring*: in the first instance exploring themselves, in how they organise their collective effort, their thinking and the value they create for all their stakeholders.

- *Energising* active choices: to move from 'more of the same' with the enterprise on autopilot, and implicit business choices, to explicit choices and how to build an approach where agility and resilience become the new 'explicitness'.

- *Facing the family*: exploring the influence of founders/leaders in shaping organisational identity, success, entrepreneurialism and their next stage of development and enabling new personal choices for founders in terms of changed business roles.

- *'Rebooting'*: renewing and re-engaging with organisational purpose.

- *Developing value*: (1) using the 'value-creating method' to explore 'value' including self-correcting leadership[9] and (2) developing a new CVP in each established organisation.[10]

- *Sharpening*: refining participants' competitive edge in ways other approaches or experiments could not.

- *Transferring*: enabling other organisations to use the models.

Next, Chapter 10 is designed to enable other organisations to use the approach. It is based on key 'developments' from the work, expressed in an innovative way.

---

9 See Chapter 10, Free Transfer: Shaping, Pruning, Seeding.
10 Examples from the three established organisations in Chapter 8, More 'Value': Some Ideas for Other Organisations in Using This Approach.

10

Free Transfer: Shaping, Pruning, Seeding

Ending With a Start – Value-creating: *A Little Yes – Because You Can*

This work ends by going back to where it started. Throughout, it attempted to create value widely, in exploring, giving breath to new ideas, mining what worked and didn't, and what emerged even while not striving for it. We know value-creating produces lift rather than depletion, and like the learning model, is crucial for development, however tiny its starting point. During many years spent as a teacher, manager, MBA tutor, consultant and coach in management development, I had a sense of the key role managers had in creating value, starting with themselves, even though *then I hadn't given it the soft embrace of 'value creating'*. With groups of managers, I often asked how frequently they said 'yes' or 'no' as a broad indicator of their receptiveness to new ideas. The majority said no *far more* – some with pride. While the worst seemed to view management as a form of training in cynicism, more worryingly, the best did not necessarily become innovators. With value-creating now I equate 'yes' as leaning towards a 'growth mindset' – *you can be more than you are* – and 'no' as leaning towards a 'fixed mindset' – *you've already reached your limits*.[1] This is why we have to change the dominant management model to ensure its role is to enable independent self-managing staff, commitment, growth and agility, as this work argues.

The final section brings together the two journeys, the ideas in the organisations, and the writer, with the purpose of enabling other organisations to use the approach here. It can be viewed as a synoptic business poem which seeks to continue to create imaginative value. Its form came from an interview

---

1   Matthew Syed 'How practice makes perfect', *Work/Guardian*, 4 June 2011.

with Jennifer Egan[2] about her latest novel, *A Visit from the Goon Squad*, which has one chapter in PowerPoint. She claimed it worked because the format underlines a structural point she was making about *brevity*, in an 'awkward, silence-imbued relationship'. On sending this chapter to her editor only on the final edit! – he couldn't open it, 'not following her instructions, immediately calling for technical support!'

This also made me realise there is a point at which writing ends, and becomes 'free'. This is when eventually it is beyond the control of its creator in both its *form*, the way it is read, in the old, less endowed software, and its *content*, the meanings, now no longer the writer's either.

How This is Structured

'Free transfer' comes with a warning: it is synoptic but less 'silence-imbued' and more 'earned'. It contains development ideas from the work expressed in the form of 'Commandments, Abandonments and Questions'. Commandments give 'guidance for care and new development', Abandonments are 'scissors for comfort-pruning', and Questions are 'growth-seeds, watering direction'. Each idea asks a challenging question for organisations seeking to use the approach.

It is introduced by a 'warm-up' question:

'How can an organisation of people you don't trust, won't engage, and won't think do better business?'

The task is for the reader to create a commandment, an abandonment and a key question.

Good luck with your journey.

---

2   Emma Brockes 'A Life in Writing', an interview with Jennifer Egan: 'I really wanted to write a chapter in epic verse because I thought … epic verse and PowerPoint in one novel, come on. Irresistible!' *The Guardian*, 7 May 2011. Jennifer Egan (2011) *A Visit from the Goon Squad*. London, Constable and Robinson Ltd.

Shaping, Pruning, Seeding

1512 The Narrative

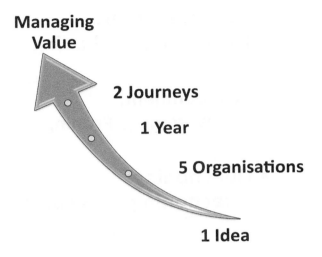

Managing
Value

2 Journeys

1 Year

5 Organisations

1 Idea

1512 The Architecture

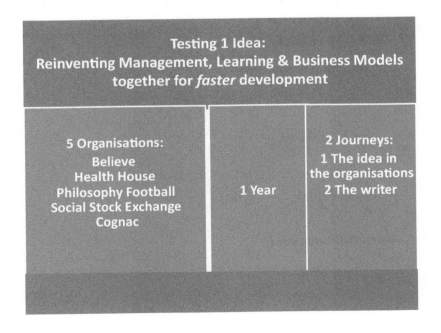

Testing 1 Idea:
Reinventing Management, Learning & Business Models
together for *faster* development

5 Organisations:
Believe
Health House
Philosophy Football
Social Stock Exchange
Cognac

1 Year

2 Journeys:
1 The idea in
the organisations
2 The writer

1512 The format

Growth by pruning and seeding

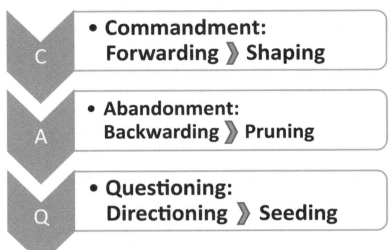

- **Commandment:**
  Forwarding ⟩ Shaping

- **Abandonment:**
  Backwarding ⟩ Pruning

- **Questioning:**
  Directioning ⟩ Seeding

Starting question – an ideas tin-opener

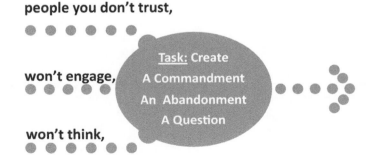

How can an organisation of

people you don't trust,

won't engage,

won't think,

do better business?

Task: Create
A Commandment
An Abandonment
A Question

Start imperfectly: make thinking *and* doing equal worlds – for all staff

Commandment

Reclaim 'research' – everyday *experiments* in looser thinking

Abandonment

Ditch the fear that we can't do it ourselves

Question

How can you embrace 'problems' as a learning journey?

Choose your theories-in-use, the models which determine how your organisation works

Commandment: Choose your backbone - your models

Question: How can you *construct* your backbone?

Abandonment: Ditch not living *on purpose*

'Learning' is *always* the first gear

Contesting the next stage of development

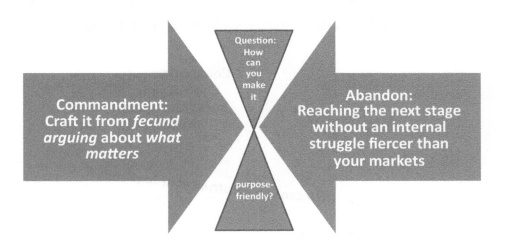

Interdependence: Management, Business and Learning - 3 rooms in the same organisation where it eats, sleeps and reproduces

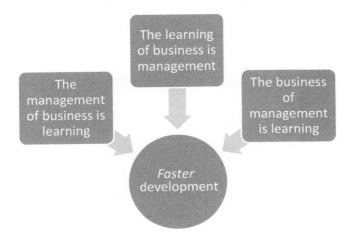

'Am I buying what you think you're selling?':
Customer 'need' and value creation

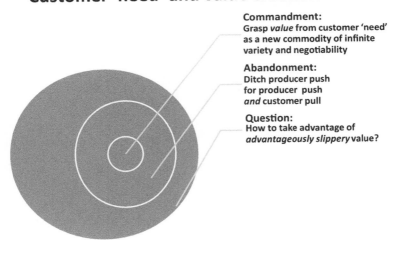

Self-correcting leadership
for uncertain times

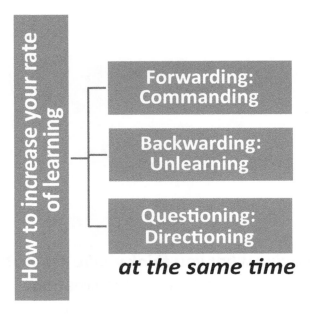

11

The Journey: Gaining an Imaginative Edge and Outtakes

Imaginative Edge for Competitive Edge

All organisations seek diverse ways of gaining competitive advantage. Writing too. Any writing journey needs persistence and energy. This can come from the necessary discipline of 'Silent Witnessing',[1] gathering and returning to evidence from participant interviews and workshops. But data-pathology is a bit stillborn. As a writer, you have to believe in this world but as the poem goes, I also 'don't believe in this world unless it is pierced by light'.[2] Some 'light' can emerge from insights about the work, a sort of marriage of fact and fancy, excellence excavated from perseverance, if you like. But there was something else: writing about business may be important but it is not *everything* – and we need more for 'any full living of our lives'.[3] So I sought ways to stimulate the writing – anything to generate a different, fuller take on the organisations – another 'edge', an imaginative one.

This Section Contains

- The journey over one year: an experiment in learning.

- Visiting the organisations: location and 'fit'.

- A musing on method (the inquiry approach).

- Outtakes: comments which fell out of the journey along the way.

---

1 See 'Silent Witness: The evidence is never silent!', p. 230 in this Chapter.
2 Anna Kamienska (2007) from *Soul Food Nourishing Poems for Starved Minds* Ed. Neil Astley and Pamela Robertson-Pearce. Northumberland, Bloodaxe Books Limited.
3 John Newton (2009) *Are God and the Gods Still There? How Poetry Still Matters*. London, Olympia. A 'wisdom-corrective' and reminder of the cost of cheap intellectual living, linking harder thinking with fuller feelings.

The Journey Over One Year: An Experiment in Learning

The journey investigates the testing out of a new idea over a limited timescale. It includes the building of the relationships necessary to construct a meaningful testing 'forum' for the idea. The testing is 'crushed' into one year because of the work demands of the participant organisations and the writer. The journey explores what could be achieved in that timescale where learning is a primary consideration, so any mistakes, oddities and inefficiencies at the point of embarking (the ideas and tools being used) can be improved along the way.

1512

Experimenting with 1 idea (using new management, learning and business models, together will enable organisations to reach the next stage of their development *faster*)

in 5 Organisations

over 1 (interrupted) year

through 2 journeys

The journey is primarily that of the idea but it is also the journey of the writer. How should this be expressed? Given that the writer is both creator and narrator, should it be 'invisible', assumed to be just part of the main trip, the idea journey? Or, if not, what form should it take? Charles Handy said that, 'organisational phenomena, *I realised*, should be explained by the kind of contextual interpretation used by an historian.'[4] It's that phrase 'I realised', that ticking *attentionising* going on in the background all the time of writing, which has a powerful shaping force. Hopefully, it can lead to insights about the main content but can also alert the writer to some concerns about the form it should take:

- *Is it the 'right' form*: in other words, might the work be better served in a completely different form, as a poem or painting, or film, music, opera, a series of Tweets, a big blog, or bits of them all?

- *How should the writer 'perfect' the chosen form*: as William Butler Yeats put it (as I remember), that if his work does not appear as 'just a moment's thought, my stitching and unstitching comes to nought' – an attention which can become corrupting, too. The more sweet-

---

4   Charles Handy (1988) *Understanding Organisations*. London, Penguin, Introduction, p. 13.

flowing and fluent the writing the more the author has devised 'a way of writing that appears to float calmly along the surface but is actually very busy paddling underneath...'[5] The 'busy paddling' is in recognition of the difficulties of actually staying afloat and creating something of value for a reader.

The journey of the writer including the doubts, are given explicitly here. They emerged from continuing reflection – maybe too much! – during and after the work. They are framed under three headings, wholemeal insights, finding (and absorbing) creative resources, and doubt removers.

WHOLEMEAL INSIGHTS

1. *Reframing*: the journey itself needed continually reframing, the last being as an 'experiment in learning over one year' to recognise how it involved risk[6] in learning and the unfinished nature of the journey (see Chapter 9,'Conclusions').

2. *Practise what you preach*: I worried, particularly early on as things seemed slow, if my rate of learning was increasing faster than the organisations. It was a form of 'will they do anything?' As coaching (one-to-one) was offered to the organisations, I got myself some too. The self-centred nature of my concerns soon became apparent –and how to tackle them.

3. *Trust what you have already created*: I needed to trust myself, and in particular, one principle of the value-creating method: 'Use learning as a bias towards action – and trust it – the first risk.'[7]

4. *Writing isn't a 'day job' it's an* everyday *job*: As one manager said about a famous one-club football player retiring in the Spring of 2011, who over a period of 15 years had won every honour and captained both club and country: 'He understood well that a big club's history starts from zero every day.' Writing is like that.

---

5   Andrew Motion reviewing Geoff Dyer's 'Working the Room', *The Guardian*, 20 February 2010.
6   This included discussions with a group of male associates whose claimed risk-taking was somehow always trumped by their defensive routines; also my own assertion that 'more of the same' is not a risk.
7   Chapter 4: Research Method or Inquiry Approach.

FINDING CREATIVE SOURCES

'The happiness in hard working'

In writing, can we tell if the will does the work of the imagination (to paraphrase WBY) – or is good writing a mixture of both? While reading 'Help!' by Oliver Burkemann[8] I was struck by how often he mentioned 'hard work': he meant the thinking which enables progress on complex, messy issues; work hard then 'flow' will come. As a result of this, my daily self-advice: tackle two complex things each day to provide discipline.

Information is beautiful

This book is a magnificent kaleidoscope of data diversely presented.[9] However apparently dull the data seems, the more imaginatively presented it shines, like finding a 'halo round the frying pan' (Nabokov). So I recreated the models in different formats as 'problems' and improvements'; the 'problems', ones the organisations were experiencing matched against 'improvements' drawn from the models. For instance: if various operational issues were experienced, improve by clarifying overall goals and direction (from the management model); and also engage in improvement conversations (from the learning model).

Silent Witness: the evidence is never silent! (BBC TV murder series)

In the BBC TV series 'Silent Witness' three forensic pathologists are given various complex murder cases to solve. In a murder case previously investigated, there is no record of a key victim on the police database which assiduously records all the details (DNA, blood type, and so on). Leo is one of the three pathologists and his nose is already twitching. *The most frequent screen action* is of him and his colleagues poring over evidence, debating, contesting and posing different questions to edge out new answers. All the time they seem to work on an intuition that something is not quite right – and though slightly different from 'something is wrong' it is usually the hunch that opens the first door, the first piece of value-creating – without which there is no pathway, no journey, no resolution (in this case) and no change.

---

8   Oliver Burkeman (2011) *Help! How to Become Slightly Happier and Get a Bit More Done.* Edinburgh, Canongate Books, pp. 11–15.
9   David McCandless (2009) *Information is Beautiful.* Harper/Collins, London.

Clearing the pathway

Perhaps 'what looks like a people problem is often a situation problem' the author of *Switch* suggests.[10] The 'situation' includes the environment, the 'path'. When you shape the pathway, you make change more likely regardless of the 'Rider' (our rational side) or the 'Elephant' (our emotional side). How should I clear a pathway?

IN PRAISE OF DOUBTING – AND 'DOUBT REMOVERS'

Does every doubt have a parent and does locating them help? The doubt clouds here included the adequacy of the models, the commitment of the organisations and early on, feeling I had the 'wrong evidence' when in fact it was an over-simplifying impatience which took the form of old models = bad, new models = Holy Grail! Even though I knew I was in good company, Charles Handy for instance, expressing doubts as mentioned before. However, I found some reassurance in the yes/no poems.[11] In the cliché, I wouldn't discover new lands without first losing sight of the shore. 'Doubt', a short powerful word, eventually gave way to a much longer, more powerful one: re-conceptualising.

I came across a comment by the 'best footballer in the world playing for the best team', Xavi Hernandez, on the first thing they teach you at Barcelona Football Club: to *think, think, think* – lift your head, move see, think, space, space, pass… Of course, I was thinking anyway, I told myself, but in a preferred mode, an anecdote, an assumption unexamined, a decent line or tale but not (at that stage) getting beyond a half story. I used Xavi as a metaphor to aid the discipline of thinking in action. So with the accumulated evidence, to think – that is, look again: to find 'space' – start from the clutter and ordinariness of what is there rather than what you want it to be; insights occur from searching again; and to 'pass' – create new angles and possibilities. For instance: was my 'evidence' just the organisations' initial impressions only? The doubts: mine or theirs? Old doubts in a new form? Only one way to find out – ask them –and find some new 'space' as a new action. Thanks Xavi!

---

10   Chip and Dan Heath (2010) *Switch*. New York, Random House Business Books, p. 18.
11   See Chapter 4, Research Method or Inquiry Approach – *Giving Method 'The Shadow': Embracing Ambiguity* text box.

DOUBT REMOVERS

These involve revisiting previous thinking, evidence and even the fundamental approach:

1. *First seek to understand* rather than refute and reload.

2. *Declutter thinking* to 'clear a pathway' through apparent obstacles the organisations were experiencing in testing the models. Displaying the models differently for easier application encouraged their adaptive use, as improvement tools, freeing action routes.

3. *Is anything missing?* To get to their next stage faster, I needed to make explicit a stage I had left out. This stage involved getting the organisations to evaluate the adequacy of their current models. Whereas we had assumed their inadequacy – *they* had to find it out for themselves. This process cannot be short-circuited.

4. *Help strengthen others' thinking*: initially, we did this by encouraging the organisations to reconnect their apparent orphans with their long-lost parents. Contrary to the claim that 'without a theory, the facts are silent',[12] in many organisations, confident 'facts' emerge through ingrained practice; these can seem independent of theory and behave like screaming orphans[13] until they are identified and brought back home. In the process of identifying and evaluating their theories-in-use, the organisations could now make stronger, conscious choices about their future models – and obviously theories.

5. *Listen louder*: as one manager said at one stage my thinking 'seemed defensive…' The writer needs to be as resilient as the ideas being tested.

Visiting the Organisations: Location and 'Fit'

In seeking a different, more comprehensive and imaginative take on the organisations, I tried different, 'impossible' questions: what would they taste

---

12 Hayek, quoted in *The Financial Times*, January 10 2011.
13 See also 7: Theories-in-use or 'Blaming the Parents' in Chapter 8, p. 201.

like, what is their song, if they were a flag what colour, what would they dress in, what if their founder was Snoop Dogg or Jay-Z, or if they were secretly funded by Diane Abbott? Or if they had different names: for example, Live Forever, Hoard Your Health-Wealth or The Beautiful Enigma??

Did I manage to get a different 'edge? On visits to each organisation (or founder) I was struck by the possible 'fit' between their offer, geographical locations, and source of customer. This section has a paragraph on the location (the office) of each participant, along with a riff on what kind of drink, song or plant each might be.

VISITING: JOURNEYING WITH THE WHOLE MIND

Visits, particularly at the starting point of a longer journey, are exciting. They then become as much an internal voyage as an external one. I've turned up at the doorstep of these organisations, dry and dishevelled in the summer sunstream, needing water, winter-frozen and transport-frustrated, needing whiskey, and most of the time feeling like I was pilfering progress, nudging margins, grateful for half concentration, lured by fragile insights, but always surprised by the welcome and the accepted invitation to think.

ORGANISATION 1: BELIEVE (THE CHARITY)

London – late November – dark and chill even when it's light. 'Meet us at our office at 48B'. The B is for basement, below a cab firm. And opposite a fast food franchise, a second-hand shop and a tyre replacement garage where the cantilevered air-hoses spill onto the pavement as if hoovering up local gossip. It's 'neighbourhood' so people stop and chat here. The local public house, not a bar, is called Rosie McCanns ('from the banks of the Bann') as the song goes, one you don't hear much anymore.

The iron steps down to the basement have an edgy rail and the front door looks like it needs protection. Down in the basement two staff have a busy, concerned shape, and are at home in their work and belonging. They always welcome a conversation.

This is not a land for small business units, the work dress code of the suburbs. The whole area to the south is a relic-ridden landscape: behind one of the city's biggest rail stations, for two square miles it was the resource-supply for Victorian industry and empire, consisting of freight-weight and more freight. This was a business model as utilitarian as the road names, Freight Way, Goods Way. Though being built on anew for Euro PLC, a large part looks like a gigantic hospital for articulated trucks. Thousands lie, in an open air garage broken down and cab-less, needing help getting round corners, they have been put to bed.

At the southern edge, new buildings shrill into view: large stores take their cue from the size of the freight-place: Bathroom Heaven, Kings Place, the Royal Canal Hub. And eventually, a trendy bar area where individual bars, too economically scared to venture out alone, together cluster. Despite the changes, some things always appear round here: Goths, trucks and drinkers. Everything fits.

If the organisation was a drink, song or plant what would this be?

Drink: Special Comfort (individually made)

Song: *A Fairy Tale of New York* The Pogues and Kirsty MacColl

Plant: A West Bank olive tree.

ORGANISATION 2: HEALTH HOUSE

Walking through the suburban streets from the British Rail station, I pass an old Triumph Herald winking its remaining headlamp, an old Singer sewing machine, and a dog sleepily ignoring me along Golden Manor. As I reach the centre I hear a hubbub of engaged, vigorous, voices with worldwide accents, healthy with interest discussing animatedly temples they can visit. They are the healthy walking group. At the front, making an uncertain appearance, is a minute welcome message to the centre itself, folding over as if self-hugging. The centre is on a corner, at 90 degrees to a private road, where a lawnmower and a wheelbarrow lie resting in the summer sun. Inside an electronic notice board displays details for patients… 'nurse practitioners can prescribe, refer and diagnose…. details of out clinicians are available at reception.' Of the four patients present, one wants to cease smoking (she said), one is overweight and one would like to get healthier – all 'preventable' conditions except for the one that isn't – ageing. I estimate we have say, 15 different languages between the five of us.

On the way back to the station, I notice an older Indian man who I'd passed earlier is now way ahead of me, nearing the station. 'How come?' I ask. 'I know a short cut,' he says. He then asked me my destination. When I tell him he frowns and says 'And you're going by *this route* –the E99 bus is far quicker.'

As I make a more visits over the next six months, I notice some changes: a large crane now struts the skyline nurturing a new construction: 'Family Mosaic', an initial block is already up and there are public notices apologising for restricting the use of the pavement for a year. Over time, the shortcut disappears because with the new building, previous public pathways are no longer so. On my next visit, I kept ringing the bell. No answer. A patient comes from behind and walks straight in. The door is always open, she says. It fits, being open.

If the organisation was a drink, song or plant what would this be?

Drink: Cucumber Cooler

Song: *I'm a Different Person* or Lola's Theme (Shapeshifters)

Plant: Evening Primrose.

ORGANISATION 3: PHILOSOPHY FOOTBALL

The sun rises in the East. It brings a perfect democracy of light. The neighbourhood is alive with alleys, lookalike streets, pavement youth-bikers, council estates and corner shops. And factories: were, want to be and one-day - how many people does it take to form a factory? One large one has been re-enlisted for storage and small businesses. We go up a narrow rocky staircase, to a small room dressed in segmented clutter; if it was a PC its capacity would have been too small years ago. The area offers challenges to businesses and it responds: a local new community restaurant, 'The Pearl' wins the Time Out award for 'Best new café' 2010. When we enter, playing softly in the background is 'Diamonds on the Soles of Her Shoes' followed by 'Common People'. Round here, they're fit for business combat.

If the organisation was a drink, song or plant what would this be?

Drink: Sapporo lager and 'Politics on the beach'

Music: *Groove is in the Heart* (Deee lite) and *Ghost Town* (The Specials)

Plant: Red Hot Poker.

ORGANISATION 4: SOCIAL STOCK EXCHANGE

Scene 1

Late September, an Indian summer in London. We are meeting at The Young Vic, at The Cut, now a thriving area in Southwark, just south of Waterloo station. This is the first time in about ten years that the Cut is *uncut*, clear of the modern stopblocks to access, hydraulic-jacks, paving stones and dumped debris, all of which linger long beyond their welcome. On the road, festering traffic cones minimise traffic access while a Stonehenge of pavement stones and red and white barrier tape deny pedestrians. Notices urge them to 'walk safely' and shunts them into the road: so ironic, they should be on stage.

On the other hand these stopblocks are the first noisy entries of the New Plan: concrete indicators of investment, a healthy sign that the previous infrastructure is now too limited for the throughput and traffic which the area will generate. They will eventually grease the palm of the cafes, bars, restaurants, shops and theatres here.

Amazing how somebody, even ten years ago, has thought through what stops an economy might also be what starts it! An Oscar for public sector investment!

Scene 2

Breezy Monday morning, more spring than winter. Even at this time the venue is bouncy and lightly packed. The regeneration investment is a springboard from the London Eye to The Tate Modern. It lifts all boats. Opposite where we talk there is evidence of the hard graft that eventually 'secures a halo round the frying pan' (we are in a theatre). The worker–actors, having rehearsed, coffee-out, in a bliss of relief, their shift ended. Iain Glen is in a conversation with a well-known actress, lately dead from 'Spooks', with lots of inward-leaning. We watch momentarily. They are *working*. Fittingly, they look in to look out better. Their objective: to change your emotional world. SSE's objective: to change the world.

If the organisation was a drink, song or plant what would this be?

Drink: Dry white wine with ice-jags

Song: *What Ya Gonna So* Plan B and *Anthem Without Nation* Nitin Sawhney

Plant: Orchids.

ORGANISATION 5: COGNAC

A private member's club for professionals, Central London: a glass-fronted ex-warehouse, large, second storey, outside-in glassed lifts, its name well publicly hung, yet still hard to find. Inside, the place is a luxury of space and light. Individuals and groups excite themselves and hubub about. Even individuals are small groups of one – networking. The windows are big enough to live out of and could be in Amsterdam or Brussels. But in London, windows have business history. Half the wallspace consists of Thatcher-windows with their purpose reversed: departed from the 1980s testosteroned and society-free, designed to escort the vision of those inside towards gazing out on all they survey and command, now their purpose is to let the outside-in: light and energy fuel individual effort to make connections. To be seen and network: networking as an anti-brand. Everything is fuelled with yes. Deals fit graciously. We talk and eat over breakfast. The conversation is worth Eggs Benedict, French toast and tea (30 varieties) – almost £30. Though no advertising is going on, something is for sale.

If they were a drink, song or plant what would this be:

Drink: Manhattan

Song: *The Only Way is Up* Yazz

Plant: Acer.

A Musing on Method (the Inquiry Approach)

This section gives another take on 'research method' or the 'inquiry approach'. The language we use is crucial here and considerable work is needed to peel away the scar tissue of preparation and make the method accessible. This is so readers *and potential users* don't feel they need to wear academic gloves when handling it, or that they are being taken up a towering yet shaky 'new research' scaffolding, only to arrive atop, breathless, in a tiny room they feel they've been in before. The inquiry approach consists of the questions we asked, the key claims, how the approach was built, the doubts we had, the thoughts we left in, and the lingering ones we thought we'd left out. The journey also consists of how all the participants improved the method as we went along.

What exactly should the relationship be between a research or inquiry method and the issues being investigated? As we were asking participant organisations to explicitly select more appropriate models rather than (probably) their current default ones even though this would be far more challenging, it occurred to us that we should be doing the same. But isn't this what every researcher *claims*?

However much it claims, most 'research' is seen by business as a cross between indulgent abstraction and academic hyperventilating. In this work, to encourage innovation and insight, we need to invent a delicate pathway between old and new, theory and practice, rigour and interest, safety and stretch, *vessel and vision*. And free of unnecessary academic shackles.

What are the default options and their limitations or strengths? What influence should 'research' have or seek? If 'research' is the front page of 'what we should be doing' in any field, then the body of the text, how it is finally expressed, is usually a monumental fistfight between theory and practice. Who wins depends on the commissioner, the author, and if there is one, the intended audience. This begs the question of who needs research and who reads it. In most cases, the commissioner (the paymaster) wins. So what sources have managers – a key intended group of this work – to usefully draw on? In current business research, Henry Mintzberg might win best prize for books most useful to managers[14] (*Managing*, 2009) but such books are rare, for a range of reasons. The key ones being:

1   TOO MUCH (OF THE WRONG KIND OF) THEORY – OR THEORISING

Business schools might be a useful source of research though not everyone thinks so. Much research 'turned out by business schools is irrelevant to business. There is no profession where the gap between researcher and practitioners is

---

14   Henry Mintzberg (2009) *Managing*. Harlow, FT/PrenticeHall.

so wide. Business schools do not command the attention of managers'.[15] The business academics' defence is that management is neither a profession nor a science and business schools, desperate for respect from other disciplines with greater claims to being more 'scientific', need to produce the sort of arcane research universities demand.

Yet they still claim that faculties engaging in research have more knowledge to pass on to students. This, according to others, is a dubious claim (along with 'passing on', as an even more dubious method) in that 'not only did business research not reach managers it wasn't even used in the classroom' (ibid.).

This issue of what exactly 'Management' is has dogged it since Frederick Winslow Taylor published *The Principles of Scientific Management* in 1911.[16] In developing a form of respectability it has made itself less valuable to those practicing it. Hence the damp response of the field to 'research'. Alternately, Henry Mintzberg has claimed that management is neither a science, a profession, nor has it changed very much over the years; it is best seen as a *communityship*, a practice, rooted in context and that 'efforts to professionalise it and turn it into a science, undermine it…'[17] It is more a craft, with a touch of art and some use of science, to inform a practice.

This is the assumption taken here; a liberating opportunity to build on its accessibility with a more diverse range of stimulants than the academy traditionally produces.

My own experience mirrors this, when, as a successful Head of Department having developed management programmes in many organisations across all sectors, and developed a Management Charter Initiative (MCI) centre, I went for interviews to teach at various business and management schools. At one I was asked what the purpose of management education was and replied that it was to make better managers. No, I was told, it was to get them onto the next academic stage (of the provider).

15 Michael Skapinker 'Why business still ignores business schools' also quoting from Freek Villen of the London Business School, *The Financial Times*, 25 January 2011.
16 Frederick Winslow Taylor (1912) *The Principles of Scientific Management*. New York, Harpers
17 Henry Mintzberg (2009) *Managing*. Harlow, FT/Prentice Hall, p. 13.

2   TOO MUCH (OF THE WRONG KIND OF) PRACTICE

This assumed a kind of 'stable verities' where other things somehow stayed the same.

In much of my (and other colleagues) consultancy work I was invariably asked to tackle organisational problems where the presenting issue was not the 'real one'. The real one was usually a more fundamental, enduring one, not too difficult to elicit but far more difficult to tackle.

Here is a typical example: the initial issue or 'problem' was the governance role in creating greater diversity in senior positions, in public sector organisations. We were asked to identify 'examples of effective practice' rather than models, and also produce hints and tips rather than theorising. Note the role of the 'commissioner' here (issuing this advice) – a sort of internalised defensiveness that because business writing produced by academics was commonly 'indulgent theorising, far removed from practice', theorising *per se* was frowned on – with the danger of producing a sort of thought-free practice. (Or, at worst, a 'let's make them do, not think'). Even 'models' – which are probably best seen as useful metaphors for a subject, a way of discussing and philosophising round the 'subject' were to be avoided. Yet surely governors need robust theories to craft their practice, for instance theories of diversity, ethics and values. Further, new models and ideas, to be of any (eventual) use, are created as a result of the limitations of current ones – once their limitations are detected. They are developed *in response to problems*[18] – in this case enduring ones in current management, learning and business models (see Chapter 6, The New Approach).

There is also another lazy assumption which many organisations have about 'identifying best practice'. There is no doubt that this can be useful but not if the context or backdrop assumes 'stable verities', that is, all other relevant variables remain the same. The key question organisations rarely pose in chasing 'best practice' is what needs to be tackled for it to have best practice itself – its *own* signature practice? Good or best practice cannot be effectively transplanted onto bad – cut flowers don't grow – unless there is a mighty argument about change as part of a sustainable change programme, to eradicate or transform the real sources of bad/poor practice. Further, good practice is invariably informed by some other good practices, usually a range of them, which overall, amount to a different approach, a different culture

---

18 Mats Alveson and Hugh Wilmott (1996) *Making Sense of Management: A Critical Introduction.* London, Sage Publications Ltd, p. 207.

and a different theory. For instance: better managers have greater expectations of their staff – that is, they put into practice different theories of motivation. So a theory without practice is superficial at best. Vice versa, it is literally headless. If 'theory' is the face behind the makeup then there are immediate limits to endlessly making a better face without eventually, changing it. And that is fundamental! In the end, for sustainable change, it's the theories and the culture they inform which needs changing.

Quite apart from the theory/practice boxing ring, there is another issue around evidence, when building a research method. Many business owners talk about key advances 'becoming' key advances but they usually do this *in retrospect*. They can be safely called that now, looking back on them. But when they were made, they were usually small, a phone call to an uninviting source, a piece of advice truculently given, something they didn't want to hear, a wired gesture, an unguarded moment when they accepted an invitation to travel through their own echo. The point is when they made that small advance, it wasn't an advance, it was *a risk*. And made while trying to desperately contain and scope a waterbed of uncertainty.

We can call this 'subjective evidence'[19] the participant emotions and gestures which inform their decisions. Much reality hovers round this enhanced 'negative capability'[20] – the byways, asides, silences, begrudgings, almosts and other approximations. Including them is risky but, without, the organisational narrative is incomplete. For research method they offer rewards, danger and promise but they need balancing with rigour: feelings are fine but performance is a key judge. So we need to ask is there evidence that the perceptions and performance are pointing in the same direction.

Outtakes (Asides from the Journey)

1.   If we are so good how come we're not more profitable? (founder)

2.   What is the healthiest way to set free a child? (metaphor for their organisation) (founder)

---

19 Lew McCreary (2010) 'Innovation on the front line', *Harvard Business Review*, September 2010, p. 92.
20 A positive quality claimed in the poetry of John Keats, that of allowing doubts to speak for themselves in his work.

3. The product team need more innovation … the IT team need needs to be more productive … sounds like you need to change your overall management model. (exchange between managers)

4. Meeting customer needs should be more than establishing a scarcity and then controlling it like orthodox capitalism… (manager)

5. We all need to join the A game: Analytics, Assessment, Attraction and Attribution … how people behave on the web … (manager)

6. We take industry awards as proof we are industry leaders whereas surveys mean we are just ahead of competitors … who are catching up. (manager 'successful' company)

7. We need to dump the traditional expectation that development would be easy. What's traditional about that? Tradition is what we call something when it doesn't work any longer. (exchange between managers)

8. Does non-profit have to mean non-risk? (staff member, participating organisation)

9. In business we need to invent the *second* wheel? (staff member)

10. Do you need new landscapes or new eyes? (manager)

Finally, one that maybe shouldn't be here:

'*Learning rhythm* takes time – where you can rely on your own thinking to solve complex problems that stay solved – can be one month, can be a year…' (founder)

12

Techniques

This section is a selection of techniques which were used during the year-long journey to advance participant thinking at an individual and collective level, and eventually enable the next stage of development to come within grasp.

They are broadly qualitative though obviously the organisations used other techniques such as business planning, resourcing, costing, partnerships and staff deployment and so on. The techniques are grouped into two broad – and probably illegitimate categories – both of which are needed to bring change nearer.

- Straight stuff: the model-grids, explanations and redesigns.

- Crooked stuff: more creative approaches including idea generating in a range of areas.

The techniques start with the management, learning and business model 'templates' used in the initial assessment.

The Straight Stuff

1 SELF ASSESSMENT: GRIDS AND EXPLANATIONS OF ALL THREE MODELS

They are given here with all their jagged flow under some principle headings, some shorthand and some absences, exactly as used with participant organisations.

Management Model

How is your management model changing?
Assess your position today and where you want to be in two year's time.
A: Today

		1	2	3	4	
Managing direction	**Hierarchy**					**Collective wisdom**
Managing means	**Bureaucracy**					**Emergence**
Managing capacity	**Today**					**Tomorrow**
Effect	**Static**					**Agile**

Guidance for Completion: This is a rough guide – really a starting point only. See below for 'Explanation of terms'. Note above where you are now (1–4) and on a separate sheet your evidence for this. We will elicit this further in discussion.

How is your management model changing?
Assess where you want to be in two year's time.
B: Two years on

		1	2	3	4	
Managing direction	**Hierarchy**					**Collective wisdom**
Managing means	**Bureaucracy**					**Emergence**
Managing capacity	**Today**					**Tomorrow**
Effect	**Static**					**Agile**

Guidance for Completion: To help you identify which boxes (1–4) you are aiming for please consider: the challenges the organisation faces, what changes may be needed, and their intended effects on organisational performance. Brief notes on separate sheet are fine. We will elicit these further in discussion.

EXPLANATION OF TERMS

Hierarchy Goals and direction are set through the authority of managers; leaders are ascribed	**Collective wisdom** In certain conditions, collective expertise of large numbers can produce better decisions and forecasts than a small number of experts; once confident, oblique principles are adopted (goals pursued indirectly); leaders emerge
Saying: *The boss/manager knows best*	**Saying:** *More open sourcing will accelerate 'wisdom' – or learning*
Bureaucracy Work is structured through formal rules ensuring consistency, maintaining tradition	**Emergence** Purposive self-organising occurs with actors working more independently, taking responsibility for co-ordinating their work
Saying: *Use the sign-off procedure –or else*	**Saying:** *Let's self-organise to get there faster*
Today Concern for control; little staff discretion; most energy consumed in daily operations; 'permission culture'; 'development' is more of the same; extrinsic motivation; works predictably	**Tomorrow** Concern for trust; staff autonomy; high improvement and innovation rate; freedom in how work is done; 'forgiveness culture'; stretching rather than striving; challenging climate; intrinsic motivation
Saying: *Limits are limits*	**Saying:** *The more challenging the goal (purpose) the more other goals will be reached*
Static Has a fading respect; traditional; inflexible; 'job for life'; comfortable; long staying staff	**Agile** Flexible, seeks continual successful market adjustment; potentially stressful; high trust leading to sustained high performance; long list of people who want to work there
Saying: *Tomorrow is more of today*	**Saying:** *With engagement, tomorrow begins today*

Learning Model

How is your learning model changing?
Assess your position today and where you want to be in two year's time.
A: Today

		1	2	3	4	
Focus for Learning	**Individual**					**Collective**
Sources of Learning	**Traditional**					**Emergent**
Type of Learning	**Superficial**					**Deep**
Effect	**Asphyxiation**					**Resilience**

Guidance for Completion: This is a rough guide – really a starting point only. See below for 'Explanation of terms'. Note above where you are now (1–4) and on a separate sheet your evidence for this. We will elicit this further in discussion.

How is your learning model changing?
Assess where you want to be in two year's time.
A: Two years on

		1	2	3	4	
Focus for Learning	**Individual**					**Collective**
Sources of Learning	**Traditional**					**Emergent**
Type of Learning	**Superficial**					**Deep**
Effect	**Asphyxiation**					**Resilience**

Guidance for Completion: To help you identify which boxes (1–4) you are aiming for please consider: the challenges the organisation faces, what changes may be needed, and their intended effects on organisational performance. Brief notes on separate sheet are fine. We will elicit these further in discussion.

EXPLANATION OF TERMS

Individual	Collective
The most powerful dispense 'knowledge'; occasional; disconnected; any sharing is based on didactic and 'subject-based' methods	'Productive interference' between individual learning and organisational practices; learning is named, claimed, shared and improvement-leveraged; connected; there is a powerful organisational learning culture informed by vision and values
Saying: *It's up to staff to learn – if they want*	**Saying:** *What can we learn from that?*
Traditional	**Emergent**
Staff are consumers of learning; restricted access; traditional training; a 'drain on budgets' yet little Return on Investment (ROI) analysis; if ROI used, no awareness of the cost of not learning; large cost in 'unlearning' needed for sustainable improvement	Staff are producers of learning; democratic access; open climate of high trust; forums emerge as problems emerge: for example, 'promising practice', creative problem-solving techniques; envisioned experiments, risk-projects led by staff; ideas into impact; managing innovation system; *skunkworks*; confident; multiple sources; many routes to 'excellence'
Saying: *Ask the experts*	**Saying:** *Here's some news we can use*
Superficial	**Deep**
Learning-lite: facts, data, top-down; useful though limiting; satisfied with first returns; learning wrong things, for example, 'unaccountable disengagement'; fearful, compliant; marginal; fire-fighting	Rate of learning increases as environment changes; acknowledges and tackles emerging issues; does more complex things better year-on-year; work is an engaged improvement conversation; iterative, persistent, challenging; all activities deeply mined for learning; transparent 'knowledge management'; future-fighting
Saying: *Didn't work before – do what we always do*	**Saying:** *Don't just try harder – learn harder*
Asphyxiation	**Resilience**
Diminishing returns; repeated failure; dependent staff; increasing costs; opportunities missed	Sustained high performance; agile; high anticipation reservoir; uncertainty-bounding; independent, politically-skilled staff; learning is organisation's oxygen; restful cerebrating
Saying: *We're always too busy to think here*	**Saying:** *The more the challenges the greater the options*

Business Model

How is your business model changing?
Assess your position today and where you want to be in two year's time.
A: Today

		1	2	3	4	
Current Business Model	**Implicit**					**Explicit**
Organisation focus	**Inside out**					**Outside in**
Value	**Value subtraction**					**Value creation**
Effect	**Stagnation and decline**					**Growth and renewal**

Guidance for Completion: This is a rough guide – really a starting point only. See below for 'Explanation of terms'. Note above where you are now (1–4) and on a separate sheet your evidence for this. We will elicit this further in discussion.

How is your business model changing?
Assess where you want to be in two year's time.
A: Two years on

		1	2	3	4	
Current Business Model	**Implicit**					**Explicit**
Organisation focus	**Inside out**					**Outside in**
Value	**Value subtraction**					**Value creation**
Effect	**Stagnation and decline**					**Growth and renewal**

Guidance for Completion: To help you identify which boxes (1–4) you are aiming for please consider: the challenges the organisation faces, what changes may be needed, and their intended effects on organisational performance. Brief notes on separate sheet are fine. We will elicit these further in discussion.

EXPLANATION OF TERMS

Implicit Limited awareness of current BM and how it works; one only, or very mature BM; 'how can we plan in such an uncertain business environment!'	**Explicit** Keen awareness of how BM delivers value; how the four BM elements cohere; BM as a 'theory of business' – flexibly; how to use it to capitalise on new opportunities; a potential white space invader'– unmapped territory outside core business
Saying: *What's wrong with more of the same?*	**Saying:** *How can we link customer value and a profit formula?* (see below 4 BM elements)
Inside-out Opaque windows – internal views dominate; environmental scanning discouraged; customers 'don't know what they really want'	**Outside-in** Sky-high overview of environment; mapping and tracking competition; customer value proposition (CVP) actively drives discussions; the job a customer 'needs to be done' (the outside) is actively internalised (brought inside); creative customer engagement
Saying: *That kind of thinking is not my job*	**Saying:** *How can we meet customer needs faster, better than they currently experience?*
Value subtraction Great barriers to 'value': staff work in silo-units, disconnected ways, attritional discourse; delays and arguments are routine; 'rules are rules'; rigid planning; improvement ideas are ignored; compliance is the greatest value	**Value creation** Sources of organisational 'wealth' are (1) the thinking (learning) of engaged staff and (2) robust customer engagement; customer unmet and unsatisfied needs are actively sought and capitalised on; whole-organisational interdependence; value-creating activities identified early on; move from company push to customer pull
Saying: *Why should we know what 'value' is?*	**Saying:** *Value is sustainable organisational wealth*
Stagnation and decline Business is at an unrecognised mature stage in the life cycle; planning is a mix of more of the same/ hope for the best'; 'the bottom line is the only line that matters in judging performance...'	**Growth and renewal** There are a number of BMs in operation; capability is developed and exploited; BM innovation is seen as a 'playbox or toolkit for conquering the unknown'
Saying: *Business models – just theory really...*	**Saying:** *If there are more opportunities than we can grasp – which are key?*

See also the four parts of the business model in Chapter 6, 'The Three Models: Facing the Future'.

2   IMPROVEMENTS FROM FEEDBACK: REFORMATTING THE MODELS IN TERMS OF KEY PRIORITIES

Management model: the choices made about how organisational effort is organised (the *how* of business).

Hierarchy/collective wisdom

1.   getting a better *balance* between any of the principles – either/and rather than either/or;

2.   as organisations develop, goals/direction are set through the 'collective wisdom' of numbers of committed staff not just the same managers;

3.   the culture is such that leaders can emerge where needed.

Bureaucracy/emergence

1.   work is structured through self-organising;

2.   staff work independently in increasingly complex tasks;

3.   consistency is maintained by staff taking greater responsibility for co-ordinating their work.

Today/tomorrow

1.   overall control is maintained through greater trust producing greater 'self-control';

2.   high improvement and innovation rate exists;

3.   a 'forgiveness rather than a permission' culture (more experimentation) exists.

Effect sought: being agile

•   seeking continual successful market adjustment (aware of its current and next stage);

- 'employer of choice' for many.

Learning model: the choices made about how organisational thinking is mobilised (the *what best next*).

Individual/collective

1. 'productive interference' between individual learning and organisational practices exists;

2. learning is named, claimed, shared and improvement-leveraged;

3. there is an organisational learning culture informed by vision and values.

Traditional/emergent

1. staff are producers of learning;

2. learning is evaluated by appropriate 'return on investment' methods;

3. 'next move' forums emerge as problems emerge, for example, 'promising practice' or managing innovation.

Superficial/deep

1. the organisational rate of learning increases as the environment changes;

2. there is a consistent movement from fire-fighting to future-fighting;

3. transparent 'knowledge management' exists (staff can 'pull' what they need).

Effect sought: being resilient

- sustained high performance (and metrics that matter);

- independent, politically-skilled staff;

- does more complex things better year on year (applies to all three models).

Business model: the choices made about how organisational value is created, delivered and captured (the *what and why* of business).

Implicit/explicit

1.   keen awareness of how it delivers value and four elements cohere (CVP, Key Resources, Key Processes, Profit Formula);

2.   business model as a 'theory of business' is used to capitalise on new opportunities;

3.   planning embraces uncertainty – includes unmapped territory outside core business.

Inside-out/outside-in

1.   strong overview of environment, mapping and tracking competition, leading networks;

2.   the CVP actively drives discussions, the job a customer 'needs to be done';

3.   creative customer engagement exists.

Value subtraction/value creation

1.   sources of organisational 'wealth' are the thinking (learning) of engaged staff and customers (see also 3 above);

2.   whole-organisational interdependence exists; value-creating activities are identified;

3.   customer pull enables greater company push (of 'products').

Effect sought: growth and renewal

- a number of business models are in operation;

- capability is continually developed and exploited.

3 DEFINITIONS AND HYPOTHESIS

Model (a working definition)

The 'models' is an inquiry approach based on key principles of 'management', 'business' and 'learning' theory used to examine and enable organisational development.

The hypothesis

Using the three models together will enable your organisation to reach the next stage of its development *faster*. Also, as necessary, (re)make explicit choices about your three models and explore new 'value'.

Management model: how organisational effort is organised

Organisation dimension	Explanation
Managing direction	How our purpose and where we are going are established and maintained
Managing means	How achieving our purpose through our performance is maintained
Managing capacity	How we develop our resources to meet our purpose and continually emerging challenges

Learning model: how organisational thinking is mobilised

Organisation dimension	Explanation
Focus for learning	Where is learning concentrated (people)?
Sources of learning	Where does learning come from?
Type of learning	How deep is the learning?

Business model: how organisational value is created, delivered and captured

Organisation dimension	Explanation
Current business model	How well is it known by staff?
Organisation focus	Is concentration on internal or on external?
Value	What is value and how is it generated?

The Crooked Stuff

4   POETICS OF MANAGEMENT

This is the inquiry approach expressed synoptically

The inquiry approach or research method is designed to:

1.   generate independence (not done *to* you);

2.   enable managers 'to improve their own condition';

3.   use learning as a bias towards action – and trust it – the first risk;

4.   create choices – for all models;

5.   be *problem* rather than 'subject' driven;

6.   be more than your brain – the lived life has contradictions;

7.   co-create value: a 'partnership' between the organisations, a continuing learning conversation hosted on Critical Difference website.

It encourages managers and organisations to:

1.   think;

2.   disrobe your relationships – practice theory anew;

3.   be imagineers: you don't have to be large to be *grand*;

4.   be reflexive: seek to improve the inquiry tools themselves;

5.   Steal creatively encouraging 'that which does not yet exist' through a mix of aspirations and activities including:
    –   assume assuming you can intelligent noticing curiosity nudging crowd wisdom;
    –   crap detecting;
    –   not letting the will do the work of the imagination. *Imagine* it first...

－   going again – like good teachers – not accepting first
     response;
－   actionable understanding – that is, understanding
     'completed' only by action.

6.   embrace the management of uncertainty – 'take risks beyond
     knowing';

7.   be experimental – practice rapid piloting and emergence; increase
     the rate of learning as their environment changes;

8.   stay open = fuel for the journey – to perceive 'gifts' we need 'new
     eyes';

9.   seek deliverable impact (take questions from the perplexed, not just
     peers);

10. begin with questions that so far, we don't know the answers to: for
     example, will the three models enable development faster? Why not
     make choices about our three models – we do about everything else?

11. start less than perfectly – engage more meaningfully.

5 HARDY IDEA TIN-OPENERS

(1) Using what we already have

Turning the principles on each side of each model into questions, for instance:

Management model:

- How are goal and direction set in your organisation?

- How does 'leadership' occur?

- Other questions: reverse this in your organisation – typical
  management methods are 'third generation managers running
  second generation organisations using first generation methods'
  (the late Sumantra Goshal, I think).

- What is needed to reinvent control in your organisation for better
  performance?

Learning model:

- How does organisational learning or 'productive interference' occur?

- How is 'knowledge' constructed and dispensed?

- Other question: how to build for ambiguity and resilience?

Business model:

- How 'mature' is your business model?

- How is 'outside-in' enabled?

- What new channels can you use?

- Business building: what is NOT being done?

(2) Turning good writing into idea tin-openers

In a blog on 'the costs of overbearing bosses' Gary Hamel said (paraphrasing):

> When authority is vested from above ... the only way for managers to retain privileges ... is to please their political patrons ... mid-level bureaucrats spend a disproportionate amount of time managing upwards ... in traditional power settings key decisions have to be approved by superiors but merely explained to subordinates.

> ...Managers can be content with compliance when they should be seeking commitment ... In an idea world an individual's institutional power would be correlated with her value-added...

(3) The questions (tin-openers):

- In your organisation how does 'authority' appear? How mixed are it sources? What benefits would come from broadening 'authority'?

- Does managing up occur? How? What are the effects?

- How are key decisions made? How can you improve/eliminate 'approving'?

- What are you asking of subordinates? In what way do you seek commitment? What decisions would you least/most want to give to staff? How?

- How do you get 'disquieting views' from direct reports?

- How can your organisation correlate a person's institutional power with value-added?

- What is 'best' decision-making? How can you deepen the judgement reservoir?

6 BUSINESS-BUILDING

- A visit from venture capitalists:

  - What have you got investing in?

  - Where do you want to be in three year's time?

- A visit to your competitors:

  - What can you learn?

  - Dump marketing.

Go back to your current/previous customers. Ask them to become your advocates. If not, seek to improve/build a new business from what they feel they didn't receive.

(One successful organisation here – not a participant – built its business from current customer advocacy regarding conventional marketing as 'customer-failure'.)

Cross-border raiding

Henry Ford based the production lines on Chicago meat stockyards. Metro, the new bank when establishing excellent service, visited not banks but firms like Zappo (shoes) who have developed world-class customer service. As for the banks, Metro asked their customers about competitor rules and practices (CRAP) which annoyed them.

In terms of your business, what borders can you 'raid across' for new ideas?

Sourcing risk

Bring new business ideas to crowd-source philanthropy sites like *Kickstarter*.

Sustaining business

Founder-trust: 'My role justifies the value I create': discuss, in an internal collective learning forum.

Business modelling – going bananas

Warm up – get out of your ordinary business mind. Imagine a business model based on a banana. Think about the banana first: what does it feel, taste and look like? Now state five new business models based on bananas in three minutes. Here's one: *to produce banana-skin moments for arrogant managers...* Once five are created, leave them and go on to this: What new business models can you 'throw over the wall into your market', to experiment? How could you experiment?

7   SOCIAL MEDIA

- build a *different* Facebook page;

- build a strategy to generate meaningful contribution (to avoid becoming a digital echo-chamber);

- how can you advocate in order to be advocated?

Using the internet, more broadly:

- Join the AAA – with web-based business what can you learn from: *Attention* (what prompts and sustain potential customer attention?); *Assessment* (use analytics to mine your own data); *Attribution* (how people make spending decisions online).

- How and what can you co-produce?

- How can being connected and sharing, create greater value?

- What has been changed by the internet in your business field?

- How can you mine your 'expert' end-users?

8   PARENTS, CHILDREN AND ORPHANS

Pick any practice in your organisation, in management, learning or business. Work back from the practice to identify the theories-in-use which informs it. Are these effective, or adequate for your new challenges? Do you need to make new choices about your theories-in-use, your models?

9   METRICS

What are the smartest tools you could use for your business now: what are the necessary elements that other metrics exclude?

Devise a metric to include: trust, risk, disruptive thinking, and prototyping and idea generating which encourages exploring before exploiting.

10   APPS

Identify two apps suitable for your business.

11   REVERSAL

An idea generator: take a problem you currently face. Reverse it – make it worse, much worse. Now reverse each worse idea, that is, make it 'better'. Be outrageous from the start.

12   'PEER BRUISING' (AKA 'A DROP OF THE HARD STUFF')

Ask a group of 'problem peers' (those sympathetic to tackling an enduring problem, regardless of status) these: If we do nothing how will this problem be in one year? What will we be saying to ourselves and each other then? What can we say to each other *now* to stiffen our resolve to address it and be more accountable to each other on this change journey?

13 TECHNIQUES TO CHALLENGE AND TRANSFORM DEFENSIVENESS

Making a critical difference

1. A responsibility rinse in high Cs;

2. Gimme five!

3. Rainbows the colour of NO.

All available from: http://www.criticaldifference.co.uk/unplugged.php or d.carroll@criticaldifference.co.uk

14 COACHING TECHNIQUE: FEEL, THINK, ACT

This is based on think, feel, act and is part of a longer sequence. Emotions can be contagious and it is important for anyone to *know* what they feel. It can be used where a customer is experiencing 'blockages' which might be unnamed yet significant, and might benefit from being made explicit along with what might need to be done as a result. This might challenge certainties. If the feelings are strong, this technique might need reusing so a fruitful customer balance is encouraged between feeling, thinking and acting. And in that sequence, particularly for recurrent feelings.

1. Feelings: what is the feeling you are referring to?

2. Think: turn a rational light on the feeling – what are its sources, dangers, benefits?

3. Act: what new actions will you now take now that you've acknowledged the feeling?

15 GOOD LOOKING QUESTIONS AND THEIR UGLY BROTHER LURKING BEHIND

Good looking questions – anticipating some troublesome issues, for example:

What's it like to work here?

Ugly question: (if so) what did you do about it? This is to identify how resilient this 'doing' was or if it fell at the first a hurdle, suggesting need to build resilience.

(See 'Making a critical difference' above.)

16   I HAVEN'T GOT TIME

In change circumstances, managers claiming they haven't got time can be a typically defensive response. In this technique ask *not* 'How much time do you need?' but 'What type of time do you need – *maintenance* time (to do more of the same 26 hours per day) or *development* time (to enable you to reflect on why you never seem to have any)?'

17   YES-ING AND NO-ING

(a) Say NO to no

'No' acts as a ground rule in idea-generating forums where all agree to link, ladder and connect rather than argue, discuss, barrister or ceregrate.

(b) Say 'yes' more

Say 'yes' rather than no in ordinary decision-making. Find ways to enable your staff to say 'yes' independent of you, and what is the impact?

18   RISKING: 'SAFETY THIRD'

> *Doing the same thing in responding to a problem is the equivalent of doing nothing.'*
>
> *Critical Difference*

Aim: To stretch manager problem-solving responses, to ease habits down the stairs, one at a time.

Please note: though this example concentrates on change, the technique can easily be amended to include other concerns around management, learning or business.

> *The best way to improve the quality of an operation is to eliminate the need to carry it out in the first place.*
>
> *Chief Executive, high performing organisation*

Many managers have a range of responses to problems they experience in their organisations. These are invariably tried and tested and may have served them well in predictable circumstances. But what happens when they don't work, half work, or give the appearance of working, or when circumstances become muddy or fluid?

Safety Third is designed to enable sustainable change by encouraging managers to 'stretch' their responses to problems, particularly stubborn or hidden ones where the temptation is to repeat attempts with doubtful potential for success. The technique can help unearth different issues, or reframe starting ones; it encourages managers to lead change effectively by making risk safe(er); develop a greater problem-solving repertoire, and a more strategic approach which recognises short- *and* long-term organisational needs.

How to use it

Starting with Box 1 identify the 'problem' you are facing currently. Then complete the related questions in this Box (as with all the boxes)

Box 2: use a conventional response, one you ordinarily use. In the related questions make sure you estimate the cost of this if it does not work.

Box 3: take your 'solution' through the five separate activities.

Box 4: complete all ten demanding questions. Now draft your optimum approach and solution to the problem you started with.

SAFETY THIRD
Cost/Effects   Changing change

Cost/Effects	Changing change

2   Doing the same
 	
Identify the organisational 'problem'
 	
Identify your common response/'solution' that is, the way you responded to it last time
 	
To gauge the success potential of doing more of the same, estimate the effects: how will it be in three, six and 12 months?
	3 Giving direction
	
	1 Identify the organisational 'problem'
	
	2 Select your 'solution'
	
	3 Take it through this change journey*
	   • Doing things anyhow
	   • Doing things well
	   • Doing things better
	   • Doing better things
	
	4 Estimate which stage your problem is now
	
	5 Create a 'solution' at least at the next stage
	
	6 Now continue examining this new 'solution' through the questions in Box 4

1   Doing nothing
 	
Identify the organisational 'problem'
 	
Estimate the effects of doing nothing: how will the 'problem' be in three, six and 12 months?
	4 Climbing barriers
	
	What barriers does your solution face:
	   • in you?
	   • in the organisation?
	
	How can these be overcome?
	
	What are the main arguments you must win?
	
	Who can help?
	
	Any sources of more 'promising practice' in this area, internally or externally?
	
	How do you generate new ideas?
	
	What networks can help? How can you develop new ones?
	
	How will you get early feedback? How will you sustain impact?
	
	How will you increase your rate of learning?
	
	Having considered each of these questions and a any others which may emerge, now draft your continuing new 'solution' (below)

> *Draft your new optimum approach for a more sustainable 'solution'*
>
> *Critical Difference*

Terms

- 'Problem': anything that concerns you that is no longer 'solved' by common organisational procedures.

- 'Solution': your approach and related actions – particularly your initial response, and then increasingly, using the 1–4 sequence here to open up more effective avenues to meet short- and long-term organisational needs for sustainable change.

- 'Direction': for instance, 'towards excellence'.

- This is based on Boydell's four stages of organisational learning but any development sequence could be used.

- 'Barriers': anything that can limit or damage the chances of your 'solution' being effective, particularly ones that may have emerged through this process and which you may not have considered previously.

The whole process should be treated as an experiment, which invites leadership, strengthens ideas, and clarifies planning through argument, action and learning.

Appendices

Appendix 1: 'Don't Try This at Home!

LESSONS FROM FACEBOOK

For organisations examining business models, Facebook seems extremely attractive. But be warned! Perhaps because of its unique (?) success based on its particular sector, circumstances and mission makes it impossible – or at least extremely difficult to imitate. Its success is clear enough: it now has over 10 per cent of the planet as users, is the equivalent of the 'third biggest country in the world'[1] and is now 'the company which creates companies' and has changed the way companies conduct their marketing. However would it have lasted this long if it was in any sector other than social networking without demonstrating convincing evidence of recovering its costs, and of making a profit? Facebook is a private company so does not have to disclose its financial performance. Facebook estimated 2010 revenue is 'between $1.1 and 2 billion' (ibid.).

To its credit, *so far*, it treats sceptically the fawning valuations it is given by – mainly – venture capitalists. Lest we forget, these are broadly the same forces which valued BEBO at almost a $1 billion when AOL bought it and then two years later sold it for less than $10 million. This intentional overvaluing of social media internet companies is a key part of the game. It was surprising, for instance, to see an article on Spotify the digital jukebox service, that it was 'raising a new round of funding of $100 million to achieve a billion dollar valuation '... *in spite of still being lossmaking.*'[2]

As will be seen with Facebook's emerging business model (above) business models are not a once and for all activity and do not last forever, just as the average lifespan of a company has reduced dramatically, the average length of time a company remained on the Sandard and Poor 500 in 1958 was 57 years, in 1983 was 30 and in 2008 was 18.

---

1   *Time Magazine*, 'Person of the Year' December 27 2010/January 3 2011.
2   Tim Bradshaw and Andrew Edgecliff-Johnson 'DST to lead funding round valuing Spotify at $1bn', *The Financial Times*, 23 February 2011.

THE EMERGING BUSINESS MODEL – OR IS IT?

In customer terms, what could be easier – a new, fashionable internet-based social network, easy to access and use, to share, indulge, self publicise... and *free*! Or is it – and who for?

Facebook began as exuberant, anarchistic free-for-all, quaintly anti-establishment, rejecting what the founders considered was corporate business. It funded the cost of maintaining its network infrastructure and large server farms through a mix of venture capital and traditional investment – with payback demands which are far from 'free'. So how did they plan to cover their costs? The film 'The Social Network' directed by David Fincher captured its beginnings in 2004, where its founder says 'No advertising – this could ruin it!' a committed position underlined in David Kirkpatrick's[3] *Facebook Effect* 'contempt for ads'. What their business model would tell us from its emerging narrative is how Facebook did an about Face.

This emerged (at least publicly) in 2007 with customer complaints about privacy. This occurred because of a rich mix of emerging issues at the core of Facebook including: the nature of the Facebook enterprise itself, social networking; the sheer volume of data users were unloading, not just in personal terms but in increasing volume, worldwide; and the range of emerging functions such a wealth of data can serve, some of which can be a purpose different from the users initial one. Key to this was how users 'publicised their privacy'. Users talked about themselves, what they wear, eat, drink, read, films they see, music they play, their orientation and status. The more 'public' – that is, shared – their 'privacy', the greater the data harvest. This is the sort of information which, once formatted, third parties such as advertisers would pay handsomely for. This could enable careful targeting, for very large groups, given the social context Facebook creates, through interaction with friends. This for marketers is the Holy Grail.[4] And in terms of scale, as Facebook developed, it was accumulating not just more individually detailed data than most countries actually had on their citizens, but in gargantuan volume. Compare this with say, Google, which serves ads on the basis of educated guesses, or Apple, analysing the purchasing history of its iTunes users.

Facebook users experienced advertising carefully targeting them (like 'permission' advertising) based on their previously expressed preferences.

---

3   David Kirkpatrick (2010) *The Facebook Effect*. USA, Virgin Books.
4   *Time Magazine*, 'Person of the Year' December 27 2011/January 3 2011.

The privacy paradox emerged: what you thought was 'your business' (how you conduct yourself in the network) now becomes 'my business' (that of the network) and then becomes 'the business' of another party. The Facebook response to user complaints was to mount a costly marketing campaign and develop a lengthy privacy code. Nonetheless, it retained strongly its vision to socialise everything, with its default setting of sharing. This seemed in large measure to regain user confidence and 'return' to users the choice they originally thought they had about the use of their own information. It restored what was, however implicitly, their initial perception of 'value' but subtly altered it too.

This change was, in retrospect, inevitable for Facebook. Its emerging business model also changed from one based around 'growing site usage'[5] to one based round digital advertising. Soon one in four of all US online display adverts would be on Facebook. However, even if identifying an explicit business model was not its key business tool until much later in its development, (according to Kirkpatrick) there are immense implications for its development here.

THE USERS: THE EMERGENCE AND CONTRADICTIONS OF VALUE

From the customer perspective, Facebook is built on an essentially narcissistic element which attracts social networkers. It is designed precisely to attract those willing to self-publicise, users who willingly disclose a wide range of personal details and preferences. They seem to accept the contradictions of 'free' – that, at an apparently technical level, the price they pay involves some surrendering of privacy, typically contact details. This is quite apart from another cost of 'free', that with the internet, whatever is said stays in the public domain *forever*. These issues are now both mundane, hardly raising a business eyebrow. But there is a deeper contradiction around 'free' concerning 'user needs'. In this, users seem to frame what they 'need' in an ambiguous yet self-advantaging way. Their privacy is somehow intact because *they* rather than someone else can 'accept or reject', ignore or link with, each individual response to their own postings. Thus, their privacy is acceptably traded; private means 'shared' as long as *I get from it what I want*. That is, until someone else (the owners) decides to share their information with others whom users don't know. Though this is not far removed from what happens with users' own individual information, they (the user) do not control it, nor have they given permission, and this leaves them with a perception that they are *not* getting from it what they want. They

---

5   David Kirkpatrick (2010) *The Facebook Effect*. USA, Virgin Books.

are somehow getting less. Their Customer Value Proposition (CVP) is of less *value* – value has been subtracted.

So how did this affect value (as in the CVP) which is essentially 'getting a job done' for customers? Their 'job to be done' was to connect with their chosen others. And Facebook is a multi-sided platform, which brings together two (or more) distinct but interdependent groups.[6]

However, in the spirit of serendipity,[7] the changing nature of value was based on the changing nature of internet-based social networking. For all concerned, 'need' was *exchangeable* in order to produce value, and value is the 'product' created mutually between producer and customer. In this way 'need', once expressed in the marketplace, becomes a new commodity.

How far is this from Karl Marx's[8] idea of exchange value – though he is clearly interested in how labour is exploited as a commodity? He shows how exchange value is the 'necessary form of the appearance of value'. For Facebook customers, privacy soon became submerged in 'value', which emerged after expressing their need, an explicit charge for it. This (delete) also involved a new channel, the internet and its 'maturing' use, moving from a playful to a more pragmatic, professionalised use. Now, if people are still individually outrageous they are invariably snapped up by businesses – the internet may well be the ultimate 'commodity'.

What emerges for organisations from this is that 'value' and need can be advantageously slippery. If 'need' is a new commodity then it is of infinite variety, infinitely negotiable and infinitely adjustable.

This recognition is included in the new business model.

---

6   Alexander Osterwalder and Yves Pigneur (2010) *Business Model Generation*. New Jersey, John Wiley, p. 77.
7   Mark Zuckerberg's and Gary Hamel 'Who's really innovative?... inventing an innovative business model is often... a matter of serendipity': http://www.managementexchange.com/blog/whos-really-innovative. Accessed 29 January 2011
8   Tom Bottomore, Ed. (1983) *A Dictionary of Marxist Thought*. Oxford, Basil Blackwell Publisher Ltd. Another angle for the work was prompted by reading Karl Marx on one of his most controversial concepts, 'value', 'use-value' and *the form it takes*. In trying to understand an attempt at 'new value' in this work, I took a few liberties in trying to apply it. The thinking went (with apologies for seeming to bowdlerise Marx): a commodity is anything produced for the purpose of exchange so a commodity has exchange-value. Customers have 'needs' but once this need enters its market it becomes a commodity. Producers or companies, meet needs through this process of exchange, which broadly determines value and there can be no a priori determination of value. The value of a commodity (by now transformed) can only be expressed after its production.

Appendix 2: Theories-in-Use

The following theories are broad brush, by no means exhaustive, and some are parts of other theories.

MANAGEMENT THEORIES

F.W. Taylor: 'Scientific management': command and control management (aka Management 1.0).

Henri Fayol and Max Weber: Administrative management and Theory of Social and Economic Organisations.

Elton Mayo: The Hawthorne Effect, 'Social' and 'rational' man.

Human Relations school: Transactional and transformational.

John Watson and B.K. Skinner: Behaviourism based on 'observable behaviour and the role of operant conditioning.

Peter Drucker: Management role and responsibilities, with an emphasis on organisational purpose.

Sociology: The study of race, sex, class and power in society and in organisations.

Psychology: Cognitive theory, mixed 'disciplines', and assumptions of what is 'rational'.

Douglas McGregor: Theory X and Y

Systems Theory: Complex nature of organisations seen as a collection of interrelated, interconnected parts, which have to be viewed as a whole.

Critical Management Theory: Hugh Willmott and Mats Alvesson; Sumantra Ghoshal

Google: self-managing, self-organising, 'disorg' which limits 'management'; 'people's sole job is innovation with transparency and ferocious product reviews to instil discipline...'[9]

---

9   Simon Caulkin 'How to make $4bn without really managing', *The Observer*, 27 July 2008.

Ricardo Semler: *Semco*, transforming organisations for higher performance based on high trust.

Contingency theory: Style of management and structure of the organisation should reflect and change with changes in its environment.

Agency theory: Designed to align the interests of senior managers with those of shareholder through a system of rewards – the same as for shareholders – increased shares, or 'stock-based compensation'.

David Pugh (and others) organisational culture and change: With occupational, political and rational-allocation systems, members of all organisations operate simultaneously in all three (DC: However most change programmes seem to recognise only the first system).

Cyert and March: Behavioural theories of organisations as coalitions of different interest groups with a variety of views, continuously bargaining for power so decision-making is inherently uncertain – contrary to assumptions of rational behaviour in 'organisation man' or 'economic man'.

Organisational development theories including organisations as coalitions of different interest groups, for example, in the case studies.

Fixed and growth mindsets: For example, Matthew Syed: how personal (and organisational) development is obstructed or enabled.

Innovation: Peter Drucker 'Discipline of innovation'; Goran Ekvall 'Developing a creative climate'; Henry Chesbrough 'Open and disruptive innovation'.

LEARNING THEORIES

Schools of psychology informing learning theory include: Behaviourism, cognitive, social constructivist, and humanist (among others).

Teaching/learning methods depending on their theory include: Rote learning, didactic transmission and reception, recipients as tabula rasa, the 'taxidermy legacy', and 'predetermined knowledge'. Independence-generating methods challenge these.

Individual cognitive styles: For example, having a learning orientation and an awareness of their own cognitive style.

Fixed (finite) or infinite 'intelligence'.

Psychology-cognitive theories and cognitive style.

Chris Argyris: Defensive routines (still the one of the best change-handles).

Carl Rogers: Freedom to Learn.

Peter Senge: Learning Organisation.

Daniel Goleman: Emotional intelligence.

PEER-PRODUCED LEARNING

Ikujiro Nonaka: Organisational knowledge creation.

OPEN AND DISRUPTIVE SYSTEMS

'Playtime': For example, Google where developers can have 15 per cent of their time for innovative projects[10] – an initiative based on high trust and learning.

Traditional theories of delivery: For example, subject-based, in receipt of, passive; academic, trickle down, conventional training, mandatory courses.

Models based on theories: (i) Boydell: Four Stages of Organisational Development; (ii) The Four stages of competence; (iii) Edmondson.

Knud Illeris: Three simultaneous dimensions of learning: a cognitive, emotional or attitudinal, and a social one.

'Knowledge', its construction and status: Some forms, for example, clinical or medical, can be seen as more 'objective' and valuable than for example, business ideas or coming from committed professionals.

---

10 Simon Caulkin 'If you want to be productive, get disorganised', *The Observer*, August 2008.

BUSINESS THEORIES

'The theory of the business' (Drucker).

Customer Value Proposition as integral part of a business model.

Stakeholder value and variations.

The balanced scorecard.

Shareholder value.

Core competences of an organisation (Hamel and Prahalad).

EFQM: The European Foundation for Quality Management 'enablers'.

Efficiency.

Finance and financial assumptions.

Business planning; design and production; contingency planning, improvement planning.

Marketing models.

Customer pull and producer push; customer-generated feedback.

Bibliography

Books and Articles

Russell L. Ackoff and Herbert J. Addison (2007) *Management f-Laws*. Axminster, Triarchy Press Ltd.

Yvon Appleby, Marie Kerwin and Sue McCulloch (2008) 'Making research', *Adults Learning*, May, p. 20.

Dan Ariely (2010) 'Why businesses don't experiment', *Harvard Business Review* April.

Chris Argyris (1994) 'Good communication that blocks learning', *Harvard Business Review* July–August.

Neil Astley and Pamela Robertson-Bruce Eds (2007) *Soul Food: Nourishing Poems for Starved Minds*. Northumberland, Bloodaxe Books.

Walter Benjamin (1977) *Understanding Brecht*. London, New Left Books.

Simon Behrman (2010) *Shostakovich, Socialism, Stalin and Symphonies*. London, Redwords.

Jonathan Birchall (2011) 'Best deal on the block' in Boldness in Business, *Financial Times* 17 March.

Julian Birkinshaw (2010) *Reinventing Management*. San Francisco, Jossey-Bass.

Julian Birkinshaw and Huw Jenkins (2009) *Risk Management Gets Personal*. London, AIM Research.

Alex Bogusky and John Winsor (2009) *Baked In*. Chicago, USA, B2 Books.

Tom Bottomore Ed. (1983) *A Dictionary of Marxist Thought*. Oxford, Basil Blackwell Publisher Ltd.

Tim Bradshaw (2011) 'The fickle value of friendship', *The Financial Times*, 31 March.

Eleanor Brazil (2010) 'Pieced together', *Guardian Society* 24 February.

David Brindle (2010) 'See you on the other side' ,*The Guardian*, Work, 23 January.

Juanita Brown with David Isaacs (2005) *The World Café*. San Francisco, Berrett-Koehler.

John Seely Brown and John Hagel 111 (2005) 'The next frontier of innovation', *The McKinsey Quarterly*, Number 3, p. 91, quoting William Gibson.

Madeleine Bunting (2011) 'Up close and personal', *The Guardian*, Society 9 February.

Fritjof Capra (2003) *The Hidden Connections*. London, Flamingo.

Donal Carroll (1981) *Don't You Believe It!* London, The Macmillan Press.

Donal Carroll (2004) 'My part of the ship is afloat', Issue 20; 'How colleges don't learn', Issue 19; 'Is that the best we can do?' Issue 18. All available from *Post-16 Educator*, 221 Firth Park Road, Sheffield S5 6WW.

Donal Carroll (2008) *Know Learning, Know Change.* London, Critical Difference, available from author.

Donal Carroll (2009) *Shovelling Mercury with a Pitchfork.* London, Critical Difference, available from author.

Simon Caulkin (1999) 'Small's no great thing', *The Observer*, 9 December.

Simon Caulkin (2002) 'Performance through people: the new people management', CIPD 2002 quoted in Donal Carroll (2008) *Know Learning, Know Change.*

Simon Caulkin (2005) 'The age of the Euro-customer', 'Management' section, *The Observer*, 26 June.

Simon Caulkin (2006) 'The job in hand: leadership', *Public Sector Management* Magazine, September.

Simon Caulkin (2010) *The Observer*, 23 August.

Simon Caulkin (2010) '7 counterintuitive truths for managers', *Vanguard Leaders' Summit* December 2010.

Peter Cheeseman of Accenture and Bruce Rayner of Choose You at Work, at MLab, London Business School, November 2009, Presentations on 'How Generation Y is changing management work' and 'Social networks and employee engagement'.

Henry Chesbrough (2003) 'The Era of Open Innovation' from *Managing Innovation and Change,* David Mayle (Ed.). London, Sage Publications and The Open University Business School.

Jim Collins (2001) *Good to Great.* London, Random House.

Jim Collins (2006) *Good to Great and the Social Sectors.* London, Random House.

David Conn (2010) 'Community champions', *The Guardian*, 18 August 2010.

Philip Crosby (1996) *Reflections on Quality.* New York, McGraw-Hill.

Cathy Davidson (2011) 'So last century', *Times Higher Education*, 28 April.

Peter Drucker (1993) *Managing for Results.* New York, Collins.

Jane Dudman (2009) 'Choosing words carefully', *The Guardian*, 13 May, quoting *'Public Sector Reform...But Not as We Know It'* by Hilary Wainwright and Mathew Little.

Henri Fayol (1930) *Industrial and General Administration*, Geneva, International Management Institute. www.redpepper.org.uk/public-service-reform-but-not-as/

Jane Dudman (2010) 'Tough Call' interview with Sir David Varney Society, *The Guardian*, 14 July.

Paulo Freire (1970) *Education for Critical Consciousness*. London, Penguin Books

Seth Godin (2009) *Meatball Sundae*. Chatham, Little, Brown Book Group.

Primyamvada Gopal (2010) 'University's mustn't again be the rich's hereditary domain', *The Guardian*, 20 August.

Lynda Gratton ((2004) *The Democratic Enterprise*. London, Pearson Education Limited.

Larry Greiner 'Dilemmas of growth' (1972) quoted in Charles Handy (1985) *Understanding Organisations*. London, Penguin.

Gary Hamel (2007) *The Future of Management*. Boston, Harvard Business School Press.

Charles Handy (1985) *Understanding Organisations*. London, Penguin Business.

Jane Henry (2006) *Creative Management and Development*. London, Sage Publications Ltd and The Open University Business School.

Andrew Hill (2011) 'Real value looks past quarterly reporting', *Financial Times*, 19 April

Sumantra Ghoshal and Heike Bruch (2006) 'Beware the busy manager', *Harvard Business Review*, Winter 2006.

Jennifer Hughes (2010) 'Tasked with tidying up Lehman: The financial fall, 2 years on', *The Financial Times*, 14 September.

Ludovic Hunter-Tiley (2010) 'Off the record', *The Financial Times Magazine*, 11/12 September.

Knud Illeris (2004) *The Three Dimensions of Learning*. Gylling, Denmark, Roskilde University Press.

Luke Johnson (2010) 'Recovery demands clear-out of old guard', *Financial Times*, 17 March.

Mark W. Johnson (2010) *Seizing the White Space: Business Model Innovation for Growth and Renewal*. Boston, MA, Harvard Business Press.

John Kay (2010) *Obliquity: Why Our Goals Are Best Achieved Indirectly*. London, Profile.

John Kay (2010) 'Why we must press on with breaking up banks', *The Financial Times*, 19 September.

Robert Kelsey (2011) 'Slow and steady', *RSA Journal*, Spring.

Peter Kingston (2008) 'No-win situation?', *Education Guardian*, 5 February.

David Kirkpatrick (2010) *The Facebook Effect*. London, Virgin Books (a Random House Group company).

James Mackintosh (2011) 'The short view', *Financial Times*, 4 February.

Roger Martin (2010) 'The age of customer capitalism', *Harvard Business Review*, January–February.

David Mayle (2006) *Managing Innovation and Change*. London, Sage Publications Ltd and The Open University Business School.

M.B. McCaskey (1988) 'Coping creatively with messes' in LR Pondy, RJ Boland, H Thonas, *Managing Ambiguity and Change*. New York: Wiley.

Carmel McConnell (2001) *Change Activist*. Harlow, Pearson Education.

Rita Gunther McGrath (2011) 'When your business model is in trouble', *Harvard Business Review*, January–February.

Steve McDermott (2002) *How To Be a Complete and Utter Failure in Life, Work and Everything: 39 ½ Steps to Lasting Underachievement*. Harlow, Prentice Hall Business.

David Meerman Scott and Brian Halligan (2010) *Marketing lessons from the Grateful Dead: What Every Business Can Learn from the Most Iconic Band in History*. New Jersey, John Wiley.

Henry Mintzberg (2009) *Managing*. Harlow, FT/PrenticeHall.

Partha Mohanran (2010) 'How to deal with new competition: adapt the business model constantly', *Financial Times*, 1 February.

John Naughton 'Are we really about to say goodbye to TV and DVDs?', *The Observer*, 24 April 2011.

Vineet Nayar (2010) *Employees First, Customers Second*. Boston, Harvard Business Press.

John Newton (2009) *Are God and the Gods Still There? How Poetry Still Matters*. London, Olympia.

Mark Ogden (2010) re-reviewing 'Sincerity and Authenticity' by Lionel Trilling, *Times Higher Education*, 7 October.

Alexander Osterwalder and Yves Pigneur (2010) *Business Model Generation*. New Jersey, John Wiley.

Martin Parker (2008) 'If only business schools wouldn't teach business', *The Observer*, Management, 30 November.

Mike Pedler, John Burgoyne and Tom Boydell (2004) *A Manager's Guide to Leadership*. Maidenhead, McGraw-Hill Professional.

Tom Peters and Robert Waterman (1982) 'In search of excellence'.

Geoffrey Petty (1998) *Teaching Today*. Cheltenham, Stanley Thornes Ltd.

Peter Preston (2010) *The Observer*, 21 March.

Proudfoot Consultancy (2005) quoted in Simon Caulkin, *The Observer*, 23 October 2005.

Ramon Casadesus-Masanelli and Joan Ricart (2011) 'How to design a winning business model', *Harvard Business Review*, January–February

Alan Rogers (2003) *What is the Difference? A New Critique of Adult Learning and Teaching*. Leicester, NIACE.

Phil Rosenzweig (2007) *The Halo Effect*. New York, Free Press.

William A. Sahlman (2008) *How to Write a Great Business Plan*. Harvard Business Review Classics, Harvard Business School Publishing Corporation.

Richard Scase (2002) *Living in the Corporate Zoo: Life and Work in 2010.* Oxford, Capstone Publishing Limited.

Richard Scase (2001) 'Why we're so clockwise', *The Observer*, 26 August.

John Seddon (2002) *I Want You to Cheat!* Buckinghamshire, Vanguard Education Ltd.

David Silverman (1974) *The Theory of Organisations.* London, Heinemann Books.

Michael Skapinker (2011) 'Why business still ignores business schools', *Financial Times*, 25 January.

Stefan Stern (2010) 'Master the mix of continuity and change', *Financial Times*, 20 January.

Henry Stewart, Cathy Busani and James Moran (2009) *Relax: A Happy Business Story.* London, Happy Publications.

Matthew Syed (2011) 'How practice makes perfect', *The Guardian*, Work, 4 June.

Studs Terkel (1974 reissued 2009) *Working.* Pantheon Books, New York.

Gillian Tett 'The very model of a modern major market influence' reviewing *Metaphors, Models and Theories* by Emanuel Derman, *Financial Times*, 24 December.

Gary Thomas (2009) 'In search of singular insight', *Times Higher Education*, 9 July.

Leon Trotsky (1968) *Literature and Revolution.* Michigan, Ann Arbor paperbacks, The University of Michigan Press.

Warwickshire College Inspection Report (2008) OFSTED.

Max Weber (1947) *The Theory of Social and Economic Organisations.* New York, Free Press.

Nicholas Wroe (2011) Interviewing John Berger, *The Guardian*, Review, 23 April.

Journals

The Chartered Institute of Personnel Development (CIPD) (2010) 'Building productive public sector workplaces'.

Commission on 2020 Public Services Trust 'From social security to social productivity' Final report, Sir Andrew Foster Chair.

The McKinsey Quarterly, 2005, Number 3.

Organisations and People (2010) 'In search of organisations that learn', *Journal of the Association of Management Education and Development*, May 2010.

Time Magazine, 'Person of the Year' December/January 2011.

Internet Sources

BITC 'The cost of disengagement', http://www.bitc.org.uk/workplace/health_
and_wellbeing/about_our_campaign.html. Accessed 15 April 2011.

Jacques Bughin and Michael Chui 'The rise of the networked enterprise: Web
2.0 finds its payday', McKinsey Global Institute, December 2010: http://
www.mckinseyquarterly.com/Organization/Strategic_Organization/
The_rise_of_the_networked_enterprise_Web_20_finds_its_payday_2716.
Accessed 2 February 2011.

Critical Difference 'Techniques to challenge and transform defensiveness' and
'Making a Critical Difference', from http://www.criticaldifference.co.uk/
unplugged.php or d.carroll@criticaldifference.co.uk.

Fast Company http://www.fastcompany.com/1724839/what-it-takes-to-be-a-
great-employer. Accessed 9 February 2011.

Gary Hamel (2011) 'Who's really innovative? Inventing an innovative business
model is often ... a matter of serendipity', http://www.managementexchange.
com/blog/whos-really-innovative. Accessed June 2011.

Jane Hart (2010) '10 steps for working smarter with social media', Centre for
Learning and Performance Technologies: http://c4lpt.co.uk/articles/10steps.
html.

Hexayurt http://hexayurt.com/. Accessed 30 May 2011.

Mckinsey Quarterly 'Mining every difference for competitive advantage',
http://www.mckinseyquarterly.com/The_power_of_storytelling_What_
nonprofits_can_teach_the_private_sector_about_social_media_2740.
Accessed June 2011.

Zopa http://uk.zopa.com/ZopaWeb/public/about-zopa/about-zopa-home.html.
Accessed 30 May 2011.

Index